World Enough and Time

Charles Bruce

A Literary Biography

Andrew Wainwright

Formac Publishing Company Limited
1988

For Marjorie
Michael and Eric, Jennifer and Alyson
yesterday, today and tomorrow

Canadian Cataloguing in Publication Data

Wainright, Andrew, 1946-

Charles Bruce

ISBN 0-88780-064-5

1. Bruce, Charles, 1906-1971 — Biography. 2. Authors,
Canadian (English) — 20th century — Biography. *
I. Title.

PS8503.R82Z938 1988   C813'.52   C88-098621-2
PR9199.3.B725Z97 1988

Cover photograph: Charles Bruce in England1944-1945
Nova Scotia Public Archives

Published with the assistance of the Nova Scotia
Department of Tourism and Culture

Formac Publishing Company Limited
5359 Inglis Street
Halifax, Nova Scotia
B3H 1J4

Printed and bound in Canada

Contents

Acknowledgements

I would like to thank:

The members of Charles Bruce's family who shared their recollections with me — Mrs. Agnes Bruce, Harry Bruce, Alan Bruce, Andrew Bruce, Harvey Bruce, Mrs. Anna MacKeen, Mrs. Carrie Macmillan, Mrs. Zoe Schulze, Miss Bessie Bruce.

Charles Bruce's friends and colleagues who remembered "Charlie" — Harold MacIntosh, Wilbur Cummings, Clayton Hart, Charles Blue, Thomas Raddall, Gillis Purcell, Jack Brayley, John Mosher.

My friends and colleagues who supported me in this project — Malcolm Ross, G.D. Killam, Alistair MacLeod, Fred Cogswell, Jim Lorimer.

The tireless three at the Dalhouse University Archives — Charles Armour, Susan Bezanson, Molly Clayden.

Norman Graham of The Canadian Press.

Donald A. Cameron, Registrar, Mount Allison University.

The Social Sciences and Humanities Research Council for its support during my sabbatical year of 1985-86.

Tina Jones, Gretchen Mosher, and Barbara Goodman for their assistance and endless patience with Wordperfect.

Last, but not least, my editor, Elizabeth Eves.

Preface

Port Shoreham is a settled stretch of road, paved in the early 1970s, on the route between Guysborough at the head of Chedabucto Bay and Mulgrave on the Strait of Canso. At one point on the road, just to the west of the old Bruce family farmhouse, there is an extraordinary view of the curving peninsula of Ragged Head and the far shore of the bay. On that proverbial clear day you may not see forever, but you do encounter water, land, and sky in intense combination of colour and circumstance. The sea especially seems in constant motion, beating before the wind against headlands, and looking in its central thrust like a river that must plunge over an inevitable precipice where, reason tells you, Guysborough quietly exists.

There are farms along the road, just as there were when Charles Bruce was a boy before the First World War, but no one makes a living from the land now; there is an old fish hut on the beach below Port Shoreham, but no two-masters are anchored behind this sandspit as they were when Will Bruce (CB's father) and others put aside their farm tools and caught herring, cod, and haddock (and, in the more distant past, mackerel) that they sold to the fish-plant boats or salted down in barrels for family use. The sense of community, once found in 'box socials,' dances, picnic days, and shared clearing of winter roads, has been watered down by the intrusions of the wide world — consolidated schools, television, a marketplace with little time for territorial self-sufficiency, values that have beaten against the strong walls of Methodist and other faiths — but such is the lack of commercial development in this area of Guysborough County and of tourist promotion, and such is the unobtrusive neighbourliness of the local inhabitants, that a remarkable blending of time past and time present occurs for the visitor. The lived experience of the transient in Port Shoreham, like that of the permanent residents, includes a future that is affected by the tangible qualities of the sea and landscape and an equally visible heritage of moral, practical, and imaginative worth. The result, as CB made clear in the best of his poetry and fiction, is a recognition of "yesterday, today, and tomorrow [as] part of a continuing whole [that puts] things in balance."

Virtually all of Charles Bruce's creative prose and a good proportion of his poetry (certainly his best poems) draw upon his experience and knowledge of life along the north shore of Chedabucto Bay. He was born in Port Shoreham in 1906 and left for university in 1923; for his remaining forty-eight years he returned to the Bruce farm only for visits and on an irregular basis. He was not a writer who, in the final end, wrote about himself; his one major attempt at a novel about his childhood years and subsequent time as a newspaperman in Toronto remains unpublished, largely because he recognized its limitations and that it did not represent the relationship between life and art he wanted to provide. But in his published work he does write about what was around him when he was a boy: the harrowing of fields; the gleam of herring in the nets; family traditions and memories, as well as community heritage and recollection, made visible through what Bruce called "hearsay history," stories handed down from generation to generation; the extraordinary in the ordinary doings of rural existence.

Since what mattered most to CB can surely be found in what he has left for literary posterity, it is worth examining not only his works but also the origins of his creative expression. Since his life in Toronto and particularly his professional life as a newspaperman were something he could not successfully integrate with his fictional vision of the north shore of Chedabucto Bay, but which paradoxically stimulated him to write of a world in which he would never live again, it is worth placing his poetry and prose within the context of such division. Since he wrote primarily about a twenty-mile stretch of territory, was concerned with depth of place and breadth of time, and was increasingly aware in his career of the supposed conflict between the regional and national in Canadian culture, it is worth considering his essays and talks on the role of the artist and the process of writing, especially his conviction that "The idea is to get across an idea, or a feeling, usually about people. Ideas are probably much the same whether they are held by people pulling herring out of the Atlantic or running a combine in Saskatchewan." Since "hearsay history" is such an integral part of his writing and of his life as an artist, it is worth listening to those story-tellers who knew Charles Bruce between 1906 and 1971 — members of his family, friends, and colleagues who weave their own versions of the flow between art and life.

CB's sisters were all considerably older than him. Bessie was born in 1891, Anna in 1893, Carrie in 1895, and Zoe in 1898. If it seems strange that they would all outlive him by a considerable number of years, it also means that they were old enough when he was a boy to have strongly-developed perceptions of him. Bessie, who died in 1986, never married, but the other three sisters are widowed now. Anna lives year-round in Boylston, about six miles from Port Shoreham, and Carrie and Zoe come from their homes in the United States to stay with her for part of each summer. When I met these four women in August of 1984 in the company of CB's son Harry, they spoke of their brother with great affection, though I can still hear the combination of love and irony in Zoe's reference to CB as "the little prince," the long-awaited boy in the family. There were no contradictions in what they told me; each picked up on what the others had said. Of course, they were speaking of family — of their mother and father, Sarah and Will, in addition to "Charlie" — but they were not over-anxious to make a good impression; rather I sensed strongly that the seventy-five years or so distance from their childhood had provided the sisters with the recognition that they were whom they perceived themselves to be in great part because of their parents and the place in which they were raised. After Will died in 1933, Sarah lived most of the rest of her life (she died in 1966 at 99 years) with Bess, who returned to the family farmhouse in the late 1950s; Anna came back east from Saskatchewan in the late 1960s; and, as has been said, Carrie and Zoe still try to come home once a year.

What kept the discussion away from the level of formal interview (for I had a list of prepared questions), and from descent into easy sentimentalizing, were Carrie's interruptions. Carrie is deaf, and in order to include her in the exchange Harry and I wrote down questions on a piece of paper. She would not always answer right away, so the rest of us would move on to other topics. Suddenly, Carrie, whose face shone with a kind of gentle intensity, would burst forth with recollection, going over old ground, but with such freshness and enthusiasm that I felt we must all want to begin again. It would be too easy and too critical to say that Carrie kept us honest; but she certainly kept us aware that we were all telling stories — about Charlie, Will, Sarah, and turn-of-the-century Port Shoreham — and that the truth included all of these tales and eliminated none.

I would very much have liked a similar gathering of CB's four sons, but instead, as they seem to lead very distinct lives, I met them separately in the summer of 1985 to ask them about their father. I spoke with the youngest first. Harvey Bruce was born in 1950, thirteen years after the last boy, Andrew. When Harvey was small his parents were in their early fifties, and he says now, "I was kind of remote to them" and that he was probably too young for much conversation. He recalls that his mother handled the day-to-day matters around the household and that CB would, about serious issues, speak his mind and then depart. But a strong sense of what it meant to be sensible was imparted in such monologues by CB, and despite their difference in age, the father was sympathetic to some of the son's youthful interests. He co-signed a bank loan for $800.00 so that Harvey could purchase a motorcycle at eighteen, and notwithstanding his apparent dislike of contemporary music, CB did not object to his teenager having a record amplifier in the house. The music connection is notable because the only such sounds CB could get worked up about, according to Harvey, were some Burl Ives sea shanties, and there was a rather "terrible opinion of music" gained from living in the house on Farnham Avenue; yet now Harvey says that he likes blues music that gives him some of the same feeling that he is sure CB worked with when writing and those blues singers "who can make you see back through their whole life — like my father." Harvey has been to Port Shoreham three times, but not since he was fifteen or sixteen. He remembers his grandmother helped to haul wood into the farmhouse when she was in her nineties, and although his father "didn't talk about roots or relatives much," Harvey does say that he feels close to the North Shore and wants to learn more about his heritage.

Andrew Bruce, born in 1937, remembers Port Shoreham very well — the big bedroom on the southwest corner of the farmhouse where Sarah slept; when he picked raspberries with his father in the summer of 1948 and the cow ate half their crop from their aluminum container; his time playing with Carl Mac-Intosh, the son of CB's closest friend. Like Harvey, Andrew cites the combination of discipline and flexibility in his father's outlook: punctuality was important, but there was also the sailboat that brother Harry got while in his teens. While Harvey insists that he did not become aware of his father's reputation as a writer until after his death, Andrew knew something of his father's stature because of the visits of other writers to Farnham Avenue, for example, Scott Young and Thomas Raddall. CB published his last imaginative work when Harvey was nine, but Andrew, who was a teenager during CB's creative heyday, emphasizes (like his older brothers, Alan and Harry) that his father did not talk within the family about his writing and that there was never much ceremony when a book was published.

Alan Bruce was born in 1931, the only Bruce boy who is a native Nova Scotian. He is today both straightforward and reticent about his father, describing him as "a man of immense character and sensitivity, often unable to communicate that to members of his family." The reticence stems from the emotional distance between father and son that Alan suggests was due to a mutual diffidence when it came to the revealing of one's feelings. But, Alan feels the possible result on CB's part was a refinement of feeling that "came out in excellent writing." Echoing Harvey and Andrew's impression, Alan states that "within the perimeter of his own moral standards [CB] was extremely liberal." His admiration for his father is seen especially when he talks of "the strength of his character" that allowed CB to beat a heavy drinking problem after the Second World War and that did not include proselytization on the subject of alcohol.

Visits to Port Shoreham were extremely important in Alan's boyhood. He first went to the North Shore in 1943, and CB's inspiration for, as well as some of the substance of, *The Flowing Summer* (1947), the poetic narrative of a boy's journey to his father's Nova Scotia home, is based upon Alan's time there. At least one piece of "hearsay history" stuck in Alan's mind from those 1940s sojourns — the fable of Will Bruce's cronies sneaking into the barn at night and twisting the pig's tail, providing Will with an excuse to leave the house "for a snort" away from Sarah's disapproving eye. When Alan was twenty-two *The Channel Shore* was published, but although CB had been preoccupied with this novel, in various forms, for almost eight years, Alan insists that no one in the family had much idea at all what the book was about until it appeared in print. He adds an important note about his father's literary reputation: when Alan was in secondary school in the 1940s there was virtually no awareness of Canadian writers among the students — Charles Bruce may have come second in the Governor-General's Awards for 1945, but he was unknown at Oakwood High.

Like his father, Harry Bruce is a newspaperman and a writer. Certainly he seems to be the son most affected by CB's love of words and the roots of Port Shoreham. Harry is his father's literary executor, knows CB's poetry and fiction like he knows the beach below the Bruce farm, has written about his relationship with his father and, above all, the sense of heritage that has been passed on; Harry is most forthcoming about the man for whom he now feels he is the "ambassador."

Like his three brothers, Harry remembers his father's standards of proper behaviour, especially when it came to obligations owed by members of the family to one another. In particular, there was the train trip CB and Harry took down to Mount Allison University in New Brunswick in May of 1952. CB was to receive an honorary doctorate, and Harry was visiting the campus that he would be attending that fall. The train was due to leave early in the morning from Toronto, and when Harry stayed out very late with his girlfriend (whom he later married),

CB was furious, so furious that he refused to speak to Harry for the entire two days of the train ride. It was an example of what Harry today refers to as the "devastating overkill" that CB applied from time to time to emotional situations. The entire episode is recounted, along with other stories of this father-son relationship, in Harry's essay "Movin' East," which appears in his book of the same title published in 1985. The other side of CB can perhaps be found in his going with Harry to advise him when he bought the sailboat he wanted so much in his teens and in his insistence that Harry should have stayed at school in order to appear in a team photo rather than have kept the eye examination appointment set up by his mother weeks before.

All the Bruce sons stress the books that were available in the Farnham Avenue house and how they were encouraged by their mother and father to read. Harvey recalls certain differences between his parents as to subject matter, but Harry insists there were no restrictions and that the main emphasis when he was young was on classics and poetry. With regards to CB's own work, Harry did read *The Flowing Summer* when it came out in 1947 and *The Channel Shore* after it almost won the Governor-General's Award for 1954, but he certainly did not see the many short stories of the 1940s and 1950s at the time they were written. CB did not blow his creative horn around the house. Only much later in life, when he was trying to complete his last work of fiction, *The Drift of Light*, did CB talk to Harry about writing. There was not much exchange about craft or technique, but CB was disturbed at the "confessional nature" of Harry's first book, *The Short Happy Walks of Max MacPherson*, especially its occasional use of raw language and references to drinking and hangovers. CB's advice to others about literature could be fairly conservative, and Harry tells of how his father was concerned that the bookmobile that came to Guysborough might carry novels by John Updike or Philip Roth of which his older sisters might disapprove, *Portnoy's Complaint*,* for example.

* However, Harry Bruce has told me that CB "found much of *Portnoy's Complaint* hilarious" and that he was aware of "a young fellow named Richler who was writing some fascinating fiction in *The Montrealer* ... long before Mordecai Richler had made any kind of name for himself."

If there was not much to broadcast at school about a father as Canadian author, there was in 1944-45 CB as war correspondent and public figure. When CB was overseas, Harry's class war poster drawing, which would normally have contained three figures representing the three branches of the armed services, had a fourth figure wearing a fedora and glasses. As for his work at the Canadian Press, Harry says that his mother told him there was a time CB would have wanted to survive as a magazine freelancer, but could not because "there were not enough magazines in those days"; Harry adds, however, that it was more likely his father felt a responsibility to his family.

Harry Bruce now divides his time between Halifax and the Bruce property, where the farmhouse still stands and a cottage has been built on a bluff above the bay. If he is a writer in some part due to his father's influence, then his return to Nova Scotia and to Port Shoreham and his obvious love for the people and country of the North Shore are due almost entirely to the sense of roots he has gained from CB's prose and poetry and from the experience CB allowed him at Port Shoreham when he was a boy. Harry first went to the Bruce farm in the summer of 1946 for a two-month visit. His aunt Zoe's children were there for part of the time, and then Harry became good friends with the MacIntosh boys who lived next door. He taught them baseball, and they showed him the woods and the beach. Once he and another boy stole out on the bay in a "borrowed" rowboat and grandmother Sarah almost sent Harry packing back to Toronto.

In his award-winning radio play for voices, *Words From An Ambassador of Dreams* (first presented on CBC Radio in 1976), a moving paean to his father's vision of the North Shore and a strong poetic statement of his own commitment to the heritage he has been handed by all his Nova Scotia ancestors, Harry writes of the magic summer when he turned twelve:

> A billion round beachstones curved three miles to the Head [Ragged Head] in this same flawless arc and, every night of my humming life, I saw the twinkle of the Queensport Light. The mornings were always as clean as the inside of this sand-scoured clam shell, and the soles of my city-soft feet toughened till I could run shoeless on these same stones, and ran like a crazy young dog under the turning gulls, and over the happy clams, and around

the sinister jellyfish, the sun-crisped cowflaps, the venerable boat sheds, the lobster pots, the old men of the sea, the dry bones of the fish, the tar, the marline, the cork, these same sea-stunted spruce, this same roily little tide gut, and all along this same cold and ceaseless Atlantic. In the summer of '46, I was the ambassador of my father's dreams.

In the play, Harry's son Alec has just asked his father, while they are standing together on the beach at Port Shoreham, what it was like when he was a kid. Harry's response is to let Alec know that past and present are bound up in the beach experience, and the future as well, since Harry's own son, it seems, will not lose the sense of heritage and will pass it on one day. The play is filled with passages of CB speaking his own poems and lines from his fictions and essays; there are, too, poems by Alec and his sister Annabel about the continuities of life. In this work, Harry Bruce has created that balance of yesterday, today, and tomorrow that his father envisaged at the heart of existence.

In 1969 Harry knew that he wanted to buy some land in Nova Scotia, but he was not thinking of the Bruce property. It was CB who reminded him of "Bruce's Island," which was actually the ten-acre peninsula of forest that ended in the half-mile long beach Harry knew so well, and who suggested that they "could work something out with Bess" (who inherited the farm after Sarah's death). The result was that in 1970 Harry bought the peninsula "for next to nothing" and built his cottage there. CB never saw the cottage, and he died some eleven or twelve years before Harry finally bought the entire farm from Bess. But somewhere in "heaven's hot July," CB, Will, and the other Bruces must be pleased that their dreams continue in their "ceaseless cadence, deep and slow./Tomorrow. Now. And years and years ago."

Nowhere is CB's reticence about his creative writing more evident than in his relationship with his wife, Agnes. When they met in Halifax in 1927, CB had already published his first book of poems, *Wild Apples*, and was writing lyrics for his second, *Tomorrow's Tide*, which would appear in 1932. When I interviewed Agnes Bruce in May of 1984 she did not mention any personal experience of these early poems, nor of those that appeared during the 1930s after she and CB were married and had moved to Toronto, including even major works, such as "Fisherman's Son" and "Words Are Never Enough," even though they focussed very strongly on Port Shoreham heritage. If Agnes realized that CB was involved with a more substantial and sustained piece of writing during the early 1940s, she had no idea that he was struggling with an autobiographical novel, *Currie Head* (335 manuscript pages), that would never see the light of day. When CB wrote at home over an eight-year period (1946-1954) in his efforts to produce *The Channel Shore*, Agnes thought but could not be sure that he was writing prose fiction. There was no one close, it seems, in whom CB confided his thoughts and feelings about his art, nor anyone to whom he seems to have read draft passages or stanzas. The extraordinary outpouring of poems and short stories between 1946 and the early 1950s apparently became visible to the family only after publication.

CB was obviously an intensely private artist who rarely, if ever, spoke about the impact of Port Shoreham experience in his life. Agnes was completely unaware of her husband's investigations, while he was in Toronto during the 1930s, of the possibility of finding work on a Maritime newspaper; a very important part of CB wanted to return to his home territory, or close to it — more than a few poems from this time suggest the sense of loss and yearning — but a drop in salary dictated against such a move; any split between the practical and creative sides of Charles Bruce was kept well-hidden. What Agnes does remember is CB's indifference to the social gatherings for writers held at the home of Macmillan publisher John Gray. He and Agnes would attend because Gray and CB were good friends, but most often CB would gravitate towards one person rather than stay in the crowd. If there were another Maritime writer present, CB did like to talk shop. This usually meant trading knowledge about history and traditions and swapping local stories.

According to Thomas Raddall, for CB writing was not something you sat and talked about, but something you had to do. Raddall first heard about CB from Andrew Merkel, poet and newspaperman for Canadian Press, in the fall of 1944 when the war correspondent from Port Shoreham was reported missing on a bombing flight over Holland. Merkel, Raddall, "a woman poet from British Columbia," and two others drove down to a pier in Halifax, and there, apparently, Merkel looked eastward across the Atlantic and intoned some verses from "Grey Ship Moving," CB's poem about a ship convoy to England. CB must have sent a copy of this poem to Merkel, though Raddall may have misremembered the Bruce "memorial" ceremony, as the first manuscript sent by CB to a publisher while he was in London in late 1944 did not contain the long narrative effort that would a few months later become the title poem of his third collection. When Raddall subsequently read this collection and other poems by CB, he was "struck first and last with the way he could describe man or place in his own home bailiwick...a worn oar or picture of a man using an oar."

The two writers were drawn to one another by their shared dislike of Toronto, their lack of connection with other authors, and by the attitude that existed at McClelland and Stewart, Raddall's publishers, that Raddall "would run dry in the little town [of Liverpool] on the South Shore of Nova Scotia." They were both amused and annoyed that the captions beneath the prints of the famous Nova Scotia photographer Wallace Mac-Askill appeared to have been written, as Raddall said, "by one of the lady poets who came out of the Halifax woodwork at the slightest smell of tea and buns" (in 1951 Raddall wrote a foreword for a book of MacAskill photos and let lines from three Bruce poems serve as commentary for several pictures). Most of all, the two writers were connected by their shared interest in Nova Scotian history — the loyalist contribution, the habits and hardships of coastal living in the 18th and 19th centuries, the facts that could contribute, if thoroughly researched, to fiction — and their mutual awareness that the rural life they each knew in their time reflected a heritage of at least two hundred years.

Between 1948 and 1970 CB and Raddall kept up a correspondence that the latter said was "rather like a pasture fence in February, a lot of empty space and a post sticking up here and there." But the "posts" were important to CB as he wrote to Raddall about his visits to Port Shoreham, his family history, his conversations with local farmers and fishermen, and asked Raddall about fishing boats, timber cruising, impressment, and many other questions, the answers to which he used in both *The Channel Shore* and *The Township of Time*. Raddall, who emphasizes CB's "absolute integrity of character" and his stories that "rang the true bell" because CB worked from actual people and events, dedicated his own collection of stories about Nova Scotia, *A Muster of Arms*, to him in 1954. Perhaps the greatest praise of one writer to another was stated by Raddall in simple terms when he responded to CB's poem "Nova Scotia Fish Hut" in 1949: he told CB that he had stood in a similar hut "yesterday or last week; but I hadn't the gift to etch the thing in words like these."

The difficulties CB had in reconciling his professional career at Canadian Press with his career as a writer of poetry and fiction are perhaps most clearly revealed in his story of Stan Currie in *Currie Head*. Stan is born and raised in a farming fishing community very much like Port Shoreham; his father, Hugh, is very much based on Will Bruce, and the relationship between fictional father and son never wanders very far from that of CB and Will. Like CB, Stan attends a New Brunswick college and then goes on to journalism in Toronto. Throughout the rat-race years dominated by his job, Stan yearns for Nova Scotia, but the significant difference between him and CB is that Stan is not a creative writer who can come to terms with lost time and place through his artistic expression. Stan eventually does return to his coastal farm home and, with his wife, attempts to raise his family there. Since CB did not do this he wrote about it instead; or perhaps because he could write about it he did not ever reach the point, like Stan, where he had to quit the daily grind and go back to a slower and more deeply-rooted existence. In either case (and they are not mutually exclusive) CB was not prepared to write about writing as a substitute for, or experience equal to, living.

Shortly before his death in 1971, CB completed the first draft of a manuscript about a journalist-writer who cannot go home again, and who tries to put down on paper what he remembers of his rural Nova Scotia boyhood. This man, Chris Harris, also attends a small New Brunswick college in his youth, and his writing there for the school newspaper is sometimes lifted verbatim from CB's own articles for Mount Allison's *The Argosy*. However, the focus of Chris's attempts to go home through fiction is never on the details of his own family life and heritage, but rather on another family down the Devon Shore (significantly different from the north shore of Chedabucto Bay and Currie Head). CB finally did try to deal with the problem of writing about what he could never live again and with the gap between what he wrote for a living and what he wrote as an artist, but the result was unsatisfactory. By allowing himself to consider what it meant for a man to distance himself from his boyhood experience precisely in order to articulate the depth and meaning of that experience, CB was coming dangerously close to what he referred to in *The Channel Shore* as "an intimate strangeness … recognition that was a kind of pain," the creative dilemma at the heart of his being. So he backed off and did not have Chris Harris work for a national news agency or write about anything that had to do with Will Bruce or Port Shoreham.

Gillis Purcell and Jack Brayley, both of whom worked closely with CB over the years at Canadian Press, remain somewhat in awe of the writing he did at the agency because, as Purcell says, "his poetry put another dimension" in the work beneath CB's byline. Although CB's colleagues at Canadian Press knew that he was a poet and fiction writer of national prominence, they knew so because of what they had read in the papers about his books and perhaps through their reading of the books themselves. CB never gave any indication of his creative efforts at the office, and when he took Purcell and Brayley down to Port Shoreham for some fishing and relaxation, he never spoke of the influence of place. But it was always evident that he was happiest "down home," and the two newspapermen, who were not given to writing poems or stories, recognized the source of artistic inspiration when they saw it.

I met with Harold MacIntosh and Wilbur Cummings, CB's two boyhood friends, on successive days in August of 1985. Harold

lives across the road from the farm that was his father's when
he was a boy, and that he inherited and then passed on to his
sons. Wilbur still lives in the farmhouse where he grew up on
the other side of the MacIntosh place from the Bruce property.
Wilbur has no children and so wonders what will happen to his
land; both he and Harold are aware that none of the young
people are interested in farming anymore — and who can blame
them as the local markets no longer need the oats, buckwheat,
and vegetables that brought in money in previous days. The two
fishing plants in Queensport across the bay, have not been in
operation since World War Two, and so there are no daily fishing smacks to pick up the herring, cod, and haddock, or even
the salmon and lobster that Harold's father and others once
caught. Harold has few illusions about the future of Port
Shoreham, and he is somewhat amused at the irony that all the
farmland last cultivated in a major way by his generation will
"go back to bush," the way it was when his ancestors and
Wilbur's and Charlie's first arrived two hundred years ago.

Both Harold and Wilbur remember vividly the Picnic Day
held in early July on the beach below the Bruce, MacIntosh, and
Cummings farms (the road down to the water runs right by
Wilbur's door) and which plays such a prominent part in *The
Channel Shore*. They remember the twelve-foot tables, the two
big spruce trees with swings between them, clam digging and
baking, sailing and rowing boats, and the enormous quantity of
cakes, pies, and biscuits. Roughly one hundred people would
turn up, the men giving up an afternoon on the farm, and not
only from the immediate neighbourhood. Harold says that this
traditional community get-together died out when he was in his
early twenties (in the 1920s), but Wilbur insists that Picnic Days
were held right up until the late 1940s when they ended because
there were "more things going on" both inside and outside Port
Shoreham. CB, who was a stickler for historical accuracy, sup-
ports Wilbur here, as the climax of his novel occurs at what he
calls "The Holiday" on the beach in 1946 (though his memory,
filtered through fiction, has the date as the second Saturday in
August).

Historical accuracy and fictional convenience (or is it merely subjective response to experience?) also seem to diverge over the question of religious and social differences between the Methodists and Catholics of the Port Shoreham area in the years after World War One. Harold and Wilbur assert that although the predominantly Catholic community five miles down the road at St. Francis Harbour was distinct in ways from its Protestant counterpart at Port Shoreham and Manchester (closer to the head of the bay), there were no real obstacles to interaction or even, except very occasionally, to intermarriage. In *The Channel Shore*, CB has his Protestants and Catholics live side by side at Currie Head, and much of the novel's plot turns around the religious gap between the Marshall and Gordon families in the summer and fall of 1919. Clayton Hart, who was twelve years younger than CB, and who has lived for years on the old Tory farm property that once belonged to CB's maternal grandfather, Robert Tory, says that if "intermarriage was frowned on a little," the trade of fish and produce and the 'box socials' and bean suppers in various houses up and down the road did a lot to break down any religious barriers. Clayton also emphasizes the importance of the local pulpwood industry that CB makes part of the world of his novel and that up until the late 1940s at least allowed for some economic self-sufficiency beyond that provided by farming and fishing at Port Shoreham.

The tremendous bond that existed between Harold MacIntosh and CB is evident in the quiet though remarkably detailed way in which Harold speaks of the boyhood chum who went on to lead such a different life, but who had "never changed one bit" when he came back from Toronto for short visits. Once when Harold was a sick boy in bed, CB dropped by with some apples and recited "a little rhyme" to make his friend laugh and feel better. There was their earlier experience together when they tried to build a small, square-sterned, flat-bottomed boat with slabs from the local mill and then launch it in the nearby river. "We pushed it out," says Harold, "and water kept coming in, so we stepped in anyway and sat down in water up to our waists." It was only later that they learned how to caulk with paint and rags. More than anything else for Harold, despite

CB's learning and experience in the wide world, Port Shoreham "was home to him," and everyone in the community knew him as "Charlie." Wilbur Cummings, who was CB's second cousin, emphasizes how "easy it was to pick up with him," sometimes after years of separation. That CB was a Port Shoreham boy through and through is revealed for Wilbur in his memory of CB telling him that he (Wilbur) "did get somewhere working in the open air" all his life while CB himself "was in a stuffy office."

Wilbur Cummings showed me a photograph of himself and CB at about age six (both were born in the same year) and taken in the winter time — two farm boys in the snow who bear no resemblance to their older selves. In the photo Wilbur is wearing a little sheepswool jacket hand-made by his mother. In *The Channel Shore*, young Alan Marshall is searching for his heritage and for that of his community by rummaging through items in his grandfather's loft: "His hands roved and probed as his eyes explored....A jumble of worn objects...linked with some aspect of life on the Channel Shore." Through these things Alan has a strong sense of "knowing the past" and of the old in a curious way being new again. When Wilbur Cummings brought out the sheepswool jacket and placed it in my hands, I understood, for a moment more forcefully than ever before, the flow between now and then, reality and fiction.

I

Heritage

One thing seems certain: James Bruce — Charles Bruce's great-great grandfather — was "killed by the fall of a tree"[1] while chopping wood for a log schoolhouse above the shores of Chedabucto Bay in the last week of March 1805. Charles Bruce did not discover this until the summer of 1946 when he chatted with his second-cousin-once-removed, Sandy Bruce, in a general store in Boylston, about four miles from his birthplace and family home in Port Shoreham, Guysborough County. Sandy told CB about the falling tree and also that James was "in the *old* burying ground, in Lipsett's pasture."[2] In a letter to the Guysborough historian Dr. A.C. Jost, CB wrote that there were no stones to mark the twenty or thirty graves that "look like cradle hills." What was odd, he said, about James's grave "was that it had been there all the time I was growing up, within sight of the road, and not a mile from home, and I had never known about it."[3] But if CB had found out about his ancestor's death and final resting place, James Bruce's origins are obscured by "a mist of time."[4]

The Chedabucto Bay region at the eastern tip of mainland Nova Scotia had been visited by Norsemen in the eleventh century, but had been occupied for countless years before that by Micmac Indians.[5] This tribe, whose territory included all of Nova Scotia, Prince Edward Island, and the coast of New Brunswick, numbered around 3500 people at the time of the first French explorations at the beginning of the 17th century. Chedabucto is a French corruption of the Micmac word that means "running far back," a reference to the twenty-mile-long bay, and the original name of the settlement that later became the town of Guysborough. In 1654, The Company of New France gave to one Nicholas Denys the region of lands and coasts around the Bay, and the Denys group, along with other French factions, traded prosperously in fish and fur with the Indians, feuding with each other, but holding the territory until the Treaty of Utrecht with the English in 1713. Seven years later, the first permanent English garrison was established at Canso at the southeastern corner of the bay mouth; however, Canso changed hands several times during the next quarter of a century as the French did not want to give up the lucrative economic ground nor allow an English presence so close to their fortress at Louisburg. After the expulsion of the Acadians from Nova Scotia,* (territory that included present-day New Brunswick), and then the victory of the British in North America in 1763, a number of Acadian families sought refuge in the bay area; but by 1771 nearly all these people had joined their compatriots in Cape Breton or in southwestern Nova Scotia.

British settlement had been hindered, meanwhile, by a decree of the Lords of Trade in London that allowed for no land grants without the territory first being surveyed and certain areas reserved for the Crown. Year-round, non-military occupation by the English of the shores of Chedabucto Bay seems to date from 1768 and to have been undertaken by Captain Joseph Hadley and his family; tradition has it that Hadley received a land grant for having commanded a transport ship against Louisburg in 1745. Nine other families (from Liverpool and Pictou) soon took up permanent residence near the Hadleys at Milford Haven, at the head of the bay. Others showed their interest, especially as the American Revolution took shape and then resulted in victory for the colonists. In 1765 the Commissioner of Customs in Boston, Benjamin Hallowell, asked and received for services rendered 20,000 acres along the north shore of the bay, not far from the Hadley settlement. Nothing was done with this sizeable plot until after the Revolution when, as adjacent sections of land began to fill up with loyalist troops and families, further immigration was expected. A town (Boylston)[6] was laid out in

* Between 1755 and 1763 "some 10,000 men, women, and children were deported .... In 1764 Acadians were once more granted the right to own land in Nova Scotia" (*The Canadian Encyclopedia*, p. 5).

sixty lots, and the remainder of the Hallowell grant was sub-divided into farms of 150 acres each.

The earliest loyalists had arrived at Annapolis in October of 1782 with agents who had detailed instructions from Sir Guy Carleton (Commander of British Forces in America) to explore Nova Scotia with a view to further settlement.[7] The peace treaty between Britain and the new United States was signed in April 1783, and in July of that year the British Parliament appointed a commission to classify the services and losses of those loyal to the Crown during the Revolution. The civilian loyalists, quite a number of whom received compensation that provided them with a measure of independence, came in their largest numbers to Shelburne in the fall of 1783 and, at the same time, to Halifax from where they then spread out along the Eastern Shore and up the roads to Windsor and Truro. This wave of immigrants also settled in Antigonish and Pictou and in Annapolis and Kings counties. Altogether there would be over 14,000 civilians, 4,000 soldiers, and almost 1,000 negro settlers in the province as a result of the loyalist migration.

However, it was not until March of 1783 that the various provincial regiments appealed to Carleton for land and for help in removing themselves from the former American colonies. Carleton promised them six months pay and at least one year's provisions and clothing. By the time these troops and their families began to arrive in Nova Scotia in the winter of 1783-84 " ... earlier immigrants had settled on the more arable and accessible land [and] other choice areas were held by those with influence What remained were such empty areas as ... Guysborough."[8] So it was that "The development of the Guysborough area seemed like an afterthought, resulting from the need for an empty area in which to place disbanded soldiers and loyalists arriving late .... "[9]

The great majority of those immigrants who came to the Chedabucto Bay region were from the remnants of the provincial regiments. There were a considerable number of Carolina troops, some of whom came via St. Augustine, Florida (48 heads of families were granted land), and others by way of Jamaica and New York (the Duke of Cumberland Regiment or Montague

Corps — 149 men, 9 women, 5 children who had spent the winter in the woods outside Halifax under very trying conditions). Those who had formed themselves into the Associated Departments of the Army and Navy included some of the British Legion and the 71st Scots Regiment, along with the Commissary Departments from New York. There was also a group from the 60th Regiment (76 men, 34 women, 19 children) "which was known most closely to resemble a foreign legion."[10] Over 1,000 persons (almost a third of whom were black) had arrived at the head of the bay by the end of the summer in 1784:

> The growing community at Chedabucto, initially christened New Manchester, had a total number of 1050 entitled to provisions. Since few of the Duke of Cumberland's Regiment remained on their holdings and the men of the 60th soon concentrated on securing their livelihood from the sea, the members of the Civil [Associated] Department became the most influential group in the town, to such an extent that the name Manchester gave way in time to that of Guysborough, after their chief patron.[11]

In the territory east of Halifax, none of the population (a total of about 2,000) was more isolated from the main centre of military strength and cultural and social life than those at the furthest end of the province. Existence was difficult even before 1787 when the supply of provisions ceased:

> The loyalist attempt at farming was not very successful. As they cleared their lands, their emphasis was less on an instant cash crop than on the necessity to feed themselves. Unfortunately, few went beyond this initial stage, and many failed to reach it. Moreover, had the land been excellent and the loyalists skilled farmers, there would still have been the major problem of lack of roads to transport their surpluses to markets. But little of the land upon which the loyalists were placed was excellent and many of them were not skilled farmers.[12]

By 1789 there was a condition of serious famine throughout British North America, and assistance had to be provided by the government to relieve the many who were below the level of self-subsistence. Before this, however, a considerable number of loyalists had begun to leave Nova Scotia where, in their opinion, "One could survive ... but one could hardly live ...."[13] By 1786 almost 2,000 loyalists had quit the province, many of them returning to the United States; well over a hundred settlers had abandoned their grants in the Chedabucto region by June of 1785.

For those who stayed by the shores of the bay, the sea supplemented their incomes. Opinions differ as to the degree. In 1821 John Morrow, Secretary of the Guysborough Agricultural Society, described the original settlers of Chedabucto Bay as having neglected their farms in favour of the fishery, especially for the mackerel that "abounded in measure." Even when the supplies of mackerel were depleted, said Morrow, the people turned to farming "only with the attention of eking out a maintenance while the chief dependence still rested on the fishery."[14] A.C. Jost writes: "Nature had most profusely lavished its wealth in the seas ... and this was being eagerly sought after at the time when our first authentic records of the district begin."[15] However, Neil Mackinnon insists that "The fisheries ... were not necessarily a source of affluence or even comfort for the average fishing community."[16] Whatever the case, by the time CB was born in 1906 there were hardly any mackerel left in the bay, and only those farmer-fishermen whose property fronted the sea left the tilling of the land and other, vital farm-work on a regular basis for the gleam of "Fat herring tangled in wet-twine ... silver-thick."[17]

James Bruce did not arrive with any of the loyalist regiments, though Thomas Raddall mentions a Major Robert Bruce whose five-acre lot in Guysborough town "was never registered, and who apparently didn't stay long." There was also "a private or NCO named George Bruce [who] had a 100-acre grant in Manchester Township, and in 1790 acquired two town lots in Guysborough itself."[18] Raddall speculates that George was CB's ancestor, as does, indirectly, A.C. Jost, who says in reference to George's name on the land grant roll for the Duke of Cumberland Regiment: "This may be a mistake in the roll, or he may have gone by the name of James Bruce."[19] CB did his own investigations in the Nova Scotia Archives and wrote to his son Harry, in 1970:

> Dr. Jost is in error .... tax-rolls of Manchester Township for 1791 show three Bruces in the area — Robert, George, and James. Whether or not they were related, it is impossible to say. Later rolls show only the name of *James*: it is likely that Robert and George moved away. James Bruce was buying bits of land in the Intervale in the early 1790s. In 1795 he bought 150 acres in Manchester, of Hallowell Grant land.[20]

CB knew this about James as early as 1955, because he mentions the 1791 tax-roll and the disappearance of Robert and George in his "The Township of Time" article. However, in 1951 he had written to A. C. Jost, telling him that James and George were two different people, but that James had not come out to Nova Scotia until 1799.[21] He had also said the same thing to Thomas Raddall the year before.[22]

CB felt that James was very probably a victim of the infamous Highland Clearances in which Scots lairds removed their tenants from their land so that sheep might safely graze and bring in lucrative profits.* In a long narrative poem, "The Standing Woods," written in the late 1940s or early 1950s, CB describes his great-great grandfather's circumstance:

> And still more Scotsmen: crofters from the west,
> Stripped of their holdings by the cautious lairds —
> Their dun fields on the hills above the Clyde.
>
> (The cautious lairds, careful and practical,
> Viewing the textile trade and knowing wool
> A far more likely crop than men and women) ... [23]

CB emphasizes in this poem that there is no way of knowing exactly where James Bruce came from; Bruce was (is) a common name in Scotland, and there were eighty parishes in Aberdeen County. The Guysborough Historical Society records have James Bruce marrying a Catherine Cadell in Aberdeen on January 30, 1798 and their son John born there. In "The Standing Woods," CB states that James and Catherine emigrated with young John "With kindred of their blood" to "that impersonal shore/Where sea curls on Nova Scotia's edge"; however, in his

---

* MacKinnon mentions that Scots settlers were beginning to arrive in the province in the late 1780s and that their settlement "would be spread over decades" (MacKinnon, p.178).

1970 letter to Harry Bruce, CB agrees with the date of James and Catherine's marriage, but mentions that Catherine Cadell was perhaps related to one Richard Morris, a land surveyor who worked in the Manchester district.

In 1809 Richard Morris conveyed a grant of land to his grandchildren, Richard, Christopher, John and Margaret Bruce. The exact relationship between Richard and Catherine is difficult to determine, especially given their different last names,[24] but the records of the Anglican Church in Guysborough for January 30, 1798 show "James Bruce, B [Bachelor] married Catherine Cadel [sic] S [Spinster]" in that church and on that day. This strongly suggests that the James Bruce who was on the 1791 tax-roll was CB's ancestor, that he met Catherine in Nova Scotia, and that their first son, John, was born there. The mists of time still swirl, however, because only two children have their births recorded in extant pages of the church record — Richard Samuel Bruce, born September 7, 1802, and Margaret Jane Bruce, born November 5, 1804. The Guysborough Historical Society has Christopher's birth occurring in 1800, though CB insisted it was in 1801; there is no record of John's birthdate.

In his poem about the Bruce family, from James down to himself, CB writes about certainties *and* their absence:

> Thus James began to sow his living here,
> In rugged ground, clearing the rough fields
> And planting. For six hard-driving years
> His hands were busy with the flashing axe.
>
> What common dreams were his of larger living
> Beyond the simplest needs of night and day
> We have no way of knowing. The act is bare.
>
> There is no way of knowing. We only know
> He joined his neighbours in the standing woods
> And chopped; and died beneath a crashing tree.[25]

The Anglican Record Book states that James was buried on March 28, 1805, having been "killed by the fall of a tree." Sandy Bruce, in his 1946 conversation with CB, is more specific, insisting that James died "at a chopping party, cutting stuff for a log schoolhouse."[26] One wonders just how Sandy knew this, but if it is true then it is fitting, because CB's first Guysborough ancestor died in the service of the community, a real-life example of the integral place of the individual in the township of time that CB created in his fiction. Mrs. Hazel Oliver of Port Hastings, Nova Scotia, a descendant of Christopher Bruce, attempts to shed more light on the Morris connection; she states that her grandmother told her that James's age when the tree caught him was forty and that his widow went to Halifax, leaving the children "with a Mr. Morris where they were brought up." There Catherine remarried — a Mr. Kilfyle — and later resettled on the land where she and James had lived in Middle Manchester. According to Mrs. Oliver, Catherine and Mr. Kilfyle died on the same day in Guysborough town, and it was supposed "they had been poisoned by the ones who had been looking after them" for money.[27] The conjecture here is obvious, but has very much to do with the genesis of much of CB's fiction, the building upon stories handed down orally through the years, what he was to call "hearsay history."

CB's mother was Sarah Jane Tory (born 1867), and her great-grandfather, James Torey [sic], arrived in Guysborough with the Associated Departments of the Army and Navy in 1784. He is recorded as taking up a grant of 70 acres fronting on the harbour;[28] James Torey's first wife, Christine Kirke, bore him six children and died in 1807. He remarried, but there were no offspring. It is difficult to trace in detail CB's maternal ancestors down to his mother, partly because CB's great interest in his family lay with the Bruce side.* It is known, however, that James's son Henry (born 1794) was CB's great-grandfather and that Henry's son, Robert Kirk Tory (born 1838) married Honora Ferguson. One of their children was Sarah Jane.[29] According to CB's sisters, Honora Tory was "a great reader," and it is recalled that when she was over ninety she asked to have a good dictionary in the house.[30] One of CB's sisters, Anna Bruce (now Mrs. Anna MacKeen), remembers reading to her grandmother Tory and spending a great deal of time with her in Guysborough after

---

* Some may say this was a result of conventional gender bias, but it certainly had to do with CB's extraordinarily strong attachment to and memory of his father, Will Bruce.

grade seven. The Torys were not a prominent family in Guys-borough until Sarah's brother James Cranwick moved up through the ranks of the Sun Life Insurance Company, became a member of the Nova Scotia Legislature (Liberal), and later Lieutenant-Governor of Nova Scotia, and Uncle Henry 'Marsh' Tory became "the principal founder of several universities ... and the National Research Council Laboratories."[31] Grandfather Tory (Robert Kirk) was a farmer on the Macpher-son Lake Road, just over a mile west of and inland from the Bruce farm above Ragged Head, the peninsula that curves out over a mile into Chedabucto Bay.

In "The Township of Time," CB writes of the heritage from his great-great grandparents in terms of "continuity":

> They left no writing, those pioneers. The wave of local history and hearsay and laughter rolls up from the memory of a man's grandparents, perhaps from a little beyond, but the waves behind roll through a mist of time .... So that, remembering tales heard in childhood, you pick it up about a hundred years ago. You see the beach and the country when the saddle-trail was being widened to a wagon road. You hear the music of the loom, the sound of your great-grandfather tapping in shoe-pegs on a lapstone, the rhyme of the spinning-wheel, the creak of labour-ing oars. You see, far off, the sails of the trading vessels, the whiskey-barrel at the cross-roads on election day, the bearded men and bonneted women on their way to church. Alive, vital, and full of hard independence.
>
> But back of that again, there is that misty wave. The grandfathers of your grandfathers .... And what you have is con-tinuity .... After looking at the tax-rolls ... and thinking of the names on the land, I had a consciousness that I was living in a township that exists not only in terms of road and hill and valley, church and farm and whaleboat; but one that has limits and boundaries in another dimension, forever opening out. A township in time.[32]

From what can be gathered, after James Bruce's demise in 1805 his sons John and Christopher "continued to occupy the 1795 land ... 150 acres of Hallowell Grant land about two miles northwest of where we are now."[33] Richard, CB's great-grand-father, acquired the present Bruce property sometime before his marriage in 1828, perhaps through the generosity of Richard Morris and his grant to his "grandchildren." The house at Port Shoreham (then Clam Harbour) was built by Richard in 1847. In 1954 CB wrote to Thomas Raddall that "the bark is still on the edges of some of the old birch beams Richard Bruce hewed out."[34] It began "as a plain square of a house, parlor, dining room (The Room), kitchen and bedroom downstairs, and four bedrooms up, each with the upper part of one wall slanted by the pitch of the roof." Later an ell (part of an abandoned schoolhouse) was added to the south side, housing a porch with an indoor well, a milk room, and a store room that led to the attic, which, CB wrote, was "a fabulous place cluttered with old hardware, magazines from the previous century, a trunk or two — the endless archives of living."[35]

CB's grandfather, Charles Joseph Bruce, "worked the growing farm,/Tended the barn, looked to the horse and cattle,/Planted and reaped and kept to the home beach."[36] CB remembers him "barely, as a wiry little old man with forked whiskers and a remarkable reputation for piety and ability in a blow."[37] The Bruce sisters recall their grandmother (Lydia McKeough Bruce — one of eight sisters)* as "a meticulous housekeeper" who let the children read books and who kept old magazines around the house. But the person from that generation who remained the most interesting to CB was his great-uncle, James Bruce, a master-mariner, who began his life at sea by building and launching a small trading schooner in the harbour at the foot of the Bruce farm, graduated to a brigantine, and then to a 150-ton brig called *The Commerce* in which he had a share and in which he disappeared with all hands while captaining a trip to Sierra Leone in 1867. This man appears as a very important minor figure in CB's fiction — as Rob Currie in *The Channel Shore*, in the short story "Reprieve" in *The Township of Time*, and in the unpublished novel *Currie Head*. In each work he passes on a heritage of romance and independence, a legend

---

* "At any rate, the eight McKeough girls all married, which helped the legend that we are related to nearly everyone in the country" (CB, "A Hill For Looking").

of the sea, to his descendants and other members of the Shore community. He is also part of "The Standing Woods":

> In the young James another impulse worked ...
> ....
> The foot of Richard's land dropped to a harbour
> Channeled behind a wooded spit of beach
> By the long action of the recurring tide.
> James had a vessel built and fitted there,
> And launched her at high water ...
> ....
> He knew the lore of water, bought a ship
> For Western Ocean work, and signed a crew
> From settlements along the quiet shore.
> What part of this was shrewd and careful trade
> And what part simple venture? No one knows.
>
> We only know the vessel weighed and sailed,
> And headed east, bound for Sierra Leone,
> And cleared the coast and vanished without trace.

CB's awareness of his heritage, his strong "sense of a relationship to past generations, a feeling of kinship of generations still to come"[38] developed slowly and at a largely unconscious level for many years of his life. He did not begin to write in earnest about the Chedabucto Bay region until he was in his mid-thirties, and he did not commit himself to the fictional Channel Shore community and an investigation of his personal roots in poetry and fiction for a few years after that. More than anything or anyone else, perhaps, as he came to realize, it was his father, Will Bruce, who took him back.

William Henry Bruce, the only son of Charles Joseph and Lydia, was born on October 30, 1863. Not much has been handed down about his boyhood, though CB in his unfinished autobiographical essay, "A Hill For Looking," states that Will did complete Grade IX ("practically a higher education for a boy in those days and circumstances"). In *Currie Head* CB describes the young Hugh Currie, whose character and experience were based very much on those of Will:

> At twenty ... he had been able to cut stave-junks, shave staves, bend hoops, measure barrel-heads, shingle a roof, replace a sill, or make a window-frame and glaze it. He could handle a two-

master, cut a sail, caulk a seam, clean and salt fish, knit and mend nets, and even make a spoked cartwheel, the trickiest job known to one-horse farming. He had known it all, cared for some of it, and had come to his highest proficiency just when the value of these skills was beginning to go out with a slowly turning tide.[39]

As has been said, only a number of family heads along the bay's north shore farmed *and* fished. When the mackerel were plentiful in the mid-19th century, Charles Joseph Bruce went to Groz Nez in Cape Breton and, for three summers in a row, caught 75 barrels of the prized fish that sold for $12-$14 a barrel. By the time Will was a young man "things changed. Big business got into fishing and everything else. The mackerel got scarcer and scarcer, and the steady supply from other fishing grounds cut into the income a man could make here." Still, in the spring there were herring, and in the fall haddock and cod (salmon were fished close to the head of the bay). This meant a man had to rise before daylight to tend the nets, clean the catch and salt it in half-barrels, and then spend the rest of the day on farm work. Of course the animals would have already been fed, but the fields had to be cleared of rocks with the aid of a stone-drag, worm and rail fences had to be repaired, there was chopping to be done for kindling and firewood, and community road-clearing to be done after winter storms. At haying time in late summer-early fall, the farmers worked until dark, except on Sundays when they "would have let the hay rot in the fields if it came to that."[40] Naturally, there were no vacations.

When Will was in his mid-twenties he left the North Shore because "The independence of simple living had died." He went to Massachusetts and worked as a carpenter in a Somerville desk factory. Although at that time "Maritimers and New Englanders moved back and forth as if there were no border,"[41] CB understates economic and possible psychological complexities in our first view of Will in "The Standing Woods," and emphasizes heritage:

> Until the call
> Of urgent blood, or restless enterprise
> While Charles was still a man of middle years,
> Awoke in Will the need to pack and go.

(Did one considered voice, in Aberdeen,
Give quiet counsel, eighty years before?)

Will married Sarah Tory in Massachusetts. According to their daughters, they had met years before in the schoolhouse almost halfway between their parents' farms. Bess Bruce was born in Somerville, Massachusetts in 1891, Anna there in 1893; Sarah came back home to have Carrie in 1895 and then returned to Somerville where Zoe was born in 1898. Meanwhile, Will left the desk factory and started up a grocery business with another man who then left for the Klondike gold rush in 1898. In a letter to Harry Bruce, CB states simply that Will "carried on alone" with the store "until things got too tough. Then he went back to the desk factory for a while" and shortly after returned to Nova Scotia.[42] In "The Standing Woods," however, there is an evocative poetic questioning about this period in Will's life that suggests a darker reality mingling with the buoyant sense of roots:

Were city streets too crowded, too intense,
Too shaken with a jostling and a clamour,
After the first flush of the Boston years?
Too fertile with the seeds of weariness,
Too distant from the lift of boyhood hills?

Or was it something else, an inner knowing
That this new venture was already old,
That fresh horizons beckoned here no more,
But opened from the purlieus of his birth?

Though well-remembered voices haunt us yet
These are the answers no one ever knows.

CB mentions to Harry that Will had business difficulties as "a hired boy had lifted $900 over a period of time."[43] A few months after this theft was discovered the grocery enterprise collapsed and Will was out of a job. Sarah was by this time (September 1900) on her home farm waiting for news and what money Will could spare. The Bruce sisters feel that Will's "health gave out" and this contributed to the decline of the store and prompted his return to the North Shore.

According to Anna (Bruce) MacKeen, Will did some carpentry work for some time, and because things were difficult Sarah went teaching "for a mere pittance in Port Shoreham and

Oyster Ponds," able to come home on weekends only.[44] In 1905 Will bought the farm from his father; even though he obviously would have paid a fair price for the family property, Will must have been a good carpenter and Sarah a teacher in demand so that money could be saved. As it was, Will did ask Sarah's brother James (the later lieutenant-governor) for a loan. James sent him a cheque for $68.00 made out to Charles Joseph, "lest Will be tempted to spend it for something else."[45] When CB was a boy helping his father pull up brush in the horse-pasture, Will told him the story of the cheque and said "absent-mindedly, 'I don't like him [James].'" It might have been when he first came back from Massachusetts that Will worked on the Tory farm at Belmont near Guysborough for 17 cents a day, but certainly at the age of forty-two he did not like being treated by James Tory as a spendthrift who could not be trusted. CB's memory of Will's dislike of James is transformed into the fiction of *Currie Head*. Here Stan Currie's father, Hugh, expresses his feelings for Stan's Uncle Steve in Will's words exactly, but with an expletive added. James must have rubbed Will somewhat raw, because those who remember Will speak only of him as "a quiet, beautiful neighbour" and a "very mild" man.[46]

Less than two years after the birth of their last daughter, William Henry Bruce was born to Will and Sarah, but died at 21 months. The only explanation of death comes from Sarah, who told CB's wife Agnes that the child had suffered fatal convulsions from eating cold cabbage.[47] When Charles Tory Bruce appeared on May 11, 1906, Sarah apparently proclaimed that "God had forgiven her," presumably for her carelessness with her first son.

In February 1901, Will Bruce and James C. Tory, along with thirty-two other men, signed a petition to the Nova Scotia House of Assembly "that the name of Clam Harbour in the County of Guysborough [be] changed to Port Shoreham."[48] This request was made by the area residents and granted by the government two months later because of the confusion caused by the existence of the better-known Clam Harbour in Halifax County. In 1967 CB provided a description of his home community that must certainly have been a fitting one when he was a boy: "Port Shoreham is not a village, but just a stretch of settled country." This "stretch" was about four miles from Boylston with (in the second decade of this century) its three general stores, blacksmith, and local councillor, and nine miles (by road) from the county seat at Guysborough. It was a close-knit community bound by a shared past, religion, and economic cooperation. James Bruce and Catherine Cadell had been married in the Anglican church, but at some point in the 19th century the Bruces became Methodists. The Port Shoreham families were all Protestants, many of whom attended service at one of the two local churches twice on Sundays. CB writes in "A Hill For Looking," "Generally speaking men were not active in church work, beyond going to church, looking after the grounds, etc. One or two would take part in the testimony — some, no doubt, as an example." But there could be no doubt where the male ministers stood: the best remembered for CB seems to have been George Fletcher Mitchell who had the Boylston circuit from 1912-15 and again from 1919-22. He was "hard-headed and stony-hearted" and is reported to have said, "They say I'm narrow; of course I'm narrow; Jesus Christ was narrow."[49]

Residents traded farm produce while growing a variety of crops for their own and their animals' consumption — oats, buckwheat, and hay. There were three cash pay-days a year: the spring and fall selling of cattle and lambs, and the end of the fishing season in the fall. While CB was growing up there were at least four fish huts on the beach below the farm — "ours; a bit to the west, Edmund MacIntosh's; then McMaster's, then Sandy Cummings'."[50] Smacks from the fishing plants in Queensport on the south shore would anchor offshore to gather and pay for the combined catch. The farmer-fishermen had rowboats stepped with a mast, called stemmers, and at least two men, including Will Bruce, had two-masted sailboats. The fish that they kept for themselves and their families would be salted down in half-barrels and stored for the winter in the cellar along with barrel-packed beef and pork and plenty of vegetables and preserves.

Port Shoreham was, in this era, still relatively isolated from the more settled areas of the province. The roads were dirt and gravel, and the main route from Boylston to Mulgrave, which ran right by the Bruce front door (no more than twenty yards away), was not paved until the early 1970s. Wilbur Cummings recalls that in 1918 it took his uncle five days to travel by car on the old roads from Lowell, Massachusetts to Port Shoreham. The main problem with road travel came after winter storms, but the solution contributed to the bonding of neighbours. Every male between 16 and 60 had to work five to six days a year on road upkeep, and in the winter the overseer appointed by the local council would call out the hand shovellers to open the roads for the mail and for local use. This effort could take two or three days, depending on the amount of snowfall, and there was no pay for the work. As Wilbur Cummings puts it, people were tough in those days and often went thirty miles, there and back, to a dance or other social occasion on winter nights.

While there was no electricity for the houses, telephones were available along the Boylston-Mulgrave road in 1916, but neighbours preferred to spend a considerable amount of time in one another's kitchens and, on more formal visits, in the parlors. Harold MacIntosh, CB's closest boyhood friend, who lived next door to the Bruce farm, paints a marvellous picture of his mother and Sarah Bruce walking back and forth between their respective gates unable to say 'good night' after an evening's visit. They finally parted half-way between the two houses. People also gathered at the post office on the other side of the Bruce farm from the MacIntosh's, and at the small store that operated out of a house nearby. The Picnic Day had been an annual event for as long as the oldest residents could remember and gave local residents the chance to socialize with those from further afield in Manchester district. However, the fairly closed geographical and social circle of CB's boyhood is emphasized by Harold MacIntosh's recollection that he and CB "once" walked all the way to Boylston, a distance of some four miles, to see some of Harold's cousins and what was in the old Attwater store there.

II

Boyhood

Because he was the only boy, and perhaps because he had not been expected by the 42-year-old Will and 39-year-old Sarah, CB was initially somewhat doted on by his parents, according to his sister Zoe. There are no reports as to what kind of a baby he was, but his sisters describe him learning the alphabet at a very young age from the letters stamped into the old WATERLOO woodburning range. Both Will and Sarah encouraged him to read, she influenced by her schoolteaching, and Will because he himself "read everything"[1] from the *Family Herald* to novels. Although the Bruce sisters recall their more religious mother taking certain books away from them as "not suitable" for young girls, it seems that CB was pretty much given the run of the literary world, at least as far as the books that were available in Port Shoreham were concerned. The mail-order catalogue was there as well to fire a boy's imagination with visions — even if they were only of air-rifles and similar items. CB was, according to Harold MacIntosh and Wilbur Cummings, a regular boy who could build leaky boats, nest apples and play lee-o with his schoolmates and fish for trout in MacPherson Lake back of the farm with shaved spruce poles and worms for bait; however, he was also slightly different because he was "always in the books." As Harold MacIntosh says, "He'd be studying and I'd be currying a horse." Two anecdotes about his other side, the creative side that was interested in words on the page and in the mind's eye, underline Harold MacIntosh's insistence that it was obvious CB was bound for a life other than farming and fishing on the North Shore.[2]

One day after school Harold dropped his books at his own house and then caught up with CB, who had walked down the road past his home gate. "Hi, where ya goin?" asked Harold. CB looked up, surprised, from his private musing. "Oh," he replied, "I was makin' a little poem and walked right by." At about the same time CB won a $1.00 prize for a limerick contest held by the Want Ads section of the Halifax *Evening Echo*. On Saturday, February 21, 1920 the following piece was published, revealing nothing about the future poet-novelist except a willingness to write:

> Farmer Johnson, he wanted a seeder,
> 'When spring comes,' he sez, 'I'll need her,'
> Through *The Echo* he bought it,
> He's glad that he got it.
> All farmers should follow their leader.

Wilbur Cummings says that except for the fact that the school-teacher was boarding that term in the Cummings home he would not have discovered his friend's talents. But the school-teacher, who read the *Echo* "cover to cover," told Wilbur about the limerick, and when Wilbur met CB on the way to school at the beginning of the week he said (with undoubtedly the same gleam in his eye that was there when he told me the story in 1985), "Good morning, Farmer Johnson!" CB, who was very shy, begged Wilbur not to tell the other children because they would only tease him. Wilbur insists that he made CB suffer for a while by telling him that it was too good a tale to keep secret and that he would have to think about CB's request. When they were almost at the school Wilbur told CB that he would not "squeal" if CB did all his hard sums for him throughout the term. For the next few months CB, who sat behind Wilbur in class, wrote down the correct figures on one side of the slate and Wilbur copied them on the other. "And that," says Wilbur, "is how I got my education." The story is a delight, but also significant because it reveals that the young CB liked to be published but did not like to talk about his writing, even at a young age.

CB's four older sisters left home well before he reached his teens — Bess and Anna, after attending Normal School in Truro for their teaching certificates, taught for a number of years in Nova Scotia before moving west, Bess to Edmonton and Anna, with her husband, to Saskatchewan. Carrie taught briefly, as did

Zoe, but both then worked as secretaries in North Sydney before moving, separately, to the United States.[3] It was while Zoe was in the office of shipping agents in North Sydney in 1919-20 that CB made her the sole subscriber (free of charge) to his "mostly-weekly newspaper," the *Shoreham Searchlight* . His lifelong involvement with journalism was launched with the following editorial on the front page of the two-page, handwritten paper:

> We hope that the reader or readers as the case may be will be pleased with the first copy of this local news journal we [sic] also hope that they will continue their patronage with the coming copys [sic]. Space will not permit to further explain this great weekly, but as was said before we are sure everyone will be doubly pleased with it.[4]

Between March 1919 and July 1920 twenty-six handwritten editions of the *Searchlight* were sent to Zoe in Sydney. If CB's early piece of doggerel — his limerick — could be associated, through the image of Farmer Johnson, with his Port Shoreham environment, then his first sustained creative output depended wholly on the people and daily life of his home region. Zoe read about the school meeting in which there was discussion about a possible tax increase and the laying of a hardwood floor in the schoolhouse; she was told in no uncertain terms by the same reporter that the Chedabucto Mutual Telephone Company "especially needs a capable manager and a new system or it will go 'punk' to use slang." As well she heard about local weddings, ice in the bay, postal service that was not up to standard, and of the comings and goings of various residents and visitors. If it is a fragmented portrait of Port Shoreham that emerges through the eyes of a 13-year-old boy, it is nevertheless a perceptive and informative portrait and vital, if youthful, journalism. CB mentions, for example, the "prominent lady of this place likely to run councellor [sic] for this district if it can be arranged for ladys [sic] to run"; he then adds, in editorial awareness of his time, "Watch out boys!" In a short, ironic list of "Things That Never Happen At Port Shoreham" the fragments do not create gaps as much as they do vignettes, a moving picture of life in the reader's mind: "The Mail On Time, Good Skating, Good Roads, Something Worthwhile, W.B. Using the Telephone." Of course, the *Shoreham Searchlight* was filled with things worthwhile, and the young CB knew it.

If the older journalist followed the cardinal Canadian Press rule of keeping his personal opinions and personal life out of his reporting, it was natural that his younger counterpart would be hard-pressed to stop talking of his own accomplishments. Thus Zoe learned of his prowess in road-running, especially the quarter-mile in which he defeated his schoolmate rivals and lowered his own mark: "The road is measured 220 yards, and turn, on a dry spot between the Post Office and William Bruce's house." Perhaps more useful information, since early photographs are difficult to come by, is provided by the statement in the issue of October 15, 1919 that this reporter-editor-publisher-runner was 5'2" tall and weighed 90 pounds.

When CB began to write he wrote about what he knew best. Throughout his life his best writing in poetry and prose was about the territory and people of the north shore of Chedabucto Bay. The links between the boy who produced the *Shoreham Searchlight* and the man who kept returning to his roots for his inspiration and subject matter are emphasized by a *Searchlight* story dated November 12, 1919. CB informed his readership of "The worst storm since the well-known August gale of many years ago …. Seventeen boats of the mackeral [sic] fishermen were lost." Fifty-two years later the retired CB wrote an article on that August gale of 1873, "the great widow-maker," in which he described the ravaged coasts of New Brunswick, Prince Edward Island, and northeastern Nova Scotia. It was, as far as can be ascertained, his last published piece of journalism.[5]

Meanwhile, Zoe had also been receiving poems from CB, or as he called them, "rhymed efforts." She showed them to Joseph Salter, her boss at the shipping agency, and he, "a kindly man who writes himself," had connections with the *North Sydney Herald*.[6] The first published work of CB appeared in the newspaper on April 9, 1919. "The Victory" is no better or worse than the poetic efforts of most twelve-year-olds, then and now, as the first few lines attest:

> Freedom's great fight is won, the Allies stand,
> Since the great war is done, conquerors on sea and land,

The fields where once great armies fought, and brave men fell,
Into a nation's service shall be brought
While groups of crosses near their stories tell.

This was followed a few months later by another patriotic piece, "Flag of Our Country," in which CB sees the Union Jack wave throughout the world, even on "the far Pacific islands/Where the great volcanoes rave." The details are not clear, but because of these poems, the prize-winning limerick, and some short essays in the Halifax *Evening Echo* "Sunshine Contest" (for example, "The Department I Like Best in Our Sunday School — the library"), CB was asked to write a poetry column for *The Family Herald and Weekly Star* published out of Montreal and carried by many newspapers across the country, including the North Sydney paper.[7] One war poem was picked up by the *Weekly Star* in September 1919, but as CB later explained, it was at this time that "a bit of realism began to crop up."[8] If the subject matter of "The Old Trail" was not exactly Port Shoreham, it was much closer to home than the fields of France:

I hit the old familiar trail
Along the margin of the lake
By greening thicket, swampy swale
My easy care-free way I take.

Most interesting in this 16-line poem is the clash between the familiar and comfortable boyhood territory on the one hand and the feelings expressed in the poems's final line: "Life's dull monotony to break." The paradox of home throughout CB's life was that while physically he could not live there, emotionally and spiritually, and in the strongest creative sense, he needed Port Shoreham to survive.

Will and Sarah's response to all this creative effort suggests both the strength of the relationship between CB's art and life and the distance he would have to travel through space and time to become the writer who could present, as he said in "The Township of Time," "the gleam of truth glimpsed through lived experience":

Mother thought it was great, despite certain reservations about poetry as a serious calling. I mentioned to her once, some years later, with indignation and as evidence of the crassness of this world, that a certain well-known expatriate couldn't make a living writing it. She remarked that maybe he should try some other line of work .... My father never made much comment. He read a lot of history and though he once explained to me an allusion in Alan Seeger ("Fit to have graced the barge that Cygnus bore.") I suspect he was more interested in it as an echo from Cleopatra's time than as poetry. However, he chuckled over a piece that compared the manner of our stormy Nova Scotia November with that of a stump-speaking politician:

> He surely has the other months all skinned
> But like the 'foresaid man — it's mostly wind.'

And I once heard him absent-mindedly mutter a line or two from one of my *Family Herald* efforts while we were hoeing-in potato seed around the burnt stumps of a new field.[9]

CB's "rhymed efforts" continued for many years, longer perhaps than they should have without variation, given the development of free verse; as well, despite a "bit of realism" the subject-matter of his poetry was mostly abstract and even ethereal right through his first book, *Wild Apples*, published in 1927. One of the main reasons for his progress as a poet somewhat apart from the modernist camp is his encounter with a book of poems (sent to Sarah by a friend in the States) by AE, George William Russell. There is some confusion as to when exactly this encounter occurred. In an article written in 1954 CB insists he was "ten or eleven by that time. Maybe twelve."[10] But a later date of 1920 is more probable because of the nature of most of his poetry after that year.

> I can still recall the tingling of the spine, discovering from the printed voice of that wonderful Irishman what men could do with words.

> *The peacock twilight rays aloft*
> *Its plumes and blooms of shadowy fire ...* [11]

AE's *The Divine Vision* , published in 1904, was certainly a particular type of nineteenth-century poetry and not at all part of the movement of poetry forward into the twentieth-century. The verses are full of "dreamy faces," "long mists of gold," and "the fathomless being of Love." Russell was an Irish Catholic whose devout faith "in the calm and proud procession of eternal things" dominated his response to the realities of the earth and his use of language. A poem entitled "The Voice of the Waters" has something of the setting and imagery of Bliss Carman's "Low Tide on Grand Pré," but nothing of the latter's intensity and focus. There is no evidence to show that CB was made aware of Carman's poetry (or, for that matter, any other Canadian poetry of quality) until he arrived at Mount Allison University in 1923. He might have moved more quickly toward the verse for which he will be remembered had he been influenced earlier by

> The while the river at our feet —
> A drowsy inland meadow stream —
> At set of sun the after-heat
> Made running gold, and in the gleam
> We freed our birch upon the stream.[12]

rather than by

> Where the silver wave with sweetness fed the tiny lives of grass
> I was bent above, my image mirrored in the fleeting glass,
> And a voice from out the water through my being seemed to pass.[13]

Of course, Carman rhymed endlessly and was too fond of a nineteenth-century perception of things ever to comprehend Pound, Eliot or even Frost. But he was concerned too with *"unelusive glories"* (my italics) such as "the scarlet of the maples" and "the frosty asters like smoke upon the hills"[14]; he liked the feel of grasses in his hands, and that tide that smacked his heart at the end of "Low Tide" was real as well as symbolic. For Russell, on the other hand, "Only God exults in silence over fields no man may reap"; for him "the magic tree of life" grew entirely behind "The Gates of Dreamland."[15]

CB later met Sir Charles G.D. Roberts and appreciated his use of concrete imagery, but criticized his nostalgia for the past; meanwhile, he was given tremendous encouragement by Russell's book because of what he took as its highly aesthetic qualities and because, unknown to him yet, he was very attracted to a particular theme of the Irish bard that he would one day make his own in a major way. Russell was concerned with a condition of innocence and magic lost with the passing of time:

"We dwindle down beneath the skies, / And from ourselves we pass away. / The paradise of memories / Grows fainter day by day."[16] In 1920 CB was not yet old enough to sense the mists of time enveloping Port Shoreham, but years later, while agreeing with Russell that "my childhood is over" and that there is a way in which "time is for ever beginning / And time is done,"[17] he would return again and again to the specifics of his Nova Scotia past and insist in his best poetry and fiction that "yesterday, today and tomorrow [are] part of a continuing whole [to] put things in balance."[18]

"At about the same time," CB writes, " I joined, or fell into, an organization called the Lone Scouts of America":

> Set up by W. D. Boyce, a Chicago publisher, who had been active in founding the boy scout movement in the States after encountering some of Baden-Powell's boys in England, LSA was supposed to reach rural areas where boy-scouting was not practicable, and incidentally to provide a corps of salesmen for Boyce's periodicals, which included a new magazine called of course *Lone Scout*. The organization turned into a vast club of amateur writers and printers. Boys wrote most of the copy for the magazine, bought hand presses and flooded the mails with amateur publications of their own. One, *The Bard* , devoted itself to verse and although Nova Scotia was a bit distant from its publication point in Dallas, I became an associated editor.[19]

Between January 1922 and June 1923 CB published at least a dozen poems in *The Bard*; late in 1923 there were several more, and the next year six appeared in *The Anthology of Lone Scout Verse*. Some of these poems were written before he joined the Lone Scouts, but with the exceptions of individual lines they are all usually of a piece and about Beauty, Dream, and such things as "far-spaced glory / Drifting with sky and sea / Never to hear the wind's wild story."[20] Occasionally, concrete images intrude: "the sails, dirt-gray and tan," "hands brown from the sun," "broken earth," and "Stone grey tide at the harbour mouth / White gulls on the bar."[21] But almost every poem written before CB went to university in the fall of 1923 is written in predictable rhyme and metre, and is a paean to a nebulous rather than an actual seascape and landscape. It was what people wanted to hear and was not much different from what all the other Lone Scouts were murmuring, except for one factor that is obvious over sixty years later: in contrast to the *always* vague and contrived settings in the verse of his peers, there are enough hills, beaches and water in CB's efforts that, despite his attempts to universalize and glorify them, have the smell and integrity of lived experience about them. In "The Ships of Home," published in April 1922, CB writes of what he has seen and touched and what he has felt within himself:

> The little ships — the sails, dirt-gray and tan —
> The fishermen, nicknamed and weather-wise. …
> The huddled huts, gray, warped beneath the sun
> Intent forever on the sea's refrain —
> Where boyhood's feet and slower steps have run
> To welcome shelter from the pelting rain.

"The ships of home … / Alert to meet the white-lipped stinging squall / Though time should plant me deep in inland loam / Time cannot change the image of them all." There is no doubt that when he wrote like this, Charles T. Bruce, as he signed himself then, was *The Bard*'s best bard.

During these years CB was also writing prose fiction — short stories. He won prizes in contests for children's writing held by the *Evening Echo* for "The Pilot's Story," "The Cat-Saucer," and "Singles or Doubles" in 1921 and 1922. The first is a tale about an elephant saving two hunters from a man-eating tiger. It is notable for its narration, somewhat redolent of Conrad, as an omniscient narrator tells the story of pilot Sam Beckwith who tells his own story to a Captain Eastman. "The Cat-Saucer," about a shrew and her less abrasive husband, and a tramp who finds the key to their house under the cat's dish, contains lively dialogue and dialect that smacks of rural Nova Scotia. The third tale is the best of the three because CB takes the time to develop the plot about two boys who are both rowing partners and opponents in a regatta. Each of the stories is plainly written by a teenager who is emulating, in one way or another, works he has read — "Singles and Doubles" has the *Youth's Companion* or *Boy's Own* formula about it. However, in June 1922 the *Family Herald and Weekly Star* published a more ambitious and original tale by Charles T. Bruce, for which he was paid $10.00 and in which are seeds of the fiction CB would begin to write over twenty years later.

The plot and characterization of "The Captain's Accounting" are fairly standard: there is a hero — Rob McLean, with his "inarticulate nature" but "crisp strength of face and figure," who rescues a ship's crew in distress — and a villain — Jarius Brome, "iron-grey of face and nature," who tries to swindle Captain McLean through an insurance fraud. Right wins out in the end, and CB closes the story sententiously, emphasizing "the ultimate harvest of Belief, the broad and flowery plain of Reward." However, what makes "The Captain's Accounting" stand out at this stage of CB's writing career is its setting "on the northern shore of the largest bay wholly contained in an eastern province" and CB's ability to convey, through obvious affection and taut, straightforward prose, the way of life in the community of Lingerlong. This "collection of fishermen's huts" with a harbour formed by a headland curving out into the bay is based on the beach below Port Shoreham and the combined geography of Ragged Head and "Bruce's Island." The strength of Rob McLean rises from his affinity with Lingerlong, its heritage of wind, water, weather, and the men who endured and handed down their boat-building skills to their descendants. "The native rocks" are sacred to Rob, and love for "crumbling soil and familiar landmarks" is transmuted by CB into a kind of faith. Above all, it is the sea that is associated with deep and abiding belief:

> In the same year the waters of our bay were shaken by hosts of the black-barred fish from the south, the mackerel that ran wild between the rocky walls that fenced them from their haunts, the green trails that lead northward. Throughout that season the gulls screamed around the boats that ever came back from the netting with full loads, that flashed like ebony and emerald and silver.
>
> Twenty yards above the old wharf, industry and patience have raised a new one. Upon the hill shine the white walls of the academy; at the head of the valley the steeple of the church.

The church here might be taken as a symbol that represents the strength of conviction CB had regarding the tangible aspects of the life he was born into and followed as a boy and about which he was writing in this story. CB carried Port Shoreham with him when he left there and wherever he went, and for many years he journeyed, unknowingly, toward a revelation of this fact in his poetry and fiction. Later in life he would emphasize the limitations of the real church: "I think I can say with truth now that while words like *faith, hope, belief* are pleasant to me, I find the word *religion* and all its variations depressing, and I can't sit still in church."[22]

Sarah Bruce taught at the local Sunday school and was superintendent of it for many years. She is described by Harold MacIntosh as "very religious" and by Wilbur Cummings as "a great woman in sickness" because of the faith and comfort she brought to her ill neighbours. Her religion certainly tempered her view of her son's creative talents: although she liked *The Channel Shore* when she read it in the mid-1950s (Sarah by then was almost ninety), she told a woman in the district she would not give it to her Sunday school class.[23] In *Currie Head* young Stan Currie is raised by his father Hugh and his Aunt Christine. The latter has a good heart, but is rather straight-laced about many things: "She was a kindly woman, but she believed the best thing for small boys was to confide all they knew. Anything else was covering up, a form of deceit." Christine wants Stan to be a minister, and while Anna (Bruce) MacKeen cannot recall her mother saying anything about the ministry to CB, the strict Methodist in Sarah Bruce was something her son found limiting.

On the other hand, as CB wrote in "A Hill for Looking", "It became an accepted fact that Will Bruce confined his church going to funerals":

> Pop usually spent the hour or so after breakfast [on Sundays] lying on the lounge in the dining room, in vest, pants, and sock feet reading the *Family Herald*. He had plenty of contact with the ministers during the Saturday nights they spent at our house among others; they liked him as a reasonable man who could talk of current events, and in general I think he liked them.

Will's independent streak was evident in the household. Every Sunday morning after breakfast Sarah would ask him if he were coming to church, and every Sunday morning Will would politely but firmly decline ("Not today, mother"). This was a sabbath ritual that CB witnessed for a long time. Once a minister dared suggest to Will that he should object to a local rum-runner's son who had run for office with the federal government. This young man was overseas in World War One when the minister spoke, and Will replied: "He may be a rum-runner's son. But he stands between you and me and the enemy. I voted for that man and I would do so again." Whatever his habits and outspokenness, Will did provide his son with a very powerful alternative to traditional Christian comforts and belief:

> ... whatever sense of heritage lived in him was liveliest when the tongued wooden needle shuttled among the torn meshes of a net, brought into the kitchen for work on a winter evening, and while he scraped flaking paint from the strakes of the *Mischief* [their two master], bottom-up on the top of the beach, and applied new putty and rags to the seams and white marine paint to the planking; and a little later when the time came to ship masts, and fix shrouds and rigging, foresail and jib, while the channel tide slipped whispering past the hull, and the sound of the bay, marching in a sou'est wind, came blowing down the beach.

CB's earliest memory is of a man called Byron Campbell, who last fished with Will in 1908, coming in from the beach and falling asleep in the fish-hut in a chair by the wall.[24] There were other memories of experiences that influenced the boy, which lived within him at the time, even though Wilbur Cummings asserts that CB "wanted to get ahead and perhaps didn't notice what went on around here." There was Will correcting himself "with a slightly apologetic laugh" after he had exclaimed "Oh, damn a dory!" when comparing dories to flats (flat-bottomed rowboats): "I mean darn." There was also Will, without apology, yelling at the old mare, Doll, after she pulled the hay cart away several times from the barn door: "What a whore of a horse!" And there was Will Bruce who, when most of his neighbours had one or two-horse mowing machines, insisted, with his son's help, on mowing the place by hand.[25] Like Hugh Currie in *Currie Head*, Will was "certain that there were still old ways that were worthwhile in new times." But like Hugh, as well, Will recognized that the value of his skills at farming and fishing, which he could pass on to his son, "was beginning to go out with a slowly turning tide."

The combination of this knowledge with an awareness of his son's talents and interests meant that Will wanted something more for CB than he had had. Perhaps the earliest direct indication of this came when CB was twelve and in need of glasses. He describes his inability to pick out clearly the steamer coming up the bay or to note "in the late October dusk when the cork-float on a trout-line went under." For some reason Sarah wanted him to go to North Sydney where Zoe lived and to have his eyes checked there by an oculist rather than by the optometrist in Guysborough. Will knew nothing of CB's difficulties with vision, and when it was suggested that he return with Zoe to Cape Breton (she had been home on vacation) for a "trip," Will said 'no' and made reference to the need to develop "saving habits" in their boy. CB despaired at this point of ever getting glasses and put his face in his hands. The response from Will was immediate and revealing: "Father was stricken. He felt for words and came out with a statement that revealed a complete misunderstanding of the only point that mattered, and at the same time a glimpse of something else: 'Look, don't worry .... You won't have to stay here and spend your life at this kind of work.'"

Will had entertained CB on winter nights beside the kitchen fire with stories of his life in Massachusetts away from the bay's north shore. These words of "enchantment," together with his own words that CB sent out to such places as North Sydney, Halifax and Dallas, and his considerable reading, sparked in him the desire to experience first-hand that world "away." Although he did not know it then, his feelings presaged a later knowledge that "There isn't a settlement among the older parts of [Canada] but has sent its flesh and blood to the newer areas [like] the community I come from ...."[26]

From grades one through ten CB attended the one-room, grey schoolhouse about half a mile from home on the MacPherson Lake Road. About 30-35 children were in attendance between 9:00 a.m. and 3:30 p.m. when they were, if Harold MacIntosh's memory serves him well, "as quiet as a mouse." In 1920-21 only CB and one girl were in the grade ten class, and the teacher had not gone beyond this level herself. "Our job," CB writes, "was not to work out the answers [in geometry] but to memorize them." He did very well in all his other subjects, but failed the provincial exam in geometry. Will, Sarah, and presumably the board at the Guysborough Academy decided that he should be given the opportunity to try grade eleven there: "It was a move usually confined to females who intended to teach [and] involved more education than most people thought useful." Although CB writes in "A Hill for Looking" that he boarded with a spinster during that academic year and was paid $3.00 a week to do some chores around the place, Anna (Bruce) MacKeen states that CB stayed with her and her husband in Guysborough "just across the corner from the Academy. He went home on weekends when the weather was fine."[27] Whatever the arrangements, CB "got the hang of geometry and learned to swear casually and without any feeling of guilt" while in grade eleven. It is not clear just when the decision was made that he go to Mount Allison University, a college in Sackville, New Brunswick, endowed by the Methodist Church of Canada, but after a summer on the farm in 1922 CB left home for Antigonish (about forty miles away) where he spent "months behind the counter of Kirk's Hardware Store," presumably to earn some money to contribute to his higher education.

A letter from Will to CB in Antigonish in September 1922 indicates that by that time there were some plans in effect for university: "If you do not like the place come home and we will chop wood and logs and you can get books and study in the evening."[28] In her letters Sarah asked her son if he had met any of "the church people," talked about her Sunday School class and worried about the parcels she had sent him. Although she said she was lonesome without him, Sarah did ask for news of his experiences, and although she addressed him as "Charlie Boy," the tone of her letters suggests an acceptance of the fact that CB had moved on in life. Will wrote "Dear Charles" and referred to their shared woods experience, chopping and trapping. It is very obvious that he missed his son and the life they had had together: "I wouldn't mind seeing that old truck once more if you were at the steering wheel and it was on the road back of our shop wall."[29]

CB wrote poetry that year in his third-floor room in Antigonish and then at home on the farm in the summer of 1923 after loading pulpwood and making hay. This was a waiting period in his life, and much later he would write of the boundaries he was leaving behind:

> My immediate world had been the north shore of Chedabucto Bay between Ragged Head and Stewart's Head. My father fished from that beach when he wasn't working the woods and fields, and for three or four boyhood summers I fished with him. And beyond this the slightly wider world of the bay itself and its opposite shore, five or six miles directly south of us ... slanting away to Queensport (where a far-off lighthouse flashed its small recurring spark in the distant night) and on to the mists of Cape Canso.[30]

The world widened when CB went to grade eleven in Guysborough, but a concrete response to the town "petered out" into a "verbal fogbank" indicative of CB's conventional attempt then to reach for meaning through abstract imagery:

> A dim voice murmurs low and is still,
> A dim light glimmers where the harbour meets
> The slumbering bay, and down the darkened streets
> The half-forgotten shadows play at will.
> Against the framework of a coaster's spars
> The sky is tangled white ....
>
> The laughter of old dream days lingers near
> The rarest music of the mystic earth
> Is sung in broken bars ...
>
> ....
>
> And faith abides, her mantle starry white;
> Unwearied still, the guardian of the night.

This poem, "Guysborough," was published in the Halifax *Morning-Chronicle* in October 1923. Half a dozen poems by Charles T. Bruce appeared in the paper between July and November of that year, poems of "thin pantheism" and CB's "trip of words and feeling." If there is too much of Beauty and Glory and "the still unchanging God of Sea and Sky,"[31] nevertheless the verse of a young Nova Scotian farm boy occupied one week the space taken up the next by Carl Sandburg or Sir Walter Scott, or by aspiring poets like himself whose work had been published in *Punch, The New York Times,* or perhaps a newspaper in Arkansas.

Such efforts by CB brought him attention that first fall at Mount Allison; words of praise from those who read poetry and those who wrote it, whose names were more widely known than that of Charles T. Bruce. CB was encouraged by these admirers, but they seemed to respond essentially to what was most imitative and clichéd in his work. It is CB's emphasis on "lyric pain" and "splendid dream" that reveal his "clean heart and courage,"[32] wrote one correspondent; and Robert Norwood, a poet and Episcopalian minister, whose hymns of praise to the spirit of God and man were vastly overrated by those who insisted the world was a bower of beauty and bliss, advised CB to "keep your body wholesome and clean as it is now and your mind as it is — normal."[33]

More valuable was Andrew Merkel, friend of Charles G. D. Roberts and his brother Theodore and acquaintance of Bliss Carman. Merkel, Atlantic Superintendent of Canadian Press and himself a published poet, would in the next few years arrange CB's move into professional journalism. Meanwhile, he took the time to commend and criticize individual lines of CB's poems rather than make general statements about the poet's character and calling. In the spring of 1924 he hired CB as a part-time Mount Allison and Sackville correspondent for Canadian Press so that graduation exercises, visits by various personalities to the campus, and sports scores could be picked up cheaply ("we pay six dollars per column"), but, as Merkel seemed to intuit, through an accurate and potentially original eye. Merkel's most memorable line to CB came in his first letter: "Where is Port Shoreham anyway?"[34]

CB states that once at university he began to read "a good deal of Bliss Carman and the Georgians, as well as Rupert Brooke." This kept him, as did the expectations of most of his middle-of-the-road readers, locked mainly into the sonnet form and predictable stress patterns and rhyme schemes. The young poet who arrived in Sackville in September 1923, and who wrote there over the next four years, was one who walked "with quickened dream and faith beguiled/Where starry winds and lyric waters flow …. "[35] As he wrote years later, "*The Wasteland* was in print by then but the poetry of disillusion had scarcely penetrated to Mount Allison and the poetry of social protest was still mostly out around the corner."

The unpublished novel *Currie Head*, written in the early 1940s, is very much an autobiographical text — too much so to make it a satisfying and durable work of fiction. Stan Currie, at seventeen about to leave the North Shore for Royal University in New Brunswick, is very much the young CB looking forward to "away," but increasingly aware of what he is both leaving and taking with him. If it is significant that if it took CB twenty years to articulate something of his 1923 state of mind, the silence on the shore in 1923 was complex and replete with creative promise. Although he did not know it then, CB's train ticket west and north was his passport into what he would eventually call "the township of time":

> Stan's mind stirred with anticipation of the future …. and with a grave excitement in its tenuous contact with the past.
>
> The land was all around him, with its reminders and its promise; for the future's pattern was traced — not precisely, in the lines of a fortune told, but in the unspecific terms of a general destiny — in the sea, curling itself lazily now on the beach, in The Head's wooded crest, in the cleared land sloping northward, in the house, and in the road.
>
> The Road — more eloquent than house or land and sea in its expression of harsh honesty, the subtle melancholy, the taciturn affection, the blunt generosity, the stubborn independence, the unnumbered threads of human impulse woven into the essential spirit of Currie Head.

Something equally clear and close to the heart remained to be articulated directly about CB's heritage and the influence of home. It finally *was* in May 1952 when CB received an honorary doctorate from Mount Allison and Will Bruce had been dead for eighteen years: "And I think of a middle-aged farmer fisherman following a spike-toothed harrow along a sidehill in the cold spring days … or salting down mackerel on the beach … and thinking of his boy away at school."[36]

III

The Bard

Mount Allison Academy opened in 1843, a Methodist institution for all denominations, but only to young men. Women began to attend a branch institution in 1854, and eight years later teaching was introduced at the college level for both sexes.[1] In CB's second year 261 students were registered, 172 of whom were in Arts and Science or Theology. Affiliated were Mount Allison Academy and Commercial College, which provided "preparation for matriculation in Arts, Law, Medicine, etc." as well as vocational and business courses, and Mount Allison Ladies College, which in 1923 was still advertising that "Our scope of instruction covers everything a girl should know from needlework to pipe organ."[2] Sackville, New Brunswick, the site of the university, overlooks the Tantramar Marshes. The area was first settled by the Acadians, who drained the marshes for farmland. After the 1755 expulsion New England and British immigrants established themselves so that by the mid to late nineteenth century the town was a thriving shipbuilding port, although later depended on two foundries and the university for its well-being. When CB arrived the town population was around 2,000 people; when he left in 1927 it was roughly the same (at the last official census in 1981 the population was 5,654).

CB entered the university grounds in a "$21 blue serge [suit] from Eaton's mail order house, fortified by the entire proceeds of a summer spent by my father cutting pulpwood — with whatever manual assistance I could give — and the first installment of money from my sister Bess, teaching school in Alberta."[3] According to his own assessment and that of his peers, CB was quite diffident that first term. He lived in a single room on the fourth floor of the men's residence "and seemed not to have grasped the necessity for mixing, or his shyness effectively concealed his real nature."[4] CB was somewhat hampered by the fact that he could speak only "colloquial Nova Scotian" (his own term) and had to take Introductory Latin at the Academy so that he could fulfill the B.A. requirement of two university years of the subject. Although he had great difficulty with Latin and had to write one supplemental examination, he handily achieved the necessary standing in French and one other foreign language — in his case, German. His English grades remained consistently high right through his senior year, only once slipping below 75 per cent. In addition to his language classes during 1923-24 he also took Mathematics, Physics, and History.

CB's social life as a freshman must have been limited by his character and by the nature of college life itself. A third-year diary note suggests that despite his increased stature on campus, CB's Port Shoreham background still kept him, at times, a young man apart:

> Ollie is pretty sore, well, so am I. When that crowd were learning to dance I was following a harrow or picking stone, or cutting wood, or piling brush. I have no illusions about the inability to play …. What have I that they have not? An incontrovertible, unassailable sense of beauty and truth in growing and inanimate things: an understanding of the Earth. The ability to find a restless quiet in the river and clouds and grass. And yet I am not at all sure that these balance the inability to navigate successfully a waxed dance floor to the syncopated time of a jazz orchestra, or to strum on a bit of wire and wood the spirit of *today*. Am I a semi-barbarian or an ultra-utopian? (For God's sake don't grow rhetorical).[5]

Despite the self-consciousness of style and tone, CB's concerns are genuine here, as acceptance of his roots and the past clashes with his desire to be in tune with the here and now. If he did find a middle ground in his third and fourth years between barbarism and the utopian ideal, it was perhaps because, as he told Thomas Raddall in 1952, Mount Allison was "a poor boy's college where you can pick up all sorts of odds and ends and tags of living." Although he became a very strong student

OCTOBER HILLS

I cannot help but dream, for dreams are all
That I may know of wonder and surprise.
They are my one response when gay stars call
From purple depths wherein all glory lies.
The quiet dusk grows deep in splendid night,
And all the silver cities flame afar—
Dim hills of home are in the fading light,
I cannot barter these for merchandise,
The rippling waters of a thousand thrills,
The stars that are the laughter in Life's eyes,
The long sweet stretches of October hills.
These are my heart of dreams, for dreams are all
That come to me of splendor past recall.

academically, CB emphasized to Raddall that "my student years were spent mostly in midnight bull-sessions, getting out the college weekly for half my room and board, doing sporting correspondence for the Halifax papers, and occasionally raising hell."[6]

For his friend, CB played down the importance of the college paper, but *The Argosy*, which had only been established in 1922-23 as a weekly,[7] quickly became the focal point of CB's expression on campus and established his reputation as "The Bard." The eight-line poem "Acadian Dreams" appeared in *The Morning Chronicle* on October 2, 1923 and four days later in *The Argosy*. No one seemed to mind the duplication; indeed, if word did filter back from Halifax it very likely added to the poet's lustre. At any rate, in this poem "the gay dreams prevail." CB's next *Argosy* contribution came the following week with a short essay entitled "The Open Road [of Thought]"; it exclaimed against fixed ideas and "opinionated scorn," something the much older CB echoed in the late 1960s when his manuscript of selected poems fell under the inflexible gaze of modernism, or perhaps post-modernism (see Chapter XI). In the same issue was the poem "October Hills," a sonnet that would appear, unchanged, as the first poem in CB's first book, *Wild Apples*, in 1927. The "Dim hills" are obviously ablaze with colour, but there is no mention of this, only of "the purple depths [of the heavens] wherein all glory lies." However, if here "dreams are all" and not a single concrete image is employed, except perhaps "The rippling waters of a thousand thrills," CB was capable not long after of somewhat off-setting "the lights of glory" with images of "the summer's fragrant hay" and "rain-gemmed grass and silver dew."[8]

Three poems that first year in *The Argosy* were old efforts from the 1922-23 editions of *The Bard*, but one, "The Ships of Home," did emphasize that CB's language did not always have to do with "splendor past recall." In the February 16th, 1924 issue "Hills Across the Harbour" was published; it had been carried in the *Chronicle* a month previously. Instead of "rain-gemmed grass" there is "life gemmed with dream — "; what is interesting, however, is the poem's major theme of the value of the inheritance of time and place. "Old laughter laughs along the guardian beach./The griefs of younger years are in the sky./The hills dream on;" but these things provide "the strength that can never depart,/ ... the single story of the years." If AE had something to do with such articulation, there was no dwelling on the loss of things once familiar, but rather an emphasis on life's continuity.

CB's most original and successful submission to *The Argosy* in 1923-24 was a short story entitled "Along Shore"(29.3.24)* about the fishermen of Lingerlong. As in "The Captain's Accounting," CB's facility with dialogue helps to create convincing characters, and (as in much later fiction about the Channel Shore) a shared sense of humour amongst the men aids in the presentation of more serious differences between them and their respective values.

In his second year CB strengthened his association with *The Argosy* by becoming a contributing editor for the Academy Residence. There is no direct reporting by CB of residence news during 1924-25, but in addition to the six poems published in his second year, he did write one editorial calling for support of the Eurhetorian Society (The Debating Team, of which he was now a member), another on the need for constructive criticism of and help for *The Argosy*, an essay on the poetry of Marjorie Pickthall, and another essay entitled "Apologie for Poetry." In the latter, he stressed that poetry is "seeking not revival, but recognition....The public...is groping for the true criterion, beginning to see with glad eyes the earthiness of spiritual things and the mysticism of the earth."[9] This is in accord with what he had to say about "the most significant poet who ever sang the romantic soul of Canada to the world."[10] He praised Marjorie Pickthall's clarity and beauty of expression as a nature poet, was attracted to her "whimsical pagan charm" and her emphasis of the enormous "spiritual strength that lies in the little things that are close to the heart of all." CB's own nature poetry at this time would have been better influenced by the often startling and

* These dates refer to the publication dates of *The Argosy*.

original images of Isabella Valancy Crawford's poems, which had first been published in a collected edition in 1905.

In "Deep in the Dusk" (11.10.24) he is still preoccupied with such images as the "silver gleams of glory in the grass" and "the drift of dreams," but he does speak of being bound "to the dusk of yesterday," to the "truth the old days knew." "Sophomore of His Ladylove" is a clever sonnet parody of Shakespeare's "Sonnet LVII," in which the poet complains that he has "nor time for English Two, till you expire" (25.10.24). "Armistice Day" on November 8, 1924 occupied the front page of *The Argosy* along with another's verse tribute to the fallen. Here CB relates, in more evident terms than usual, what the dead soldiers have lost and preserved for us: "The wild whisper of black October wind..../The cool dark grass, and the blinded stars — rain-driven,/And the life that stirs in the breast of the broken sod."

It is in two poems especially — "Aftergrass"(1.11.24) and "Surf"(15.11.24) — that CB reveals he can write of the earth and sea without dreamy moralizing and in images that represent the things themselves. The former poem had been previously published in a Lone Scout collection (*The Bohemian*, no date) and its strength lies in individual phrases ("the smell of broken earth," "the coolness of the aftergrass"), but "Surf" deserves to be quoted in full, as it is only the occasional word or image that interferes with the poem's concrete unity:

> Far down the beach the gay surf still lifts white;
> Wind driven scud breaks south across the sky —
> Rain ripples down, and gathering gulls in flight
> Dip tired wings, and voice the old, wild cry
> Against the dusk.
> The gray cloud-levels reach
> Far down beyond the range of capes, to hide
> From those who linger on the lonely beach
> The white-winged sisters of returning tide.

The beach is still general in terms of actual place; CB had yet to let his readers know that he was speaking of Chedabucto Bay's north shore, and he had yet to people his poems with the convincing characters he could put in his Lingerlong fiction.

In *The Argosy* Literary Competition, which provided a maximum of three points for a poem or article, five points for a story, and required a minimum of twenty points for a gold-inscribed pin for Literary Distinction, CB led at the end of the first term in 1924-25 and was tied for second place with 24-1/2 points with only two numbers of the paper to be published before the academic year was over; unfortunately, no record of the final results seems to exist.

The Debating Team provided a higher profile for The Bard: as a member of the three-man squad he helped defend the resolution that "modern democracies adequately promote human welfare." The paper reported him as speaking of the opportunities for intellectual freedom under modern democracies, and as stressing the better methods of education and types of national character found under such a system of government. The debates were held against other universities once a year (St. Francis Xavier was the victim of Mount Allison's fourth consecutive victory on March 25, 1925) and were front-page news in *The Argosy*. There were photographs of each team member and individual plaudits. CB's "wonderful vocabulary" and "fine delivery of words" were cited.

The perception of CB as a nineteen-year-old Junior is helped by a diary he kept that has survived intact. It contains mainly personal news and reveals a great preoccupation with young women: there is considerable reference to "necking" with various girls, but I have been assured by Charles Blue, who knew CB quite well that year and the next, that this term meant "a love affair for an evening, or even a few minutes, but *not* sexual intercourse!"[11] Given the social climate of Mount Allison and Sackville and CB's own conservative moral background, we can assume that he indulged in hand-holding and perhaps some passionate kissing, but no more. He writes of sleeping-in and missing classes, of skipping classes, and of further problems with Latin. His attitude here — rather matter-of-fact and unconcerned — is somewhat surprising, as in the previous year his marks had fallen rather drastically (even in English, from 87 to 75), prompting a letter from President Trueman to Will Bruce about a 3rd in Latin and a failure in Mathematics in the first term:

"Will you kindly talk over Charles' work with him … a man of his ability should do much better than this."[12] CB did, in fact, bring all his grades up to second or first-class standing in his Junior year, but his extra-curricular activities seem to have forced him to work "like hell" in concentrated periods. Charles Blue describes him as an "English student more than anything else" and says that any shyness he may have had was gone by then.

More important to his future than his social life were his favourable impressions of Charles G. D. Roberts when the famous poet visited the campus on October 20, 1925, and his continuing correspondence with Andrew Merkel, who discussed more of CB's poetry, encouraged him to submit to *The Dalhousie Review*, and mentioned the possibility of inclusion in a Nova Scotia anthology. CB was writing fewer poems at this point (or at least having fewer published) but more essays on the nature of poetry and one essay on his Port Shoreham heritage.

On October 17, 1925 the now Assistant-Editor-in-Chief of *The Argosy* published a short prose piece, "October," with an epigraph by Bliss Carman (from his "Vagabond Song"): "There is something in October that is native to my blood." In prose CB obviously had the inspiration and ability to portray his home territory and to convey what it meant to him. His poetic models restrained him and did not allow him to write of the "black crows cawing in wind-shaken trees," of "old snake-fences," of the "hard and bitter wind" that sweeps across an October beach. This would have been poetry, had CB written it thus, redolent of A.J.M. Smith and F. R. Scott's verse, but CB was either ignorant of these poets or else uninterested in their efforts. Nor could he yet incorporate into his verse word-portraits of those farmer-fishemen whom he knew so well, or say of them in a poem, "It seems to me that the broken brown soil, the dancing sun, and the gray rain of October are peculiarly theirs: typical of these forthright, brave-hearted people, who preserve through the passing years the individual austerity of their lonely life."

In a much longer essay a month later CB wrote on "Love of life" in which he referred to the "concrete specific preferences" found in Rupert Brooke's poems — for example, "wet roofs beneath the lamplight," "Moist black earthen mould," "Shining pools on grass". The life of the senses and the creative response to such a life, CB asserts, "is far deeper than mere sentiment": "The concrete things that affect you are not only parts of what you see and think and do; they are part of the you that other people meet, and without them, you are another personality." CB then places himself firmly in the midst of his Port Shoreham experience, both in terms of his own experience and as a writer (the part of himself that his audience is meeting):

> The most utterly contented hours I have ever known ... were those sunny summer days during which I crouched, ankle-deep in water, and passed lumber up over the side of a Danish tramp.
> Places where little brawling books have suddenly widened out into placid pools affect me like the quiet chuckle of an understanding friend after the departure of a noisy woman .... I have as keen an appreciation of sunsets as anyone, but I don't want to look at them at someone else's invitation ... I don't particularly want to talk about them. Emotion repeatedly expressed in words seems to me to be rather cheap .... Attempted expression that fails is pitiful(14.11.25).

What is both interesting and ironic here is that CB's reader can sense strongly the loom of the Danish tramp, the sound and sight of the wandering brook, and, because of other definite descriptions in "October," stand on the beach with the author amongst the fish-huts, boats, and lobster pots.

CB's expression in these two essays does not fail because the real world conveyed evokes emotional response without proclaiming it. In contrast, in most of his poetry CB was still saying to his reader, "Come and look at my sunset! This is what *I* and you *should* feel." Thus in "Sea Sense" (3.10.25) the first six lines of the sonnet offer trees and reefs and "torn surf lifting," but the last eight lines speak of dreams and, ultimately, "A splendor, fugitive and frail and fair." "Sea Windows" (17.10.25) is somewhat better, but only because the tangible seascape and landscape dissolve into personification rather than into abstraction. "Altar Fires" (31.10.25) informs the reader that what can be seen and heard and smelled and touched are "altars [of] faith against the sun." No other poems appear for almost six months. "The Seer of Saving Beauty" (17.4.26) is a message poem in which "the gray cold beach" at the centre of things is only a metaphor for a larger vision, vague and simplistic in its unquestioning assertion: the Earth remains "ungrieved by sorrow, unscarred by pain .... /While beauty laughs from the hills of Heaven/To save men's souls from the Hells of Hate."

Because of his position on the paper, CB was not eligible for the Literary Competition in 1926 and, indeed, the April 24th issue of *The Argosy* announced that he had been elected unanimously to the position of Editor-in-Chief for 1926-27. Once more in March he was second speaker on the Debating Team and contributed to its 5th consecutive victory, this time against Dalhousie and on the subject of the Dominion's role in the foreign policy of the British Empire. His poetic prowess now seemed to play as much of a role in his campus stature as his public speaking: the summary of his performance beneath his *Argosy* photograph on March 13, 1926 begins by calling CB "the bard."

During this academic year his feelings about the Bruce home (as opposed to the Port Shoreham environment) seem to have caused him some distress. Perhaps he had not kept up his correspondence with his parents or had indicated that he might not want to return home for Christmas. On December 15 his diary reports, "Got letter from Anna that made me feel rotten. Will go home tomorrow if money comes." The next day he apparently borrowed $15.00 and headed for the North Shore, where his difficulty was obvious: "Here an interim of two weeks in which I cut wood and watched for mail."

Mount Allison was a place where he was forging a reputation and was independent, no doubt, of the role of "Charlie Boy"; it was also the first place where he lived away from home that allowed him the time and space to create a perspective of where he had come from. Bound up in his sense of himself as a writer must have been an awareness that he had changed, was changing, and that to comprehend the strengths of farmer-fishermen and the extraordinary quality of their experience and environment was something very different from actually living their life and being unable to perceive it in relative terms. In his diary, in which he had extolled his own "understanding of the Earth," his "ability to find a restless quiet in the river and clouds and grass," he revealed at the end of the school year his need to imagine himself at Port Shoreham before he was actually there: "left for home — and spent a summer in the woods and in the Ford."

CB's diary entries in his senior year number only eight days in the first term. Undoubtedly he was very busy as editor of *The Argosy* and with his course work in which he obtained two firsts and three seconds. He also appears to have been very involved with another Mount Allison student, Vera Campbell. Although his diary contains the names of thirty-nine young women, with a check mark beside seventeen of them (and a '0' beside four names), virtually every one of the eight entries has a reference to Vera Campbell, and the first, on September 20, 1926, suggests that he wrote his poem "To a Wild Kind Girl" about her. On October 3, 1926 he seems distressed that he is so involved ("This is a hell of a mess to get into at just this time"), but by November 11 he announces that they have "split." Certainly this relationship did matter to CB, because he corresponded with Vera Campbell in later years, writing her in Boston (for the last time) several months before his death in 1971 to say that she was one of a small group of Mount Allison alumni with whom he still kept in touch.[13] In addition to his university work and love life, CB was also sending various reports down to Canadian Press in Halifax. Andrew Merkel was apparently telephoning his campus reporter from time to time with instructions.

In his prose CB continued to strip away the considerable veneer of abstraction and even escapism that dominated so much of his poetry. "The Tree" (2.10.26) is a short story without dialogue that attempts, through the mythic quality of its narrative and its representative, living forces — the Boy, the Tree — to convey the essence of man's relationship with the natural world as found in immediate, local experience. The Boy watches the Tree through a classroom window (in History class), feeling at first its uniqueness, but then, because of his sense of kinship

with it, "a curious significance in all growing and living things."
As the seasons pass, the *reality* of the Tree (as well as the usual
abstractions — its "strength, and beauty and truth and grace")
causes the Boy to come to terms with the tangible aspects of his
own life:

> He thought of his home, a place for which he had never had
> any particular affection, in a new way. He heard the low whisper
> of wind through the pipe-organ of the hills; caught the swift
> white crash of surf on the beaches over which he had wandered,
> and suddenly knew that he had always loved them.

If the Boy escapes History he merges with something larger and
yet substantive — "the whole earth." The ending of the tale
leaves the boy in such *touch* with the world that it recalls
Hemingway's adage from *The Sun Also Rises* (there is a strong
strain of *Ecclesiastes* in parts of CB's work): "I did not care what
it was all about. All I wanted to know was how to live in it.
Maybe if you found out how to live in it you learned from that
what it was all about."[14]

The essay "Laughter" (16.10.26) indicates that CB was not
given to blind idealization of Port Shoreham or of similar communities: " ... so many good people have forgotten how to
laugh! Whenever I drop into the home town, a fear strikes me
that some aspect of a naughty deed will seem to me funny, and
that I'll be ticketed thereafter among the damned." He goes on
to talk of a student who spent summers with people who were
"literally, salt of the earth, yet whose lives were simply a succession of superstitions and inhibitions; political, moral, religious."
That student followed the conventional roles, but used to slip
away to the wharves "where hardened old sinners swapped sea
lies for chewing tobacco. That was where the sunshine was, and
a great peace reigned."

However, CB's poetry was still influenced by the role models
he encountered — either through reading or direct contact —
that were set in their ways. On January 26, 1927 Canada's
self-proclaimed national bard, Wilson MacDonald, read his
poetry at Mount Allison. CB had already reviewed
MacDonald's most recent book, *Out of the Wilderness*, two weeks

previously and had, in *The Argosy* (15.1.27) called him "truly great," citing as evidence lines such as the following:

> The gardens of heaven are lonely for men —
> The stars almost plead for a glance from your eyes
> And though this that passes comes never again
> Yet no one goes weeping when loneliness dies.
> There are wings in the air
> Which the lowly may wear.
> There are harps in the wind everywhere.

CB's effusive, uncritical response to a poet whose work he saw "crystallizing" the beauty of Canada reminds us of how distanced he was from changes that were occurring in modern Canadian poetry. MacDonald viewed himself as the equal, at least, of Keats and Shelley, and much of his poetry was designed consciously to support his romantic self-perception as a ladies' man and the nation's poetic saviour. Whatever talent he may have had was dissipated by his preoccupations with his private myths and public image.[15] CB vastly overestimated MacDonald's work and influence, and nearly all of the six poems he published in *The Argosy* in 1926-27 strain toward that "transcendental loneliness" that so limits them. Four of these poems appeared in *Wild Apples*, what CB later referred to as "a rather neat little cardboard-covered book into which went the wind and the stars and the girls."[16] Interestingly enough, one poem that was not considered (appropriate) for *Wild Apples* was "Beach Children" (27.11.26). Here CB presents his major theme of later work that "yesterday, today, and tomorrow [are] part of a continuing whole," together with word-pictures of familiar territory: "Go back where the skies are gray;/They are ploughing there — /And the smell of the earth is sweet on the autumn air./ …. /And the old time things that are always new shall rise/Across our spray-swept eyes."

By the spring of 1927 Andrew Merkel had determined that CB would be in journalism, and before he left Mount Allison CB knew that he would be working as a reporter full-time in Halifax for the *Chronicle*. Although they are not signed, it is difficult to believe that anyone other than CB wrote *The Argosy* editorials "The Open Road" (29.1.27) and "Books" (12.3.27). Each is measured in tone and seeks to convince rather than cajole readers as to the merit of its argument. These pieces come to mind when one reads CB's later journalistic efforts written almost entirely outside the managerial boundaries of his position at Canadian Press. In *Currie Head*, a wise newspaperman suggests to Stan Currie, about to join a news agency similar to Canadian Press, that being a good editorial page man is the step below "real creative writing." But Stan is on his way up to an administrative position where he will be trapped for years. Fortunately, unlike Stan, CB was able to make art in the distances between the news agency "rat-race" and "remembered earth." It is no slander of that art, however, to mourn the loss of CB as an editor and the impact he might have had in that role on public opinion and political action in this country.

Undoubtedly because of his way with words and his prominence in the public life of the university CB was chosen by his Mount Allison classmates a valedictorian. But perhaps the fact that he was once fined 75 cents for yelling "Why?" in the college dining room when the President of the Student Council was in the middle of an announcement, or that he always had ingenious excuses for avoiding penalties for skipping chapel, had something to do with it. As for his speech at the commencement exercises, if it is at all memorable, it is for its turns of phrase, its celebration of a "Sense of Humor," and "the appreciation of Laughter" encouraged by Mount Allison, rather than for its conventional appeal to tradition, "Loyalty," and "the nobility and grace that are redeeming threads in the tapestry of life."[17] In his 1952 speech, upon receiving his honorary doctorate from his alma mater, CB looked back at that valedictorian through the experience of twenty-five years of the "tapestry" and writing about it as a journalist, poet, and short story author:

> What [he] had to say, perhaps in terms a bit stilted — because he was under the influence of a half-course in English prose, and used to veer in style all the way from Macaulay to Richard Jeffries — was that the members of his class had come under the influence of certain things at Mount A .... an appreciation for things that are true, and for things which are beautiful. He hadn't quite realized then, I imagine, that Keats' famous phrase about truth and beauty is merely a quotable cliché; that there is no such

thing as abstract truth or abstract beauty; that there are simply acts, words, people, scenes that strike you with conviction or recognition, and that to the feelings they arouse we have pinned these inadequate and abstract words. [18]

CB now moved even further away from the North Shore — within two years he married and within four he was a father. He worked for the Halifax *Morning-Chronicle* during 1927-28 and then for the New York Bureau of the Canadian Press news agency for eight months. From 1928-33 he was on the CP editorial staff in Halifax and then transferred to Toronto where he worked and resided for the rest of his life. [19] It is significant that when he left Sackville in the spring of 1927 he was more "homesick" than at any other point in his life. Mount Allison had been in so many ways another world from Port Shoreham, but it was only a day away by train or car, and CB went home every summer until his graduation. At university he experienced a life of freedom and dependence, and he was leaving this combination behind: the freedom to be away from Port Shoreham, but to consider it in creative terms from not very far away in time and space; the dependence on what in some of his *Argosy* pieces he did not mind admitting, but which, until his 1952 Alumni Dinner speech, he did not seem to allow had permeated his college years: the image of Will, "following a spike-toothed harrow … thinking of his boy away at school. That, too, is Mount Allison."

The Sackville *Tribune*, which printed *The Argosy*, published 250 copies of *Wild Apples* at CB's expense (cost would be covered if the run sold out at 75 cents a copy). Although there is no specific record of sales, CB writes, "I didn't quite break even on this piece of vanity publication"; irony is suggested here, but not certain — there were only slightly over 250 students at the university. The "Introductory Note" to the book by none other than Robert Norwood is surprisingly perceptive, though perhaps for the wrong reasons. When Norwood commends CB because "His songs are always lilting catches of those mystical perturbations without which there can be no poetry," we should be wary of what he means by "As [CB] learns simplicity and dares more and more to be himself … " he will become a fine poet. Nine of the thirteen poems in the book had appeared in *The Argosy*. The first, "October Hills," as has been said, was from his freshman year; the only alterations CB made had to do with the addition or deletion of commas and semi-colons. CB changed some punctuation in "Sea Sense," from the autumn of 1925, but more important he revised two lines: the end of the octave had the vague "And all loved things, across the cool grass drifting" replaced by the more substantial, though rather common, "And shadowy clouds, across the cool grass drifting." In the sestet the change was not at all positive, as "spray-washed wind" yielded to "wistful wind." The lament "Rupert Brooke" (13.2.26) kept its "Faith," "Glory," and "Beauty," but now added capital letters to "*V*alleys of the Sun" and "*L*ove and *L*aughter"; the ironic result is that mimetic terms become allegorical and Brooke's death less real. "Queen's Jester," which had not appeared previously, is a forgettable sonnet from the poet to his dark college lady. In "The Immortals" (13.11.26) CB had plainly striven for effect and created a strained mythic mask that must have been difficult for the editor of *The Argosy* to wear: "This intimate swift madness of desire/Has gathered me close to a thousand things;/Found the keen rapture of my own heart's fire/In poetry, and the hush of breathless wings." However, in the book's title poem (2.10.26) CB does not end up "wistful at the call/Of gay and transient beauty" or add more abstractions, as he did so often in his undergraduate poetry; rather he concludes, without peroration, "I've seen the fall/Of silvery petals; and an orchard moon — /Or swaying shadows on the midnight wall;/And branches, tranquil in the sun at noon."

In the second section of *Wild Apples* CB leaves his sonnets behind. "In Praise of Earth"(9.10.26) is best captured by the "pantheism"[20] of its opening stanza of sixteen: "Before the world's dim altars,/All men of righteous birth/Bow down in deep thanksgiving./I pray to Mother Earth." "Altar Fires" (31.10.25) and "The Seer of Saving Beauty" (17.4.26) have already been considered. "To a Wild Kind Girl" (seemingly Vera Campbell) is better than the dark lady sonnet, but there is too much clichéd talk of "the blazing trumpets of desire" and "all who follow Beauty's flying feet — " to make the poem memorable. "The Song of Snow" has an "elfin clearness" that wakes "the lyric prisoners of death" and so is nothing new from CB. In later years CB referred to "Infidel" (15.1.27) as "mildly satirical," his "rebellion ... still concerned with the organized and the orthodox."[21] The final stanza is a lyrical but strong statement, though, against repressive bonds, and what satire there is must come from CB's sense of his own *real* limitations: "The cry of morning, and the dusky dress/Wherein the flowering buds of night are caught,/ Have called him from enduring righteousness./He has gone mad with beauty; touch him not." At the last, in "Masquerade," CB speaks of his "careless eyes, with new gods possessed" and of his turning away from "the constant faith of sky and sea." Much of this seems an anti-romantic pose, if only because the entire poem is a series of romantic images and platitudes. But it is significant that the final published poem of CB's university days should contain the fear of forgetting "hills at nightfall, and the gray unrest/Of wistful fields beneath October rain." He had carried Port Shoreham away with him for four years. Now the long road was waiting, would the new gods let him remember?

IV

On The Road

CB worked for the Halifax *Morning-Chronicle* from May 1927 until the end of that year. Just what his exact duties were is not clear, but perhaps Stan Currie's experience on the Halifax *Globe* in *Currie Head* during the same period (after leaving university and before moving to a news agency) can serve as a guide. Stan worked several years at his paper, so CB would not have made parallel progress from "cub to run-of-the-mill reporter" in his eight months at the *Chronicle*. But the low salary[1] must have discouraged him as it did Stan, and one can imagine the young and eager CB hanging "around the news room at all hours in the hope of finding something to do." One can also imagine the eager ex-editor of *The Argosy*, sent to cover commencement exercises at Mount St. Vincent University, waxing eloquent about the Catholic ceremony and comparisons of this college to his alma mater. On reading Stan Currie's story about the commencement the news editor of the *Globe* tells Stan to forget it because the sisters usually provide a "yarn" and a reporter is sent to the exercises only to represent the paper.

While his limited time on the *Chronicle* gave CB the necessary experience of professional journalism, Andrew Merkel was obviously keeping an eye on his development. Merkel wrote to J.F.B. Livesay, General Manager of Canadian Press, on November 28, 1927: "There is an extremely promising reporter on the staff of *The Morning Chronicle* in the person of Charles T. Bruce … I am firmly convinced he is going very far in journalism and I think if you knew of his work at first hand you would agree with me that he should be in our service."[2] Livesay seemed concerned, in his response to Merkel, about the salary to be paid the young staffer, but CB joined the CP's New York Bureau on January 9, 1928 at $40.00 a week.

Before this move CB had met his future wife, Agnes King. She had been born and raised in Vancouver where her father practiced law. The King family had long roots in Windsor, Nova Scotia, while Agnes's mother was a New Englander who grew up in Boston. After receiving her B.A. from the University of British Columbia, Agnes came to Dalhousie University in Halifax (where her father had studied law) for graduate work; during 1927-28 she completed her M.A. thesis on the poetry of Edna St. Vincent Millay under the supervision of Archibald MacMechan. She is not sure when exactly she met CB, but says that it must have been in the fall of 1927 as she was living in Shirreff Hall at that time. She does recall that she and CB did not go out much together in Halifax and that he left for Canadian Press in New York early in January 1928. When Agnes completed her M.A. she moved to New York, where she had relatives, and worked for the Bell Telephone Company. The two Canadians with Nova Scotia roots then began to see a lot of one another.[3]

CB at first lived at the Hotel Clendening on 103rd Street and later shared a sublet apartment with a Columbia University chemistry student on West 13th Street. His favourite eating spot seems to have been a place at 50th and 7th "with wicker backs to its stools ... where [he] used to get chicken-a-la-king on toast for $.50 after the hockey games." For an equal amount he could go to Eva La Gallienne's 14th Street playhouse, put on a dinner jacket, and sit in the gallery. The Cotton Club is also mentioned in his notes and the backroom drinking establishment of an Italian restaurant.[4] After eight months on the editorial staff in New York CB was transferred to the CP night staff in Halifax where he would handle "sea and storm largely." Agnes, apparently, did not return for some time, and the result was a strong poetic response on CB's part to their courtship.

An important outlet for his verse was *Song Fishermen's Song Sheet*. CB writes in "The Back of the Book" that Andrew Merkel "came up with the idea ... of publishing printed broadsheets through which the verse written by a small group of Nova Scotians would (they hoped) reach a slightly wider public than was likely to see them on the backs of old envelopes." Two or three issues of these broadsheets, with poems by such luminaries as Charles G. D. Roberts and Bliss Carman, as well as Theodore Goodridge Roberts and Robert Norwood, were released "under the imprint of a mythical publishing house called the Abanaki Press." Broadsheet promotional material described the Abanaki as "the original 100 per cent Nova Scotians [who] by the tribes not blessed with residence on the sea's verge ... were given their name — Children of the Rising Sun."

In October 1928 their poetry-writing descendants announced that they were neglecting "to bother about anything but water and wind and weeds and the human heart; [we] have gone back to a Nova Scotia that existed hundreds of years before the Inter-Colonial. And [we] have not entirely failed to strip the smothering garments of prude politics and hypocritical litera-ture from the lovely body of [our] land."[5] However, the land's populace did not respond as hoped, and the broadsheets were reduced to song sheets that were run off on the CP mimeograph machine. In "The Back of the Book" CB recalled that

> The song fishermen were a mixed crowd: writers, teachers, housewives, clergymen; mostly Halifax people but with a few coming in by correspondence from various points in the Maritimes and elsewhere and most of us trying to work up some fun. Some liked to stab the establishment (though I don't think that term had been yet devised) and some were members of it. At least a couple thought Moscow meant salvation. One or two preached a kind of mystical love for everything. Actually not much clashing philosophy got into the sheets, the contents of which ranged from deliberate doggerel to some fair verse. I like to think that though we never made it to the river we sometimes got within sound of the falls.

As CB explains it, he himself "had no political convictions; only enthusiasms ... A personal disinclination to line up with either the philistines or the angels kept working its way out in the verse I wrote." He had a definite reluctance to translate into poetry life that lay outside his personal experience, and this showed in his various contributions to the broadsheets and then the song sheets (which only lasted a year or two before they "merged into a short-lived magazine called *Acadie*, produced by Thede Roberts"). His initial effort for the first edition of the broadsheet in October 1928 dealt with advice CB had received (perhaps from his more worldly fellow-poets) to cease worrying about love and his "urgent heart." The implication at the end of this poem (which was published as "Caution" in *Tomorrow's Tide* in 1932) is that love is lost unless one seizes the day, and this obviously has to do with the absent Agnes in New York.

That autumn CB visited Port Shoreham; the result was "Resurrection in October," a poetic tribute to the connection between the people who lived and died there and the natural world, but with an emphasis that love is "alive" and finds "no peace" in pantheistic musings. CB may still have been expressing himself with his usual iambic rhythms and set rhymes, but the Glory and the Dream were fading away.

This movement away from the association of the "urgent heart" with the "splendid dream" is continued in "Rainfire," at least to some extent. When the dream is lost, CB writes, "grim heaven" provides only "The archaic tumult of relentless rain" as escape. The rain is real, but the language and images with which CB describes it keep him far from any modernist articulation of reality: "In the rain's beat are restless ghosts athrong;/Down the swart strakes of unremembered ships/Full tide makes gutteral song." The poet's life experience, though, is a comment upon his *art's* archaic tumult as his urgent heart requires "Some word more quick than rain." In "Not Now" the poet states quite clearly that the natural world cannot provide the necessary sustenance for his love-sick spirit. Despite the personification, however, the sea and earth and sky he denies are just themselves and not part of some vague territory of dream, so the reader's and poet's knowledge that love-sickness will pass means that the tangible natural world will be encountered again. What CB later thought of this work is emphasized by his providing the comment of a Halifax friend at the time that it was "passable bedroom verse, meaning it was no great shakes."

Much more interesting because it is a free-verse experiment CB was not very often to repeat in his poetic career is "Brooklyn." It is not an especially good poem, but its voice, tone, and setting are so unique in the CB canon that it is worth quoting in full:

> Do you remember
> How we used to leave the subway
> At Kingston Avenue,
> And walk 'round the corner
> To nine-fifty.
> When the smoky moon
> Or the windy sun
> Was making the Eastern Parkway
> A good place for love?
>
> And that Sunday morning
> We had canteloupes and coffee,
> And read the *Times* and the *Herald-Trib*,
> With an eye on the door
> For your aunt coming back from Philly?
>
> One night before you went away to Maine
> You said
> "This is not the end. It can't be."
>
> But there have been a dozen tragic endings
> Since then;
> And thirteen lovely beginnings.[6]

Here the poet focusses entirely on himself and his lover; the poem is not really written for anyone else to read, and its form and content could not be more distant from "the blowing trumpetsof desire" or the poet "gone mad with beauty." However, nothing in CB's background in Port Shoreham or at Mount Allison had encouraged any kind of self-attention that could last; CB and Agnes King were married on Friday, December 13, 1929 in the chapel of the Anglican cathedral in Halifax. "Brooklyn" is ultimately significant because, although when his love-life settled[7] and his focus shifted elsewhere CB continued to depend on conventional poetic form to a considerable extent, "the mystic earth" began to emerge from its very real, untransmuted features and the equally substantial experience of its inhabitants. CB was not a city boy, although he lived in the city for the rest of his life. From roughly 1930 on, his finest creative efforts were based on his Port Shoreham heritage, but were as firm and of a piece as Brooklyn concrete.

His job as an editor at CP (he was eventually transferred to the day shift) meant that CB watched the news copy as it came in from around the region and helped determine what was worth pursuing further and what could be sent out to member newspapers immediately. Gillis Purcell, who later became General Manager (Canada) of the agency, suggests that CB probably also served as a "rewrite man," that is, he would tone up and flesh out the submissions of reporters in the field. Purcell recalls meeting CB around 1930 in the Halifax Bureau office; he describes CB as a "ruffle-headed, carelessly-dressed young guy [who was] quiet and modest."[8] Purcell, who had heard a lot about CB from J.F.B. Livesay, Dorothy Livesay's father, admired his poetry, and admits that he felt a certain amount of envy for a young man who could not only write verse but superior journalistic pieces as well.

CB, as an editor, did not get too many opportunities to be original in his journalism, but two efforts from the early 1930s indicate his talents and presage his future creative concerns. In late January 1931, a Lunenburg fishing boat, which was carrying rum to the prohibition-bound U.S., was fired upon by the American Coast Guard in lower New York Bay. The captain of the *Josephine K*, William Cluett, was killed. Perhaps CB was sent to cover the funeral, but, more likely, he volunteered to do so, sensing in the story something of his heritage. He filed a 650-word report in which he let events and people speak for themselves, but shaped the articulation into an eloquent questioning of the need for Captain Cluett to die. CB's portrait of a Lunenburg town that buried one of its own, yet was united by so much more than an individual death, is the epitome of passionate restraint. The reader hears the Anglican minister at the funeral understate the facts that resulted in the Coast Guard fusillade: "Captain Cluett was simply the commander of a supply boat carrying a commodity demanded by the people of the United States." The reporter does not allow the human elements of this complex issue to be shrouded by legal or ethical debate. Rather, he provides omniscient narration that elevates an anecdotal piece to the level of parable more concerned with simple truths than with moral lessons: "Consideration of the ethics of carrying liquor were far from [the] minds [of Lunenburgers]. Friendship and sympathy transcend the cold logic of international law. William Cluett was a good man to sail with, a good man to sail under." At the heart of the story is the reality of Lunenburg, rather than some abstract celebration of the town. Ideas, heritage, and vision are found in things as they are:

> ... the fleet is in. The harbour is thronged with the masts of shipping, low lying motor craft, fishing vessels, rakish and graceful, and the squat hulls of four-masters, in with salt from Turk's Island, their burdened rigging stark against the winter white of the basin shore.

The New York Times carried what CB had written, without a by-line, on February 1, 1931. This prompted a letter, almost twice as long as the item itself, from a New York lawyer, Alexander Rorke. He wrote the *Times* extolling the "sheer literary beauty" of the article, calling it "a literary gem, deserving of equal mark with those classics" of journalism, and suggested that, regarding prohibition, "It may become ... what 'Uncle Tom's Cabin' was to the adherents of human slavery." Rorke later sent a copy of his letter to CB, and the Canadian Press published a small booklet that contained CB's piece, the Rorke missive to the *Times*, and Rorke's note to the author in which he said, "There are very many people here in New York City who felt as I did about your report."[9] Gillis Purcell states flatly of the Cluett report, "Nobody else wrote like that," and over fifty years later, Jack Brayley, who joined CP in 1935, could still remember the impact CB's prose had on him.[10]

If CB seemed to realize instinctively that he had no need to resort to fine writing or to transmute human experience into abstract sentiment in order to convey its essence in a newspaper story, he simultaneously found a straightforward and unadorned way in which to write a poem, which was not in the casual and prosaic style of "Brooklyn." In February 1931, "Lunenburg" appeared in *The Open Gateway*, the monthly publication of the Halifax Harbour Commission. In form it is a conventional sonnet, but CB writes entirely of tangibles, a poetry that years later he described as "simple and stirring and understandable without drifting into banality; using the con-

LUNENBURG

Tomorrow's wind shall bring the spars alive
That mark this haven's use for throttled steam;
Tall spars and straining duck, to lift and drive
Sheer hulls—and not a funnel in the stream.
Now to the darkened wharves a man goes down
With the sure tide's own granite in his face,
And in his hands the future of a town,
And in his walk the sea's unconscious grace.

Here is a laughing challenge, not for us
Who spend the suns at cage and desk and vault.
Never to change for minus signs and plus
Black rubber boots and jersies bleached with salt.
Only with shaken heads we answer it—
"We's goin' out tomorrow; comin' wit'?"

crete terms of life .... "[11] In such poetry, he insisted, "The thing
is to see whether you can make [readers] feel the same thing by
setting up imaginatively before them not what you feel but the
concrete things that made you feel that way."[12]

In the quatrain CB presents "Tomorrow's wind," "Tall spars"
and "Sheer hulls," and the fisherman "With the sure tide's own
granite in his face" who represents the constant past that is "the
future of a town." In the sestet, rather than provide an abstract
commentary on the distinction he sets up between such a man
and those of us who are caged indoors at our work, CB allows
the dialect of the Lunenburger to be the poet's articulation of
meaning in the poem: "We's goin' out tomorrow; comin' wit'?"[13]
When he was twenty-five CB was capable of writing about the
people and experience he knew best with virtually the same
strength, conviction, and ability he displayed two decades later
in *The Mulgrave Road*.

Port and Province was a monthly "with the object of promot-
ing the port of Halifax and the progress and prosperity of the
province of Nova Scotia."[14] In the spring of 1932 CB produced
a piece for it in which he discussed the constant emigration of
Nova Scotians to other provinces and, indeed, to other parts of
the world. It was a theme he returned to in the fiction of *The
Township of Time* and a seminal two-part essay published in the
CBC Times in 1956.[15] The May 1932 article, "Land of Home-
Loving Wanderers," is interesting not only because CB makes
an attractive case for Nova Scotia being "the greatest little ex-
porter of brains we know of today" (the province, apparently, is
not big enough to hold all those who want to achieve and profit
"to the limit of human recognition"), but also because of a narrative technique that he could not employ in the more stringent
confines of Canadian Press. The essay takes the form of a story
within a story in which the frame tale is of two Nova Scotians
who try to explain to a rather ignorant American that their
province is more than "just rocks." This conversation prompts
the first-person singular narrator later to ask an acquaintance
from Pictou about Nova Scotia's human exports. The remainder
of the article is a monologue by the Pictou man (who now lives
in a city far from Nova Scotia) about the uniqueness of the

province and its people, to which the narrator adds a final "Amen." This figure of the local met beyond provincial borders is a prototype for other, future characters in CB's essays and fiction and poetry, men and women who remind the narrator of home and whose movement "away" suggests to him the heritage of his own itinerant nature.

Meanwhile, CB's reputation as a poet was growing. In the 1930 anthology titled *Modern Canadian Poetry* there were six poems from *Wild Apples* and in *Songs of the Maritimes* in 1931 two more.[16] There is a letter to CB written in December 1932 from the Assistant-Editor-in-Chief of the Montreal *Daily Star* that refers to the "poem regarding Christmas ... used ... on Saturday last."[17] This may well have been a verse included in Christmas cards sent out by Agnes Bruce that year, in which CB recalls a small red pig he received from Santa in 1910. The memory of the tin pig breaks down "the walls between Today and Then" much as it does in a prose piece CB wrote much later for *Canadian Homes and Gardens*, entitled "Tin Pigs and Raisins," in which his central metaphor is "the Pool of Now and Then."[18]

Certainly Andrew Merkel was prepared to push the reputation of the poet he had first read almost ten years previously. Early in the winter of 1932 Hugh Eayrs, president of Macmillan of Canada, came to Halifax, and Merkel had him read a manuscript of twenty-five lyrics and sonnets that CB had compiled since 1927. " ... Hugh decided he would publish them under his practice of recognizing that there were books that should be published, even when there was no chance of their making money."[19] Whatever the story behind the scenes, CB was soon no longer a poet with only one vanity press book to his credit. He was very proud of *Tomorrow's Tide* and would walk by Allen's Bookstore on Granville Street to admire the two framed pictures of himself — one in a dinner-jacket and the other in a Mount Allison sweater — surrounded by copies of his book. A friend who worked at Allen's told CB one day that things were looking up as two women had come in to price the picture frames. CB recalled that a royalty cheque of $13.75 was the highest of the two or three he received.

Tomorrow's Tide[20] is a mixed collection from a young poet who continued to depend to a considerable extent on past poetic models, but whose increasingly complex life experience allowed for a more original expression and perception of things. Most of the love poems in the volume have been discussed. CB could still write what might be called his inductive nature poems, such as "Ragwort": "Sombre and wise and mellow/The dark weed grew,/To mark in pensive yellow/The truth we still know:/'Tomorrow's high alluring/In today goes past;/Desire goes on enduring/As long as dreams last.'" His celebrations of the earth could still be archaic in tone and language, as in "The Bystanders": "The young moon lifts a bloodless knife,/The ploughman drives his burning share;/And fain of half-remembered life,/The wistful deities are there."

When Bliss Carman died in June, 1929, CB's tribute to the poet, "Reinforcement for the City under the Star," was couched in language more indicative of his comfort with certain imagery than it was admirable emulation of Carman himself: "But the voice echoed with an elfin thunder/Of aching need behind the city's gates — /A need of dusty grace, of lyric wonder,/A need of singing clay: 'Shamballah waits.'"

There were also CB's more rhetorical efforts in which he separated himself from the political convictions of some of the committed contributors to the *Song Fishermen's Song Sheet*. In "Essay on Sociology" he states, "No heart is in me for the swarming breed/With party cause to urge or faith to swear," but his alternative is rather high-sounding and undefined: "My trust is in the marrow of the man." More effective because it is less evasive is CB's symbolic employment of the rose in "Parable on Peace." A rose makes a contract with the earth and sun that she will bloom until "Gabriel's quaking trumpet hailed them home." On that Judgement Day Jehovah does not recognize such a thing as a rose. However, the potentially modern moral that happiness is something that must be striven for and earned, in a world where pacts of self-interest are all too common, is undercut by such terms as "throve" and "ruddy foam" and the generally fanciful nature of the poem.

By far the best poem in which CB attempts to place the new politics in perspective is "Tomorrow's Tide." Here he invokes a place-name from his Port Shoreham experience for the first time in his verse and sets up a contrast between political plans and compromises on the one hand and, on the other, the meeting ground of man and the natural world on the beach near Ragged Head. In the first stanza of eight lines CB describes the beach before dawn without adornment: "Not yet, behind the bluffs of Ragged Head,/Red light has lifted, nor the wind astir/Made the bay quick with breath. The beach is still/" But he does feel it necessary to elevate the common scene: "Night lies with us and we are used to her/But the pulse beats; and a relentless will/Forswears the velvet lover." It is in the second stanza that CB pays most precise attention to the simple life he would have offset political activity; but historical, religious, and insubstantial images result in a crowded situation. The "Brief scraping as the weathered boats go down" is a strong individual line, but has trouble being heard.

CB later wrote of this poem, "What poetry there is ... exists elsewhere than in the didactic element. The 'brief scraping,' the 'rasp of stem and strake through furrowed gravel' and the 'gutteral hiss of water streaming in the shoreward wake' [stanza three] are authentic experience." This is so, but in the last twenty lines of "Tomorrow's Tide" there is too much of the poet telling us such things as "No treaty binds the shifting squall,/With wind there is no compromise," and not enough of the sound and feel of "the surf that breaks on Ragged Head." CB admitted, looking back over thirty years at the poem, that there is too much of a lapse into admonition or argument.

"Lunenberg" is part of this collection, and here CB proves, without saying, as he does in "Tomorrow's Tide," that "The faith we leave you and the word we give" are of life's unornamented experience. In "Spirit of a Province" he asks, "How shall a word, in changing sound, express/A thing grown tangible through furrowed clay ... ?" If he can suggest that "The rugged stress of sea on stone may give you wit to guess" — thus using words to summon sound and sight — he is still aware that often "words

TOMORROW'S TIDE

Not yet, behind the bluffs of Ragged Head,
Red light has lifted, nor the wind astir
Made the bay quick with breath. The beach is still.
Night lies with us and we are wed to her.
But the pulse beats; and a relentless will
Forswears the velvet lover. In her stead
Slow tides of grey set the sharp dark ablur,
Before the morning swell is ringed with red.

Not now the sleep encircled night may drown
This early lamplight pale against the pane,
Nor woodsmoke drowsing in the tranquil dusk.
Now stubborn kinsmen of the viking strain
Join crisp and thrifty greeting with a brusque
Brief scraping, as the weathered boats go down
To meet dark water in the need to gain
This day the daily bread of no renown.

Caught from the common rasp of stem and strake
Through furrowed gravel, and the guttural hiss
Of water streaming in the shoreward wake,
The word they leave you in the sand is this:

"Tommorrow's tide is deaf to call,
Without recourse the daylight dies;
No treaty binds the shifting squall,
With wind there is no compromise."

Life's urge exploited, statesmen shape the truss
Of ribboned foolscap in a distant room,
And wait new wars behind the terms of peace.
Here on the beach the seeds of struggle bloom
Beyond the need for militant release;
Hazard is never second-hand to us—
Though millions ache to wear its crimson plume,
Here on the beach we are not troubled thus.

While simple strength and rugged beauty live,
Unmarked of splendor crowned or glory sped,
The faith we leave you and word we give
Beats in the surf that breaks on Ragged Head:

"Let go the signed and sealed excuse
That nourishes maturing spoil;
And turn your thirsting millions loose
On hill and forest, sea and soil.

Unchecked, the rainwet troopers ride,
The sunlight-feathered arrow flies;
Implacable as creeping tide,
With wind there is no compromise."

avail not," but that it is essentially abstract words that do not do justice to the occasion.

In the final poem of the book, "Recapitulation," CB writes of death, "when the last brief word is said," and asserts that what remains for the living, and is rediscovered by those of spirit only, is the strength of "shingles under pounding rain" and the faith found in "The light that moves on bending wheat/The song of gutters under eaves." The language of reality — as provided by the poet in simple, concrete imagery — was, for CB, the result of articulations *in* reality: the sounds of sea on stone, the even softer speech of light and wind in a field of grain. "To Harold Raine" best illustrates how far CB had come from his mother's perception of "the hills of After" and Robert Norwood's view of how these hills should be presented in verse. Raine, General Superintendent of Canadian Press, was killed in a plane crash in 1931, and CB eulogized his colleague as follows:

> I wonder now — up some far cosmic stair
> A cigarette butt smoulders on the floor;
> And cherub copy-boys are soon aware
> Of a new voice behind the dingy door,
> To laugh and swear and hum an earthy tune —
> And shoot crisp bulletins to sun and moon.

Reviews of *Tomorrow's Tide* were generally positive. What is interesting is the comparison, by some critics, of CB with his poetic contemporaries. One states her approval that "the note of futility, bitterness, and decadence so dear to most of our young moderns is conspicuously absent."[21] Another calmly points out that "If we do not find the variety of metrical experiment usual in younger poets, there is a freedom and mastery of the forms used which is not usual at any age."[22] *The Commonwealth* strikes a Norwoodian note when it praises the "wholesome personality" revealed in the poems, but also emphasizes "an admirable willingness to experiment."[23] The book was reviewed alongside Dorothy Livesay's second collection, *Signposts*, in the Toronto *Mail and Empire* and, possibly because of CB's Canadian Press connections, in *The New York Herald Tribune* (which appreciated the sharpening, by an ironic under-

tone, of "the otherwise conventional edge of certain of his sonnets.")[24]

That conventional edge was also honed by CB's insistence in
a decade of political turmoil and shifting commitments that the
heart of the world's matter is found in "Slow tides of grey which
set the sharp dark ablur,/Before the morning swell is ringed
with red."[25] One of his rewards was a letter from Charles G. D.
Roberts, editor-in-chief of *The Canadian Who's Who*, asking him
to write up "half a dozen" biographical sketches at $2.00 each.
Roberts' criterion for inclusion was " ... any career presenting
any feature which justifies its preservation from oblivion."[26]
There is no indication here from Roberts as to whether CB was
himself to be saved from the void (and, in fact, CB did not appear in this edition of *Who's Who*).

In September 1933, after five years with CP Halifax, CB was
transferred to the editorial staff of the Toronto CP bureau on
Adelaide Street. Within three years he was appointed News
Editor and then, in 1937, General News Editor for all of Canada.
Obviously his duties and responsibilities within the organization were increasing; these, together with a growing awareness
that he was farther from his roots and familiar territory than he
wished to be, seem to have prompted him to investigate a return
to Maritimes journalism. In August 1934 he wrote to President
George J. Trueman at Mount Allison that he was interested in a
"rejuvenation of the Sackville Post."[27] He felt that the
newspaper plant could be obtained for around $10,000 and told
Trueman, "My own interest is a gradually growing desire to get
out of big cities and take a hand in building something for which
I would be directly responsible. If I had [the money] I shouldn't
hesitate to buy the *Post* and go to it, win or lose." Trueman
replied a few days later, saying that he did not see much of a future for the editor of the paper and generally discouraging CB.
However, Herbert M. Wood of Sackville did tell CB that " ....
with your talent and ability, I feel you should be able to make a
success of it."[28] Wood also mentions that CB's political per-
suasions would stand him in good stead for some government
patronage after the 1935 federal and provincial elections, though

just what Wood meant by this is not clear since at no point in his letters or published or unpublished work does CB admit of a "political persuasion."

Trueman's opinion seems to have won out, and there is no more correspondence about the Sackville paper. But a year later, in August 1935, CB wrote to R.A. Jodrey regarding Jodrey's possible purchase of the *Windsor Tribune* in Nova Scotia, and indicated that he would be willing to take a reduction in pay in order to be able to work in his home province. When Jodrey, in November 1935, asked CB if he were still looking for a job, CB hedged and suggested he would need "$50.00 a week to run the editorial and news end of it." Again, such correspondence ends without any decisions being made, or at least publicly stated. Perhaps CB had wind of his impending appointment as General News Editor when, in April 1937, C.A. Munro, publisher of the St. John *Citizen* (only a few months old), offered him a position on the recommendation of Andrew Merkel. CB's interest in returning to the Maritimes might have been negatively influenced by his responsibilities to a growing family — Alan was born in October 1931, Harry in July 1934, and Andrew in January 1937. CB's reply to Munro reveals a certain sense of being caught and unable to move: "Under other circumstances your tentative proposition would be more than welcome, but as things are I feel it would be a mistake for me to make any change or commitment at this time …."[29]

Of what was CB thinking during those first years in Toronto? Even without comparison to his Sackville and Halifax outpourings of the previous decade, he wrote very little verse — only seven or eight poems. One, "An Ear to the Ground," reveals what was missing in his urban, punch-clock existence:

> An ear to the ground — and wait
> You hear the chuckle and slap
> Of chop in the surly strait
> A thousand miles by the map?
>
> Oh no; it is only a fault
> Engrained in the rock of the mind;
> Remembered grace to the halt,
> Remembered sight to the blind.

Whatever the world becomes,
They will not leave you alone —
The old impersonal drums
Of leisurely surf on stone.

An echo, following still,
A silence gathered and drowned
In tides of a restless will
To live again with the sound.[30]

Will Bruce died in October 1934, four days short of his seventy-first birthday, and this undoubtedly caused CB to gaze eastward and back into time. He wrote "Fisherman's Son," a double sonnet, in the months immediately following his father's death; it was accepted for publication by *The Canadian* in July 1935.[31] Here CB speaks of the physical experience of fishing on the bay with Will — "the trenchant bite/Of cold salt water," "the brief recurrent shock/Of bodies braced against a plunging line." The emotional and mental bonding of father and son that occurred when CB was a boy was based on such reality and provides strength years later:

Now at its need the weakened mind shall turn
An oilskin to the dictatorial rain.
What shall a little wind of words avail
Against a heart close-hauled, with shortened sail?

Then it is Will's turn to speak of his lack of surprise, but embarrassment that "his son,/Learned in a gentle way of thought and speech,/Should still consider where the mackerel run/And three gray fish-huts on a windy beach." Will knows of the "kinship" that is "More eloquent than blood" and that was tempered in the wind of Chedabucto Bay. In Will's sestet, CB grabs the net of abstractions with both hands and pulls it *down* from the depths to what is known:

Lord, I address myself to you: be kind,
Thoughtful of how the cosmic current sets;
Though immortality be a state of mind,
Let there be clean firm bottom for the nets.
When it is time for this quick flesh to die
Let herring school through Heaven's hot July.[32]

FISHERMAN'S SON

I

Now I am thankful this unbroken flesh
Has known hard rowing, and the trenchant bite
Of cold salt water, as reluctant mesh
Came up at sunrise from the tidal night.
Wisdom was in the brief recurrent shock
Of bodies braced against a plunging line;
Familiar meaning in the liquid knock
Of building swell concerned with buoyant pine.

Only in some black biting hour we learn
How strength and wit lie dreaming in the brain...
Now at its need the wakened mind shall turn
An oilskin to the dictatorial rain:
What shall a little wind or words avail
Against a heart close-hauled, with shortened sail?

II

This ghost is much embarrassed that his son,
Learned in a gentler way of thought and speech,
Should still consider where the mackerel run
And three grey fish huts on a windy beach.
Embarrassed but unsurprised. His heart has known
That kinship tempered in an offshore blow,
More eloquent than blood to mark its own,
Pulsed always in us. And he knows I know.

Lord, I address myself to you: be kind;
Mindful of how the cosmic current sets.
Though immortality be a state of mind,
Let there be clean firm bottom for the nets.
When it is time for this quick flesh to die
Let herring school through heaven's hot July.

WORDS ARE NEVER ENOUGH

These are the fellows who smell of salt to the prairie,
Keep the back country informed of crumbling swell
That buckles the international course off Halifax
After a night of wind:

Angus Walters and Ben Pine, carrying on for Tommy
    Himmelman and Marty Welch;
Heading up the tough men who get into the news,
Heading up the hard men of Lunenburg and Gloucester,
Keeping the cities bordered with grass and grain
Forever mindful that something wet and salt
Creeps and loafs and marches round the continent,
Careless of time, careless of change, obeying the moon.

Listen to little Angus, squinting at the Bluenose:
"The timber that'll beat her still stands in the woods."
Yes, these are the fellows who remind you again of the sea.

But one town, or two,
Are never enough to keep the salt in the blood.

I haven't seen Queensport Light over the loom of Ragged
    Head in years,
And never a smell of rollers coming up the bay from Canso.
No one ever heard of Queensport outside the bait report;
No one ever saw the name of Ragged Head anywhere.

Off that obscure beach, Will Bruce and George McMaster
Set their herring nets, and went farther out for mackerel.

The mackerel never ran, but in July
Fat herring tangled in wet twine were silver-thick,
And the flat low in the water as we hauled around
To head back for the huts;
In full daylight now,
After the grey dusk of a windless morning;
After the bay, gently stirring in half darkness,
Tipped down again to blush at the sun's rim.

Cleaning fish is a joy you would balk at;
But nothing is mean with gulls hovering down,

Sun brighter than life on glistening eelgrass,
The bay crawling again in a quickening southwest wind.

There was always time, after the wash-barrels were empty,
After hand-barrows were lugged up the beach to the hut,
And herring lay behind hand-wrought staves,
    clean with salt.

Time to lie on warm stone and listen,
While the sting went out of crooked fingers and thighs
    ceased to ache;
Time to hear men's voices, coming quietly through
    a colored cloth of sound
Woven in the slap of water on fluent gravel.

Their talk was slow and quiet, of fish and men
And fields back on the hill with fences down,
Hay to be made through long hot days with never
    a splash on the oilskins
Or the lift of water awake under half-inch pine.

The mackerel never ran; and if the herring
Had been only a story, a legend for midnight telling,
These would have launched their flats and tended
    the empty nets.

I know it now, remembering now the calm;
Remembering now the lowering care that lifted
From a face turned to the wind off Ragged Head.
These are the fellows who keep the salt in the blood.
Knowing it fresh in themselves, needful as hope,
They give to the cities bordered with woods and grass
A few homesick men, walking an alien street;
A few women, remembering misty stars
And the long grumbling sigh of the bay at night.

Words are never enough; these are aware
Somewhere deep in the soundless well of knowing,
That sea, in the flesh and nerves and puzzling mind
Of children born to the long grip of its tide,
Must always wash the land's remotest heart.
These are the fellows who keep the salt in the blood.

As a paean to a way of life and to the person who best represented that life for the poet, this poem can stand with any in
Canadian literature.

Early in 1938, CB sent J.F.B. Livesay a long, free-verse poem
that his then General-Manager thought deserved a better title
than "Salt in the Blood."[33] The reference is to "Words Are Never
Enough," a tribute to those men and women who have travelled
inland in Canada, but are "Forever mindful that something wet
and salt/Creeps and loafs and marches round the continent,/Careless of time, careless of change, obeying the
moon."[34] CB is, of course, one of these people who admits he
has not "seen Queensport Light over the loom of Ragged Head
in years," but he remembers that "obscure beach" where his
father and others launched their boats and cleaned their fish. In
one central stanza, life is simply worth living because "nothing
is mean with gulls hovering down,/Sun brighter than life on
glistening eelgrass,/The bay crawling again in a quickening
southwest wind." The fishermen's voices and stories are
"Woven in the slap of water on fluent gravel," and speakers and
listeners are more human for the salt in the blood of narratives
and in themselves. The sea is without and within us — it is
where we came from as a species and, in the womb's solution,
as individuals. It is the element of heritage that, as we travel
away from our roots, "Must always wash [our] land's remotest
heart." CB emphasizes, as he has before, that "Words are never
enough" to convey and keep the truths of existence. But what
he writes of here is alive "deep in the soundless well of knowing" in himself and in those simple men and women who are
artists in their own way, capable of communicating our shared
beginnings.

"Words Are Never Enough" was published in *Canadian
Poetry Magazine* in July 1939 and later appeared in two anthologies — Ralph Gustafson's *Anthology of Canadian Poetry*
(1942) and A. J. M. Smith's *Book of Canadian Poetry* (1943).[35] The
poem also won CB $100.00 for first prize in a contest sponsored
by the Women's Canadian Club of Toronto and for which E. J.
Pratt was one of the judges. Just what those on the supposedly

leading edge of Canadian poetry thought of CB might best be found in what the prominent Montreal poet Leo Kennedy wrote in an article for *New Frontier* in 1936 called "Direction for Canadian Poets": " … Bruce of Halifax writes convincingly of the sea and ships, but his poetry carries the personal, insular emotion of one still unaware of immediates."[36] Although Kennedy later insisted to CB that "immediates" had been a typographical error for "political immediacies,"[37] his essential criticism was no different. At the time CB did not think so much as sense that

> … the poet's business is with insights flashed from his own experience. Insights that may … begin to weave a frail web of human kinship. Is it not where kinship has failed, or never been, that all hostilities come to monstrous flower?Torture, murder, rape, war, and all the malice and indifference and indignity with which mankind corrupts itself? ("The Back of the Book")

Poetry, he felt, could only combat such horror not by moralizing over it, but by attempting to convey "the gleam of truth glimpsed through lived experience." He fired off two poems to Kennedy: in "Immediates" he asserts that justice and injustice come "Not from the system but the man" and that the translation of "the inexplicit earth" for the human race comes through such things as "The bite of salt through sodden wool," "the roofless beach," and "The open cut, the healing scar." In "Alternative" CB would have "Protest and studied invective" follow only from an understanding of life's basic "seam so woven that fabric and thread are one."[38]

Leo Kennedy did take CB's poetry seriously, whatever he may have thought of its political naiveté. In January 1937 he wrote CB lamenting his omission from the *Brooker Yearbook of the Arts in Canada* and telling him that he, A.J.M. Smith, and F.R. Scott "are now working on another book of poetry to follow *New Provinces* [1936]." Kennedy invited CB to join them "in the new venture."[39] CB's reply emphasizes the limitations on his creative writing and perhaps too his own sense of distance from the Montreal poets: " … I don't think so, this year. Ever since leaving the Atlantic Coast three years ago I've been up to my ears in work and anything I've written is lying around on the backs of envelopes."[40] When Kennedy requested some of this "envelope" poetry, CB sent him "Deep Cove"; it appeared in *New Frontier* in June 1937.

"Deep Cove" is a 212-line narrative poem about a sculptor named John Black who returns, after years of absence, to the seaside village of his youth, looking for inspiration. He finds the familiar surf and tranquillity, but also a disillusion with the ideal place of his memory — the village has changed, city slang and "new and duller ways" have intruded; "only the echoing ghost" of kinship and the flow of life remains. The single inhabitant in whom flesh and spirit are one is a young woman named Mary: "Some recrudescent and archaic strain ... /Lived in the breast she bore against the rain,/The brown young face she lifted to the sun." Black learns from her that his work is not done, that he must sculpt life not as it is, "But as it can be." There follows a long monologue by the sculptor, who articulates one of the emerging central themes of CB's *oeuvre*:

> Here are the things Deep Cove will live by then:
> The day and the moment and a man's own strength;
> A man's conviction that the man next door
> And the one next to him, and he himself,
> Are all joined branches in the growth of life;
> That no one living can be set apart
> From any other living — even the dead
> Live on in us through strange and tenuous threads.[41]

The problem is that this important message is addressed to Mary, who has just asked Black to take her with him, and he has refused, advising her to remain in the village as a symbol "Of telling beauty." In the poem, Mary stoically accepts his decision, thus allowing the sculptor's sense of vision and purpose to remain intact.

CB later wrote: "The story-line is nonsense. If Mary is such a catalyst of light and life that she can rejuvenate the cove, how has it got into the shape it's in now? And John, while he has good instincts and some insight, must be essentially a fool to leave her to it. I saw quite soon that I had written some fair lines in an absurd context." But the context is significant because it is not perhaps so far removed from CB's own situation of heart and

IMMEDIATES

IMMEDIATES? Let us take for text
The bite of salt through sodden wool,
And place a running headrope next
Ink by the pen or bucketful.

Two cents for haddock, one for cod;
Weather a chance, and wind a guess—
But no allegiance to the god
Of unavailing bitterness.

Here on the roofless beach they know
The fallibility of plan,
That justice and injustice grow
Not from the system but the man.

An ageless land and sea conspire
To smooth the imperfect mould of birth;
While freezing spray and dryng fire
Translate the inexplicit earth.

"Get understanding first of these:
The open cut, the healing scar;
Before you flick prophetic keys
To tell us what immediates are."

RETURN AND INTRODUCTION

Eight years or ten are time enough to lay
Uneasy change along the rutted track:
Ploughed fields are bush, and russet roofs are grey,
And time has moved the wagon and the stack.
Or is it only that remembering eyes,
Once keen to spring's return and summer's going,
Tricked by the town's insistent symmetries
Have lost their old discernment, never knowing?

Two roads go hither, and two hills are thrust
Into the shining of a double sun;
And I—uncertain if the earthy crust
Of sober truth envelops either one—
Go aimless, questioning in which of these
Lives the lost friendliness I came to seize.

II

He was polite to strangers, but his mind
Was fixed on other matters and his pride
Walked in the future privately, to find
A cavalier with triumph in his stride.
I, who am nice to strangers, meet him so:
Go reaching back t beach and field and hill
Without regret or jubilance, to know
The boy who looked beyond tomorrow still.

Wordless, I question him: And is your thought
Familiar with this bearing and this face?
Does this design the quickening years have wrought
Wake no reuturn of time, no hint of place?
Not yet has any fire of greeting starred
The grave politeness in his clam regard.

mind in the late 1930s. He could write "Fisherman's Son" as a celebration of the past and "Words Are Never Enough" as a tribute to those who remember their heritage, and he could long "To live again with the sound" of surf on stone, but he could not go back to Port Shoreham to live and write there. "Deep Cove" as it stands is about the separation between art and life as much as it is about the connection. If CB literally could not go home again, he had to find a way in his art to convey "the living stream [of yesterday, today, and tomorrow]/That flows in us and everything we know."

That he was questioning the relationship between past and present and struggling with divisions in time, rather than the flow of time is evident from another double sonnet of the late l930s, "Return and Introduction."[42] In the opening octave CB seems to present himself visiting Port Shoreham "Eight years or ten" after he first left home on a permanent basis. This self, in his mid-twenties, wonders if the old territory of boyhood has changed, or is it only that his "remembering eyes" influenced "by the town's insistent symmetries" cannot see the place clearly? The result in the sestet is that he is "aimless," lost somewhere between reality and the perception of it, a position complicated by time past, passing, and to come. In the second sonnet the narrator is in his mid-thirties and writes of " … reaching back to beach and field and hill" to meet his earlier self. The younger CB and the older one are strangers, despite the complicated reversal of time's usually-perceived flow, when the older asks the younger, "Does this design the quickening years have wrought/Wake no return of time, no hint of place?" What deepens the confrontation and the question is the fact that CB "had [probably] not been back to eastern Nova Scotia in years."[43] In other words, this double sonnet was written by a man who wrote of return in the past because he could not, for whatever reasons, return in the present. If the quality of the poem obviously indicates that CB was not "aimless," his subject-matter strongly suggests problems with the actual loss of Port Shoreham as a home and with the dependence on memory at the heart of his creative vision and production.

Much older, through a commentary on Charles G.D. Roberts' "Tantramar Revisited," CB revealed that he had come to terms with such difficulties: " ... it seems to me that [Roberts] fell into an artificial sentiment when in [the poem's] closing lines, after some unforgettable images of the Westmoreland Shore, he turns away, refusing to come near lest he 'spy at their task even here the hands of chance and change'":

> The interplay of chance and change with the old and known, the play of time on the remembered and the half-forgotten, with its intimations of a fluid continuity, is for me an endless fascination. Only an unchanging world would be intolerable. Along with this is the curious fact that long separation from things once familiar can create something like the hankering we have for the unknown and new ("The Back of the Book").

In the 1940s CB wrote a poem in which memory was only one element in his perception of the past, and the past was always itself and part of the future as well. "In The Long Evenings Of Long Summers"[44] contains images of the north shore of Chedabucto Bay from "years ago, and lives away" and describes how far shores once dreamed of ("Vancouver ... Demerara ... Finisterre") have now been reached. But there is no division between then and now, nor a simple linear progression "away," because now from those far shores " ... a lost landfall beckons to the reach/Of the heart's ardor" — the old becomes the new, the past the future, and precisely because there is a movement *on*, not back, to what is known and familiar, the progression is cyclical as well. The resultant creative matrix is what Roberts called in his poem "Life and Art", "The mystery of my memories/And all I long to be."[45]

In 1936 CB was promoted from Assistant News Editor to News Editor at CP because, as Livesay said, it " ... is a fitting recognition of his consistent good work and the broad view he takes of the service as a whole, from coast to coast and overseas."[46] The next year his seniority within the organization was firmly established as he became General News Editor for the entire country. Shortly after the war broke out in September 1939 he was transferred to the vital New York Bureau as Acting Superintendent there. The CP office was in Rockefeller Plaza in Manhattan, and CB commuted from Flushing near the site of the World's Fair (where, Agnes Bruce recalls, Sibelius's "Finlandia" was played "about nine times a day"). The stories he cabled to Toronto included those about the average American's attitude towards the war ("New York Women Make Bundles for Britain," "Most Americans Realize Day For Showdown Near") and hard political items (the U.S. General Election, "Canadian-U.S. Joint Defense Board"). In the spring of 1940 he wrote personally to Livesay that there was great difficulty in discovering the truth about ship losses in the North Atlantic "when probably the Admiralty itself didn't know."

Apparently, despite his senior position and responsibility, CB was not happy. In August 1940 he wrote Livesay, " ... there is a certain amount of discouragement in doing what I know to have been a pretty good job [at CP] and ... getting no reputation out of it that would serve me anywhere except in CP ... I have none [of the loyalties] that would cause me any heart-wrenching at leaving off."[47] Livesay had already written to him about a possible job to head CBC Radio News,[48] but Canadian Press recognized CB's value, and when Gillis Purcell was granted a leave of absence to serve as Public Relations Officer for the Canadian Army overseas, CB was recalled from New York and appointed Acting General Superintendent, one rank below the top administrative position in the organization. According to Purcell, the General Superintendent was really an Assistant General Manager who would not be on the news desk "unless something happened on the wire." Then he would tell the local news bureau how to handle the news gathering (usually by "lighting a fire under the bureau chief.")[49] Jack Brayley, who after joining CP in London in 1935, moved to the Montreal Office and a stint with the National Press Gallery in Ottawa, and then became CB's Atlantic Bureau Chief in 1946, remembers that while CB "was not aggressive or opinionated .... He wouldn't tolerate any b.s. or bunches of adjectives in his stories, but wanted writing that was clear and crisp."[50]

In particular, one New York letter to Livesay reveals that CB still kept time for literature and for the relationship between art and life:

> I got that Henry James stuff you mentioned from Leon [Edel] and have just finished "The Lesson of the Master." Funny thing, I can't always tell when HJ is serious or having fun. For instance, in that story, it seems to me both St. George and the young novelist are off-balance. It strikes me that the experience of marriage with all its major responsibilities and minor irritations, and heart-breaking emotional debacles, is necessary to a person who wants to see anything whole and write about it — that the freedom to write, economically and so on, that comes to the man who escapes it, is just a bit barren. The trouble is you can't have the experience for 10 years or so and then shed the responsibilities, except by the accident of death, or unless there is plenty of money back of you. And in that case, you probably wouldn't have had the necessary worry to mature a perceptive and resilient mind anyway ... So I think that men of genius are accidents of fortune.[51]

Certainly there is more than general commentary here. CB was close to Livesay and seemed to be sharing with him some of his personal commitments as a man and writer. *Home* in Toronto, with all of its attendant responsibilities, was where CB wrote his poetry and fiction about Port Shoreham, but if this home and writing there were a great distance from CP administrative duties, Port Shoreham as home (and any creative possibilities there) were even further: "I've had a plan in my mind for some time to put a good concrete cellar under the old house down there (built about 1845) and a bathroom in it, for a GHQ, if I ever find it advisable to say 'To Hell With This.'"[52]

CB had first met Leon Edel, the future James biographer, at CP in Toronto in 1938.[53] Edel was cable-desk man for CP New York from 1939-42, and he and CB had ample opportunity for literary discussions during the latter's New York year. They kept in touch after CB had returned to Toronto, and Edel, aware that A.J.M. Smith had a Guggenheim Fellowship to enable him to put together an anthology of Canadian poetry, warned CB " .... there may be a danger that Smith will be partial to the disciples of W.B. Yeats on the one hand and T. S. Eliot on the other, he being very much a product of both."[54] Whatever Smith's leanings he did include four poems by CB in the *Book of Canadian Poetry* and praised CB's "Sincerity and .... forthright solidity of feeling."[55] In one long letter to Edel, CB offered more thoughts on James (he was "concerned with the bark and the sap, and didn't profess to see things whole") and praised Conrad as "The only fellow I ever read who gave me the impression of being able to do a hell of a job on a sweeping picture and at the same time a good piece of work on the little, indicative angles ...."[56]

The family (Agnes and the three boys) was settled in 1941 in a large house on Farnham Avenue in Toronto, where CB lived for the rest of his life. His professional career, however, was still unsettled. In 1942 Gillis Purcell returned to CP as General Superintendent and CB went back to being General News Editor. In this capacity he visited London in August and September 1942 and almost immediately filed reports on the Canadian catastrophe at Dieppe (CB interviewed survivors of the raid at a "south coast port") in addition to other pieces on the war effort. After another year and a half in Toronto he was named CP London Superintendent; he was in England from March 1944 until July 1945. Meanwhile, through the late 1930s and early 1940s CB continued to write poetry, and in one extraordinary sustained effort he produced the manuscript of a novel.

In 1938 CB won a Canadian Authors' Association competition for a sonnet written to Andrew Merkel, "Finds Former Poet in Editor's Chair." In the poem he compares the way he and Merkel have had to make a living and their long silences about their own poetry: "We never swapped iambic overtures — /Do swearing seamen leave the creaking brace/To chronicle each other's hardihood?/Our log is written where the traffic roars ... "[57] That he was writing verse, although not a great deal was published, is evident from his correspondence with Dorothy Livesay in May and June of 1941. She wrote asking him for contributions to "Poetry Quarterly," which was to be edited by Alan Crawley, "all for the love of raising the deplorable standard set by *Canadian Poetry Magazine* and the like ilk."[58] There is some irony to this as *CPM* was once the official organ of the rather staid Canadian Authors' Association (and the connection lingered) and CB had published in it, would continue to do so, and would become an executive member of the CAA. At the time, however, he replied, "I've got a young protégé, believe it or not, who is writing some great-looking stuff and I will try to corner some of the old envelopes he writes on and see if there is anything on them that might get past you. The guy has read too much Alfred Noyes .... But that was 2 or 3 years ago and I believe since then he has come along to handle words to some purpose."[59] CB was obviously having some fun at his own expense, but the creation of a *doppleganger* again suggests his feeling of distance from poetic centres and perhaps a diffidence about his own work still. Part of what he must have had in mind when he referred to the "old envelopes" was his 138-line ode to the progression of the brotherhood of man and in this progression the example and glory of Britain.

"Personal Note," said CB, was written "to express the belief of one individual and is published with the idea that others may be interested and may perhaps find some purpose in seeking to define for themselves their own faith."[60] He further stated that it was not a war poem, "but is meant to apply to living generally." Obviously, though, the inspiration came from the British stand against the Nazis and CB's belief that such a stand was rooted in the history of "this small island."[61] There are echoes of Pratt in the early images — "Consider now the road we took in time,/ From brackish waters through the ancient swamps/Towards this mammalian stature and the tribe" — but the most important aspect of the poem is the emerging major theme that dominated CB's writing in the 1940s and 1950s: "Survival in the whole/Through the long hand-in-hand of each to each." The essential perceived link now between the kinship of local experience and "humankind's goodwill," "Between the interest of all and the interest of one," is found in images that may in the past have been juxtaposed for purposes of contrast, but here are joined: "The neighbour's horse, borrowed for your ploughing,/The *Jervis Bay* taking the plunging shells/Into her side — these are the same in essence." CB is still very much against "systems" and asserts that "Life is where man lends heart and strength to man/Of his own will." However, his testimonial to British justice and truth through a reductive historical view of things makes "Personal Note" a systems poem:

> There is nothing essential in the name Britain
> Germany could be just as good a name.
>
> ...
>
> But the virtue of names is what they mean to mankind —
> The pulse they wake in its throat
> The dream they shape in its heart
> The strength they give its arm.[62]

Although he did not lose his attachment to Britain, CB wrote much later that this poem (and his 1945 narrative poem, "Grey Ship Moving") was "topical editorial matter and topical reporting." Poetry, or the writing of it, he said, must be "accident-prone," and the "obvious" nature of "Personal Note" meant that it had not "been touched by enough accidents of the desired kind." All this is somewhat euphemistic. Brief references to Florence Nightingale, Sir Philip Sydney, Nelson, Drake, Thomas à Becket, *et al.*, together with too many abstract terms — "goodwill," "justice and truth and kindliness," "valour and humour," "dream," "faith" — resulted in a kind of propaganda that CB may not have so obviously intended, but which was taken as such by most of his (admiring) readers. The poem was included in *Voices of Victory: Representative Canadian Poetry in War Time* (1941)[63] and reviewed alongside Pratt's "Dunkirk."[64] The word "patriotic" was emphasized, as was CB's "eloquence appropriate to this hour." Perhaps one of the most telling responses to "Personal Note" came from CB's uncle, James C. Tory: "From my standpoint, but knowing so little about poetry, I consider it the best work you have done in that line."[65]

Macmillan had turned down the idea of publishing the poem in pamphlet form as a companion piece to Charles G.D. Roberts's "Canada Speaks of Britain," but Ryerson Press did bring out 250 copies at $.75 each under the contract that CB himself would take 150 copies. Whatever royalties he received CB gave to the Navy League of Canada to provide for the welfare of merchant seamen.

It is interesting that "The Steelyards," written soon after the ode to Britain, stands in some contrast to it in tone and message, though this later poem is very much influenced by the world of conflagration.[66] Will had brought home from Boston a set of steelyards from his grocery store. This was a portable balance for weighing purposes, and it sat in the Bruce pantry at Port Shoreham. The central metaphor of the poem is dependent on *known* reality (as opposed to the learned and reported reality of "Personal Note") and involves no translation of life outside personal experience. There are "the scales of reason" to tell you certain things, "reason (mass-produced in units)/Or a march played to the tune of love and hate" — all this while France is falling and tax-sale notices are nailed to the barn next door. But in the end there is "The balance tallied in the single you." In this poem CB is critical of mass response, but is not an advocate of isolated behaviour. He looks ahead to what he would have to say in the next two decades of his best creative writing, as is shown by his emphasis on "the wakened mind ... /The blood and breath and the nerve, the recorded experience/Traced in the metal of flesh." In the midst of the war's collective experience, CB was ready to use his own life as an example of how " the single you" is forged and moves toward a balance with the world at large. He was ready to trace in the metal of his own flesh his novel.

V

Homeward Bound I

Exactly when CB began to write *Currie Head* is difficult to ascertain, but he seems to have completed a considerable portion of it before he left for London, England and over a year's duty there from March 1944 to July 1945. In August 1946 CB sent *The Atlantic Monthly Press* either one short story or a group of stories under the title "On the North Shore."[1] The fiction editor at the press was enthusiastic, but expressed greater interest in a novel: "The skill with which you suggested the beauty of the countryside of Nova Scotia and some of the adept characterization in your story seemed extraordinary to me."[2] CB replied that he was working on a "trilogy" and that he had already written a section of the third book, though large amounts of the whole effort would have to be revised. A few days after this letter he sent the fiction editor further comments on his novel:

[The] ms. of *Currie Head* is being mailed to you today. I haven't read it as an entirety since I put it away three years ago.

1) I had originally planned a novelette of 30,000 words or so. As a consequence, the action and characterization are nearly all from the point of view of the central character, Stan Currie. He becomes almost identified with the narrator, though the story is not essentially autobiographical. I don't know whether I should try to develop the point of view of other characters.

2) In some spots the corn is too green. There is a certain quality of unction here and there that should be eliminated. Long conversations in one or two places almost become orations.

3) Some incidents should probably be eliminated. Toward the end there should be more about Currie Head and probably less about Toronto and the problems of a news agency in war time. The news agency business is one I know from the ground up, but it's questionable in my own mind whether I've made it interesting to read about, or whether it can be made interesting. But the tedium of

any such profession to a character like the one I'm trying to draw is essential to the story.

4) The story itself — the cumulative influence of a place on successive generations, and of the place and the people on one person who is at the same time sensitive and mentally tough — is probably not certainly implicit.

5) Because of the novelette method adapted at the start, some chapters in outlining the impact of continuing situations skip back and forth over a period of a couple of years. I'm not sure about the permissibility of this sort of structure.[3]

The Atlantic Monthly Press certainly turned down *Currie Head*, although there is no record of the fiction editor's response to the manuscript, because seven months later CB sent to *Harper's* magazine "a portion of a novel" about a child's world and with a protagonist named Stan Currie. CB told *Harper's* that he intended to finish this novel called *Currie Head*.[4] This was April 1947, but when correspondence about a CB novel next turns up in January 1949 it is about a manuscript called *The Channel Shore*, and it seems to be a very different story from that of Stan Currie. It seems likely that between early 1941 (when he had resettled in Toronto after his New York stint) and early 1944 (when he left Toronto for CP London), CB produced the 355 page, typed manuscript entitled *Currie Head*.[5] What he attempted to explain to *The Atlantic* fiction editor relates specifically to this work: the action and characterization are nearly all from Stan Currie's point of view. Stan does become virtually identifiable with the narrator, though the question of autobiography must be closely examined. There is at times a little too much fervour about the way of life depicted, and the essential narrative problem has to do with too much talk and not enough action. The balance between Currie Head and the news agency in Toronto is perhaps better achieved than CB suspects, though the movement back and forth in time is not always smooth. As for the influence of place on successive generations and of place and people on one person, these are very powerfully if not always consistently presented.

Despite CB's denial *Currie Head* is a very autobiographical work. It draws heavily for its themes, characters and action on his boyhood in Port Shoreham, his years at Mount Allison, and his career as a journalist/newsman. It is not an autobiography because certain significant details of CB's life are altered in the fiction and important fictional details are part of the story that is being told. The novel is very much an attempt by CB to come to terms with who he was (and *is*, at the time of writing) and where he came from. It offers a thinly-disguised portrait of Will Bruce; CB had already touched upon Will's tremendous influence on him in "Fisherman's Son," but now he had much more to say about the profound and lasting qualities of their father-son relationship. Perhaps he realized that he had written his strongest and most original verse about the people and place of Port Shoreham and yet had only scratched the surface of heritage. Perhaps some of the dissatisfactions he had with his profession and with his distance from Nova Scotia prompted him to ask questions in fiction that he literally could not afford to ask in life. Perhaps by creating a Stan Currie so closely modelled upon himself he could not only articulate a personal vision of the past and present, but explore the possibililites of a personal future as well. In "Deep Cove" he had, in the end, insisted on a distinction between art and life, and portraying his protagonist as an artist in this poem had allowed him to do so. The one important difference between Stan Currie and CB, so many other things being equal, is that Stan is not a poet — he is not a man who has been able to create art out of memory and the growing distance between past and present. In *Currie Head* CB does so create, but the result is not the "separate strength" of John Black's sculpture; in its failure to cohere and convince as a novel, however, *Currie Head* reveals the life framework upon which all of CB's essential creativity rests.

As the manuscript begins, Stan Currie is taking a train to a place called the North Shore, which, purely in terms of geography first of all, has had an impact on him:

> Just talking about it, the country was coming to life in his mind in detail, a landscape remembered in the general terms of sometimes harsh and frequently gentle beauty, colored now with the specific slant of a beach, the sweep of a nearby hilltop. Strong country, with small brooks running through it toward salt water,

their steep wooded valleys breaking the long coastal slope into individual hills and promontories, but not bothered with too much symmetry.

There are people too, "men and women shrewd and generous and friendly, easy-going and independent," to whom he is returning. The place, the people and the incidents of his boyhood that Stan recalls have their importance "in the relationship of the motives, the impulses, the action of the time they recorded, to the living present here in the moving train." Stan, as well, has a strong sense of "tomorrow" flowing from this past and present.

Stan's great-great grandfather emigrated from Scotland, his grandparents were called Joe and Lydia, and his great-uncle, Rob Currie, disappeared while captain of a boat bound for Africa. Like Will Bruce, Hugh Currie worked in Boston for a number of years, married there, and started a family before returning to Nova Scotia to work the family farm and fish in the bay. Although Stan's mother died in Boston, she bore a son before Stan who died in infancy. If CB could base the life and character of Hugh so much on Will, who was dead, he apparently had qualms about creating a fictional mother based on Sarah Bruce, who was very much alive. Thus, in *Currie Head*, Aunt Christine helps in the raising of Stan, but Hugh's unmarried sister is a former schoolteacher with strong religious convictions.

In his autobiographical sketch, "A Hill For Looking," CB describes the heritage that "was liveliest" in his father when he mended nets on winter evenings and when he fished off Ragged Head. Stan remembers "through winter days and nights the smell of the summer beach lingering in the coils of a dark brown net... watching his father's fingers along the line" and seeing him launch his boat in the morning, not knowing whether he had "just a splash of salt water over the gunnels or a run of fish that'll break your back hauling it off the bottom." CB recalls the Sunday morning exchanges between Will and Sarah about church attendance, while Hugh tells Christine every Sabbath, "No, I don't think I will [go to church] today."

The very problem of Hugh's characterization in the manuscript, that he is more talked about than revealed through his own words and actions, emphasizes the degree to which CB was relying on memory and refusing to remake his father for the purposes of fiction. The interdependence of CB's art and life, as far as Will and Hugh are concerned, is perhaps best illustrated by the following, almost-identical passages. The first is from the fiction of *Currie Head*, written in the early 1940s; the second is from the autobiographical material in "A Hill For Looking," produced much later:

> [On Sunday morning] Hugh reclin[ed] on the lounge in clean white tie-less shirt and the old vest and trousers, reading the Family Herald ... moving gently from side to side one grey-stock-inged toe ....

> Pop usually spent the hour or so after breakfast [on Sundays] lying on the couch in the diningroom, in vest, pants, and sock feet, reading the Family Herald.

Similarly, both Hugh and Will have* good relationships with the ministers who spend Saturday nights at their respective homes; they both mow their farms by hand; and each has strong differences with a close family member — Will's brother-in-law, Hugh's brother — who has more money and about whom each says, "I don't like him."[6] If so much of Hugh is Will, then it is not so difficult to surmise that a great deal of Will must be Hugh. If the Sunday morning scene in *Currie Head* reveals life flowing into art, there is no reason to believe that the reverse flow does not occur when CB writes and Stan thinks, "The fact was that Hugh [Will], in the phrase of the region, 'believed,' but his belief was so pervasive, so much a part of living, that he could not reduce it to the definite tangibles of hymn, prayer, and sermon, or feel that he made acknowledgement ... by an hour and a half in church." The stories Hugh tells to Stan about his ancestors, and the effect they have upon the boy (and subsequently the remembering man) are most probably based upon the stories

* The only convenient way in which to speak of Hugh and Will simultaneously is to use the present tense.

Will told to CB, who is later compelled to write about them, albeit in fictional form:

> These stories lived only in the changing book of the mind, fading and always renewed, a fact or detail lost, here and there; a fact or detail added as the years marched; the fluent, common, continuing tradition of Currie Head [Port Shoreham] and the North Shore …. The story of Currie Head and the story of Hugh [Will] were there, becoming part of himself, to be heard now as yarns and realized later as blood and sinew and bone of his own flesh and nerves and habit.

Stan returns to Currie Head in the first years of World War Two, and it is his physical movement towards the place that releases the flood of his memories. He has reached a point in his life where he has to return home to find the connections between who he was and is. CB went back to Port Shoreham by writing about it; he did so to come to terms with aspects of his life because he could not literally go home to live. Stan does not have the release of writing nor the ability to clarify life through art, but his memories are very similar to those of CB and serve the same purpose of allowing him to go on, deeper into life at Currie Head, much as CB would venture deeper into the "lived experience" of his poetry and prose fiction. On the train (for Stan) and in the process of writing *Currie Head* (for CB), "the natural current of thought [in] his mind turned up other memories, which had stayed with him through the strenuous years and returned to him at intervals without the evoking influence of familiar land and sea."

Not only do the Currie-Bruce ancestors and the presence of Hugh-Will suggest the connections between Stan and CB, so do the following in *Currie Head*: activities with Stan's two boyhood chums from neighbouring farms, Dan Graham and Harry Neill (like those with Harold MacIntosh and Wilbur Cummings); Stan's "continual reading," which began to separate him from his friends "even while the greater part of his day-to-day life and activity were identical with theirs"; his boarding in "Town" for the year of school before university and going home on weekends; his riding the old mare in the pasture and fishing in the lake back of the farm; his fishing on the bay with his father, trapping for fur, chopping wood, and clearing stones from ploughed fields.

One thing that does distinguish author from character, as far as boyhood experience is concerned, is CB's writing poetry and other items. However, CB's resultant links with the outside world — sending the *Shoreham Searchlight* to Zoe in Sydney, having his work published there and in Halifax, and being an editor of a boys' magazine issued in Dallas — (which must have prompted him to consider life and a future beyond Port Shoreham), have their parallel in Stan's constant dream of "the road," "of a life worked out away from The Head, somewhere in cities."

The complexities of 'going away' that CB describes in his story in "A Hill for Looking" of his near-sightedness and Will's misunderstanding of the proposed trip to Sydney ("You won't have to stay here and spend your life at this kind of work") is also dealt with in the novel: Hugh keeps the money that Stan has earned from trapping muskrat, and there is a misunderstanding between father and son as to why — Hugh is saving funds for Stan's university education — that concludes with Hugh announcing, "I'll never see [you] tied down to the kind of work I'm doing for a living." Some of Stan's experience is wholly invented: Anna (Bruce) MacKeen cannot remember her mother ever saying that she would like CB to be a minister, as Christine says to her nephew; there is no evidence that CB was ever offered the opportunity to board with or work for one of his uncles, while Stan declines such an arrangement proposed by Christine; surely in one of his reports about his boyhood CB would have described drifting helplessly out in the bay with either Harold or Wilbur — Stan has such an adventure with Dan Graham. However, when Stan does follow "the road" to the marshlands of southern New Brunswick and Royal University, a Methodist institution, what he carries with him of Currie Head is certainly in essence what CB held in his head and heart as he moved towards Sackville and Mount Allison.

The problem with the first part of the novel (some 100 pages) is that CB describes events and character too much, rather than dramatizes them, and he shifts from vignette to vignette of

Stan's experiences, which are not linked except by continuity of people and place. Movement through time is presented abruptly and arbitrarily, and it is not easy to discern Stan's age at any particular point. A host of minor characters frequent these pages, sometimes only for a single scene and sometimes appearing and disappearing without any preparation. Part of what the *Harper's* fiction editor had to say about the way in which Stan's boyhood is conveyed is accurate:

> You have very successfully evoked a child's world, with a feeling for place and people. The writing has a sensitivity and richness. But from a dramatic point of view there is a certain monotony. The mood is so quiet, unvaried, there are so few peaks and and valleys .... Stan never quite captures the imagination ....[7]

Stan's failure to capture the reader's imagination comes from the fact that the young Stan is very much a product of memory — his own and CB's — and does not emerge as a distinctive character until the final seventy pages or so of the novel when the past catches up with the present and Stan acts rather than remembers. CB was aware of the validity of the *Harper's* comments when he answered them: "I have been conscious of the fact that Part I is largely below the level of dramatic action. The truth is, I imagine, that I've been trying to work the thing out according to a sort of inner logic that at times has disregarded domestic interest in favour of an instinctive 'this is the way it would be.'"[8] What makes the next two parts of the novel interesting is CB's continued reliance on the facts of his own life and the inclusion of a great deal of material that seems to be a significant blend of "lived experience" and artistic invention.

Not a great deal of attention is given by CB to Stan's years at Royal University. Like Stan's, CB's "self-consciousness was gone" when he became a sophomore. The words in the Royal *Yearbook* of Stan's senior year that describe his "amazing metamorphosis" from freshman to sophomore are exactly the same as those in the October 1927 edition of *The Argosy* that refer to the change in CB between April and September of 1924.[9] If CB, unlike Stan, did not seem able to admit to himself at the time that this "metamorphosis" was due, at least partially, to a "renewed, deeper affinity" with his home territory, it could be that such an admission was simply not made in the same way. If Stan feels "By God, I was Stan Currie, son of old Hugh, grand-nephew of Rob, who'd sailed a three-master out of the strait and never came back," he does not write in the university newspaper about his heritage. CB, whose university diaries and notes contain only one directly articulated sense of North Shore self, nevertheless wrote in *The Argosy* about where he came from. In the early 1940s the writing of *Currie Head* does flow back into life so that CB can declare he did, in the fall of 1924, return to Mount Allison as the son of old Will, grand-nephew of James, who had sailed a three-master to Sierra Leone and had never come back.

What helps Stan in his six years as reporter at the Halifax *Globe* (as compared to CB's eight months at the *Chronicle*) is a sense of life that he has brought with him from Currie Head: "Yourself and people; everything narrowed down in the end to that relationship." As for the Head itself, "It was only when he was away from it that a strong sense of belonging lived in his mind." He meets Janet Moore, whom he will eventually marry, who lives in Halifax with her big family, and CB's fiction begins in earnest. Certainly Janet is not based on Agnes King, except perhaps in terms of a strong and attractive personality, and there is no way of knowing whether there was a rich young woman, comparable to Pauline Daley in Stan's life, who complicated CB's existence before his marriage. It seems unlikely: CB invented Aunt Christine because his mother was still alive; there is no doubt that *Currie Head* was intended for publication, and CB was not about to display his own love life so directly. The story line about Stan's involvement with Janet and Pauline is rather predictable and conventional; CB is unfortunately at his best when he talks about the two women rather than when he attempts to develop them as characters through dialogue and action. For example, of Pauline: "The subtle difference expressed in outlook and manner, translating the actual differences of money, of background, of social habits and ways of thinking, would not be understood along the road from Morgan's Harbour to Queenston." There is one sustained exchange between Stan and Janet with ripples of joy and discontent that does presage something of the master of dialogue and plot development in *The Channel Shore*.

What do ring true are the portraits of the newsroom at the *Globe*, Stan's colleagues, and his journalistic experience, which is based on what CB knew by the early 1940s as a result of almost fifteen years in news work. As well, the young CB, making his transition from the *Chronicle* to Canadian Press, had not yet articulated, either as a journalist or an artist, the idea expressed in *Currie Head* that we should listen to the "hearthstone conversation [that] is the only true history of any country." Unlike Stan he had not yet begun to envision the "tapestry woven out of memory, a magic background to the picture of the present." This tapestry would emerge in detail in the 1950s with such essays as "The Township of Time" and the short stories that would make up the volume with the same title. But the CB who was writing *Currie Head* had written "Lunenburg," "Fisherman's Son," and "Words Are Never Enough." He had explored human connections through time in "Deep Cove." Stan, therefore, is based on the experience of a creator who was roughly ten years ahead of him in time.

That CB was writing Stan Currie very much as he himself was in the early 1940s, when it came to an awareness of Nova Scotia heritage and an ability to articulate the connections between the past and the present, is revealed in Stan's story for the *Globe* of a rum-runner's funeral. Stan meets Captain Jeff Parks at a Halifax poker game, and it is a North Shore fisherman as well as a Lunenburg seaman whom he describes: "It was the look of a complete realist, who does not discount the romantic in life, but takes it as a matter of course; a look reflecting the mature innocence of accepted experience." Jeff Parks is killed by the U.S. Coast Guard while running rum, and the discription of his funeral, as reported by Stan for the *Globe*, is word for word that of Captain William Cluett's funeral as written by CB for Canadian Press. If Stan's story lands him a job with Dominion Services, a news agency based on Canadian Press, it also earns him some advice from the *Globe's* editor-in-chief, which is essentially that he not get himself killed off as a creative writer doing the kind of desk work he is going to do. CB could not make it more clear that the problems Stan encounters at "the rat-race of Dominion Service ... the slow erosion, by the years and economics, of [his] integrity" have to do with the gap between the essence of the Parks funeral story (and all its North Shore connections) and "the driving necessities of the competitive medium that ... trapped him personally." Stan has years to go before he will extract himself from the "rat-race" and return to Currie Head to live; the only way out and on for CB was to remember and to write.

Stan arrives at Dominion Services in Toronto in 1933, the same year CB was transferred to Canadian Press there. Within a few years, like CB, Stan becomes a news editor, and from what Gillis Purcell has to say much of his daily news agency experience was CB's own, from the time schedule for filling the wire to the style of a teletype flash, and especially the supervisory aspects of the job. Certain newsroom characters in *Currie Head* are lifted from life with virtually no attempt at disguise, while others are composite figures, either more or less recognizable.[10] Stan quickly feels trapped by the "blue-printed" aspects of the work, by the fact that there is no room for "artistry or craftmanship" and that "there isn't enough real interchange between the city and the country. The traffic's all one way." The rest of his dissatisfactions, even before he is prepared to come to grips with them, can only be expressed in terms of The Head: "What [his job] was worth he wasn't sure. There was no fun in digging sheep manure out of the shed in the spring, either. But it was there to be done."

Less than a year after his transfer to Toronto, CB had written to George Trueman in Sackville of his "gradually growing desire to get out of big cities" and, since he was looking for small-town newspaper work, out of CP as well. As well, after Will's death he had made his enquiries to R.A. Jodrey of the *Windsor Tribune*. Until 1945, when he abruptly quit drinking, CB was a heavy drinker,[11] and at least some of the pressures of his job contributed to his need for alcohol. The more administrative responsibilities he took on, the further away from writing the news he got, and although he seems to have spoken about his discontent to very few people, Gillis Purcell attests to the fact that CB did not like where he was headed in CP, despite the prestige and added income.[12] Neither did he speak to anyone about his work enquiries elsewhere. The letters to George J. Trueman and R.A. Jodrey and the declining of C.A. Munro's offer were not known by his family and certainly not at CP. Just as he rarely spoke to Agnes or others about his creative writing, he did not reveal many of the feelings he had during this time about Port Shoreham and how he measured so much of his life by the people and experience there. Some of these feelings are certainly evident in his novel as Stan's professional and personal life unfolds.

When Stan is promoted to the position of news editor he responds by thinking he will spend six months on the main desk and then leave, either for the *Globe* in Halifax again or else the Pacific coast, but the birth of a second son puts off any hard decisions. A few months after Dave Currie is born, Hugh Currie dies, just as Will Bruce died in October 1934 after Harry Bruce was born that July. Stan returns to The Head for the funeral and is "completely at ease" there for the first time since his boyhood, somehow joined to time and place by his most immediate ancestor's union with earlier Curries. If Stan is next in line in the eternal scheme of things, he has a strong sense that eternity has not to do with "garish Heaven," but with days like this one "under September's blue and amber" on the North Shore. Back in Toronto the negative side of existence is again captured by a metaphor from The Head: "… it seemed to him that he had been at the end of a crosscut saw for a long time." Stan drinks considerably now to dull the pain of a soul-killing job, but it is the memory of Hugh that halts his journey down. Riding back to Toronto from Niagara Falls on a lake boat reminds Stan of the old steamer on his home bay, and he thinks of his father who "wouldn't let himself be driven past a certain point … of an inner independence that stood up sharply against the crowding demands that continually encroached on human dignity and human fellowship." Before him is the example of Hugh, who had the courage to leave Boston and return to the old ways and wisdom after a twenty-year absence, who "would never have placed ambition ahead of self-respect."

Why had CB begun *Currie Head* in the first place? The original novelette plan meant that what he had in mind, first of all, was Stan Currie's boyhood — the roughly 30,000 words or so that constitute Part I of the manuscript. Because he deals with the Royal University years in such brief terms, CB perhaps reveals that he had not considered what was to happen to his protagonist after he left The Head. The quick narrative jump to the *Globe* years suggests that the "trilogy" concept came rather late in the scheme of things, as did the idea of proceeding with the novel with the central dependence of the development of Stan's life on the facts of CB's own professional progress and certain personal tensions during the 1930s. But the challenge implicit in Stan's choices to CB's own existence is extraordinary.

Stan does not possess his creator's ability to fill the gaps between memory and present reality with poetry or thinly-disguised fiction, so he chooses to give up journalism and return home to work the family farm. CB writes fiction entirely and seems to separate art from life in the final seventy pages of the manuscript. What he is actually doing here, however, is emphasizing the exchange between art and life. Through convincing dialogue, characterization, and action that do not depend upon the narrative voice for their dramatic unity and purpose, CB portrays Stan as an ex-journalist who sheds the skin of his interim years in Halifax and Toronto and discovers "the sinews of integrity" beneath. He creates a protagonist who can give up the news agency life, but who can do so only because, first of all, CB himself knew "The essential thing was … a known road to remembered earth." Known because of Will, Port Shoreham, and the memories that were alive in CB's art both before and in *Currie Head*. Stan accepts "the truth that [for him] words are never enough"; what CB attempted to make enough, not only for himself but for potential readers of his novel, is the complex combination of words and lived / imagined experience in his fiction that emerged from fact. That he realized he had not quite done so is emphasized by his putting away the manuscript for three years, by his subsequent revisions of it, and then by his recognition that what was needed was not fiction that emerged from fact, but fiction that was more true than fact, a combination of words that received its inspiration from personal life, but which did not reflect such life so completely. The next two decades of CB's creativity would tell this type of tale in poetry, short story, and novel form.

What Stan discovers in building his new life and encountering help and understanding from those who have always lived at The Head is that "The immediate yesterday was gone. Tomorrow and the day after, blending curiously with an earlier time, absorbed him now." There is a sense of completion, of confidence, and of satisfaction in the simple achievements gained by working with his hands and accepting "the harsh but flexible demands of the earth, the sea, and the seasons ... the old common relationship of neighbourly equality." A pattern of living emerges whose fabric of heritage and blood is generations old: "He knew now that he would never act entirely on his own responsibility, that no one ever did .... You could act, a single individual and you turned to find at your shoulder a singing host." Above all for Stan there is the memory and example of Hugh and the accompanying recognition that he will never live and work alone, but be dependent on the love, strength, and experience of others and have them dependent in a similar manner on him.

There is, admittedly, one note to this portrait of Currie Head, as Stan finds everything there he hoped to find — the complexities of adulthood (How will his wife respond to his desire to return? Is it simply a matter of going home again?) are presented as little different from the innocent experience of boyhood. However, it seemed necessary at the time he wrote his first novel for CB to deal primarily with the final distinction between his protagonist and himself — Stan does go home to live. What he finds there was for CB the inherence of the North Shore, if not the sometimes rougher lessons that come from trying to match reality with vision. Later in *The Channel Shore* and *The Township of Time*, the fragilities and the vagaries of life through time and in one place would be shown mingling with the strengths and constancies. But even in these two books, with CB at the height of his artistic powers as far as his fiction is concerned, the rougher lessons would be absorbed and subsumed by the affirming essence and pattern of Shore experience.

Meanwhile, by granting Stan his fictional freedom, CB both freed himself from a dependence in his fiction and poetry on his own memory of place and time and allied himself with the perception and employment of memory as a vital but single aspect of the re-creation of time and place. As a writer, he might very well live and work alone in important respects, but by accepting who he was through finally portraying Stan Currie as someone other than himself, yet not distinguishing between his narrative voice and Stan's view of the pattern of living, CB became more aware of the complex kinship of the artist, his subject matter, and his audience. Out of the quarrel with himself, a sometimes moving and integral work of prose fiction, but an essentially limited novel emerged. In the end, Stan is not trapped idealistically at The Head; he volunteers for the Merchant Marine in order to help win the war and senses that when the war is over strong muscles and a sense of heritage might not enable him to keep the farm up in a changing world. He might have to leave again for periods of time so that his family, inheritors and ancestors both, can stay. There is resolution here but no closure for CB. *Currie Head* was a book he had to write; now he could move on to fiction that was "a telling pantomime of action and not a tame chapter of sounds."[13]

When CB put *Currie Head* away in 1943, it would be another eleven years before *The Channel Shore* was published. He did not know it yet, but contained in Stan's story were the seeds of his later classic. When Stan returns to The Head early in the war he learns

> ... that Fred's [Graham] cousin Grant, living in a comparatively new house just east of the Currie place, was the husband of a girl from The Islands; that Grant's eldest son Alan, by his first wife, Hazel Mackie, was already in the army; that Chance Gordon, the dark engaging wild one who had vanished from The Head in Nineteen Nineteen, while Stan was still a boy, had never turned up anywhere.

Stewart and Josie Gordon are mentioned, as is Professor Andrew Graham, "one of those country boys who leave the farm and never think of it again"; Andrew's son Bill "had spent a couple of summers at The Head years ago."[14] Present when Stan is a boy are the strict, religious farmer John Marshall, the young schoolteacher Renie Fraser, the trouble-making Riley boys whose father runs the local store, and Vangie Murphy, the loose woman on the edge of the community's conscience, together with her illegitimate son (or so he seems) Tarsh.

The reason that *Currie Head* was resurrected from CB's shelves was that editors at both *The Atlantic Monthly* and *Harper's* asked him in 1946 if he were working on a novel or had one in mind. Elizabeth Lawrence at *Harper's* suggested, after reading "On the North Shore," that CB expand upon his themes of religious conflict and communal thinking. That CB had put *Currie Head* aside in a fairly permanent way and was looking for different articulations of his home territory is indicated by his reply to Lawrence:

> For nearly twenty years the only writing I did outside the day's work was the occasional poem. In the last few months I've been doing some evening and Sunday slugging at imaginative prose, mainly to see how it turns out. "On the North Shore" is the only fairly tangible result so far ...
>
> My chief difficulty is, of course, time. Eight or ten hours a day in an office are fine discipline and background for writing after you finally escape. I haven't escaped yet.[15]

There followed several months of correspondence about *Currie Head* with both magazines, as "On the North Shore" seems to have faded into the background. In the spring of 1947 CB wrote Elizabeth Lawrence that he hoped to get the novel "cleared up ... by early summer."[16] The criticisms of the manuscript provided by *The Atlantic Monthly* and *Harper's* were not, apparently, overcome by CB's rewriting. By January 1949 CB's literary agent in New York, Howard Moorepark, had received a synopsis of a novel called *The Channel Shore*, and over the next five years CB shaped, rewrote, and polished the story of Anna, Grant, Hazel and Anse.

CB, however, was not yet finished with *Currie Head*; after *The Channel Shore* was published in 1954, he went back over the manuscript of his earlier novel and brought everything in it into line with what the public now knew of the North Shore. Thus John Marshall became James Marshall, Chance became Anse, the Mackie family — Richard, Eva, Hazel — became the Mc-Kees, and the Rileys became the Katens. Place names too had to be consistent: The Corner was changed to The Bridge; Little Pond to Forester's Pond; Kingsway to Princeport; The Village to Stoneville, and of course the North Shore to the Channel Shore. Perhaps CB had hopes that Stan Currie's story could now be published. Stan is a minor but nevertheless important figure in *The Channel Shore*, the one who left and then returned to stay, and who at the novel's end is allowed to articulate the sense of heritage that is not his alone. It is more likely, though, that CB was willing to let the manuscript lie (no correspondence about it exists after 1947) and that what he was concerned with in his revisions was that there be no conflict "in the record of the mind."

VI

Interlude

In February 1944 the *Canadian Printer and Publisher* announced that CB was temporarily leaving his position as General News Editor at CP Toronto to become Superintendent of the London England Bureau: "In London it will be Bruce's job to guide CP's European staff through the transition from war coverage to the task of reporting the aftermath and its effect in Britain and European countries."[1] This statement certainly represented some confidence about the state and direction of the war, but as CB discovered there was a great deal of war coverage to be handled before any peace treaties were to be signed.

He arrived in London on March 15, 1944, stayed briefly at the Mount Royal Hotel near Marble Arch, and then moved into a flat with a colleague. In his first letter to Purcell he wrote, "The Americans are over-running this place [London] like a sort of benevolent pestilence."[2] The staff at the London Bureau as of April 1945 consisted of Superintendent, News Editor, Late Day Editor, Night Editor, a reporter for Troopships, three men covering the Canadian Army, and one general position. A considerable number of reports were filed under the heading "London Letter" and about events away from the front: the I.L.O. Convention in London in January 1945; the Commonwealth Relations Conference; "From a People's War to a People's Peace." But most important was direct news of Canadian troops and, in June 1944, their participation in the D-Day landings. "We've been manning the office 24 hours a day since three days before D-Day .... I'm getting in 9-10 [a.m.] and trying to get out by midnight."[3]

One thing that did concern CB greatly was "This whole matter of the fair use of words [in war-time journalism]." CB wrote to Purcell about the use by the Associated Press of such terms as "their share of the *spoils*," in regard to allied territorial arrangements, and "approving of an *itch* for territory on the part of the allies." He was worried about an undue influencing of the reader's judgement through this type of language: "After all, words are the brush and the paint we use to give the picture, and I think it's just as important to use the finest of brushes and the truest point as it is to see freely what we're painting for other folks to look at."[4]

CB himself was obviously a strong supporter of the Allies in their fight against fascism, but he saved his personal opinions for his private notebook and reported in concise, straightforward prose on Vice-Admiral Percy Nelles of the RCN mission in London and on "How Britain's Human Torpedoes Work,"[5] among other things. Just how the farmer-fisherman's son from Port Shoreham saw the enemy is perhaps best revealed in an undated extract from a London notebook:

> ... is [it] possible for a man enamoured of power (evil) to get the pleasure out of rain, sky, sea, earth as such that one sensitive to these things does [?] Conversely, whether it is possible for one who loves these things to be cruel, dishonest — whether it is possible to consider the things which dishonesty and cruelty [make] important in a man of that type .... It is easy to fake religious feeling, but not ... love of nature. For that reason if you find a man [having] satisfaction in nature it's a good bet he's a good man.

Certainly there was one report filed by CB in which his subjective and creative response to the war was evident. In September 1944 he was asked by the Air Ministry if he would like to cover personally the flights that were dropping supplies to Allied airborne troops in Holland (after the big parachute drop of men at Arnheim). On September 20, 1944 he wrote about his one and only flight over enemy territory:

> Our pilot, Doug Robertson, took his big plane straight and low over the dropping zone through a literal hell of flak. The bomb-aimer, Norman Roseblade, let go the cannisters, "bang-on." Robbie pulled her nose up and to port, heading out of the area. In a moment the navigator, Lem Prowse, would be calling in a course for home. Then the flak slammed into us. It smacked "P for Peter" with the shock of a giant fist. For a split second the

aircraft seemed steady on her course. Then she went into a screaming nosedive.[6]

By the time the pilot had pulled the plane out of its dive, it was too close to the ground for a safe exit by parachute. Besides, they were still very much above enemy territory. After a hour of "cursing, cajoling, and muscling the ship along" the crew belly-landed in Belgium: "We ran a few yards in case the ship caught fire, and then knelt down and kissed the earth. There was a good deal of rough reverence in that gesture." A signal was sent through to home base announcing that all were safe, but it did not get through, and when CB filed a dispatch from Brussels it did not reach London until after he walked into his office in London on September 22. The result had been a missing plane and the beginnings of an obituary for CB. As if he would later need reminding of how close death had come, Robertson, Roseblade, and Prowse were killed in action some months after the incident over Arnheim. Prior to their deaths, CB had written a letter to the officer commanding the fliers' home base in which he lauded their performance; after the war he paid a private visit to Roseblade's parents in Toronto.

CB settled into a flat in London's West End and found time to see John Gielgud in Congreve's "Love for Love"; he entertained Canadian M.P. Paul Martin when Martin visited the city, kept notes on British expressions ("say when," "melancholy as a stage whore"), and compared London to Canadian centres: "The smell of leaves in Lincoln's Inn Fields is much the same as in Sackville or Toronto." Writing to Purcell, he said, "I can't see wanting to stay in this country, but doubtless I haven't seen it at its best from the point of view of comfortable living."[7] In May 1945 he wrote Purcell that he had not had a drink since March, "with the exception of V-E week," but looked forward to pulling "a cold bottle of black horse out of that lake up around Scotia Junction." Something that he wrote his mother in July 1944 suggests CB's ambivalent attitude about his role as war correspondent: "We're having interesting times these days ... lots of work and excitement .... Despite all the interest there is in running this office in times like these there are times when I wish I were just a few years younger and not near-sighted. And others when I wish it would all get over and I could go back to normal living, in Canada, and play ball with the kids in the back yard. I must be feeling sentimental today." To his son Harry he sent news of buzz bombs hitting London, the high cost of clothes, playing tennis in Regent's Park, and even mentioned a brief landing in France after D-Day.[8] In return, his mother and sister Bess, who were living in Edmonton, kept him abreast of Port Shoreham people and events. Bess spoke of retiring to the farm within a few years and debated with CB about the Scottish origins of the Bruces. She told him that Uncle James Tory had died in June 1944 and left the bulk of his estate to the Dalhousie University Medical School; each of his nieces and nephews received $5,000. Harry Bruce told his father about school marks, books he was reading, and about the annual family holiday at Sand Lake in the Haliburton region of southern Ontario.[9] In particular, CB's letters to his son reveal his considerable attention to what Harry has told him about home life and a genuine effort to describe something of his experience in England.

While in London CB was also writing reviews and poetry and making himself known to the British Authors' Association, the British Poetry Society, and *The Poetry Review*. For Canadian Press, early in 1945, he reviewed a book of poems by a member of the Canadian Army, S. J. Downham. There was, he said, "good concrete writing mixed in places with the most utter banality .... All through the book hackneyed phrases ... rub up against authentic lyric poetry."[10] But he must have been sufficiently impressed because he told Purcell to call the book to the attention of the Toronto *Globe and Mail*'s book editor, W. A. Deacon. Meanwhile, Downham's verse had received the attention of *The Poetry Review*. CB wrote to the Secretary of the British Poetry Society objecting to the use in the journal's review of Downham's book of the term "colonial vernacular" because the poet "was born in the independent sovereign nation of Canada."[11]

CB must have been taken seriously in England as a Canadian nationalist and as a poet, since in April 1945 he was invited by the Poetry Society, on Andrew Merkel's recommendation, to read his own work. He did accept and on May 18 read several "very brief lyrics from the earlier book *Tomorrow's Tide* and then got into a bit of unpublished stuff."[12] He was asked at either this or another Poetry Society meeting if he were a traditionalist or a modernist. All he could do in response, CB said, was grunt: "The distinction meant nothing to me. I just use the verse form that fits the idea."[13]

During his time in London CB did write at least two war-poems — two, at least, that would see the light of day. "For All Who Remember"[14] contains three, four-line stanzas with regular rhyme scheme and iambic metre. Images of the sea, the war's front line, and parachuted supplies represent the three armed services, but in contrast to the war are isolated lines at the end of each stanza that contain images of home life and peace in the natural world. The intent and result of the poem is rather obvious, though simply presented and not at all strained or naive in its juxtaposition of a man's experiences.

More ambitious was a long (263 lines) five-part narrative poem about an Atlantic crossing of a troopship. "Grey Ship Moving" is CB's tribute to the Canadian war effort. Four lieutenants are on their way to Europe in a converted pleasure ship, the *Sappho* (modelled on the *Andes*, a Royal Mail ship with a perhaps less evocative name) — "Stephen Clare of Toronto, in Education;/Felix Lane, an exuberant engineer/Fresh from the apple lands of the Okanagan;/An ordnance man, Jack Dunn, from the Eastern Townships,/And Glen Maguire, the gunner from Saskatoon."[15] With the emphasis on names and places, it seems as if the poem will interweave four individual stories, but such is not the case. The themes of comradeship and the unified force of the common man are presented essentially through the limiting inner conflicts and growing vision of Stephen Clare. He is somewhat based on CB, "a bookish, near-sighted scribbler" whose great-uncle took "a fore-and-aft three master" to Africa and disappeared in the late nineteenth century, and he is "not exactly in combat category." But through talking to his mates about his personal difficulties (mainly his failing marriage) and sharing in their experiences, he realizes the strength and conviction of the communal spirit and benefits from it. Essentially, the thread that binds them all is that "You can't stay out of the show.

No choice in the matter." The ship carries life against death, and the voyage is, like all living, an "endless venture." Stephen even writes a sonnet that reminds the reader of an early CB poem where the abstract and concrete collide and complement one another at the same time and do not yet display the union of the idea and reality to which the poet aspires. The forced idealism of "Grey Ship Moving" clanks a little like the *Sappho*'s anchor as she turns in the Mersey tide and moves again toward the north Atlantic. The poem is, like "Personal Note," very much message verse and, like the ode to Britain, "topical editorial matter and topical reporting .... coloured by the obvious."[16] What does linger in the mind is "the sight and sound of the usual" — simple descriptions of the ship and everyday life on it during the seven-day journey, fairly ordinary except for the ship's destination.

In late December 1944 or early January 1945 CB began negotiations with the British Authors' Press to bring out an edition of his more recent poetry. Edith Frye of the Press had written to him of "so many disappointments in trying to bring literature produced in the Dominions before the public in this island."[17] But she did feel that poems about the sea would sell in England, and CB accordingly agreed that his collection could be titled *Fisherman's Son* or *Salt in the Blood*; he also told her that his poem "Words Are Never Enough" had won a national poetry prize in 1939. At this time he must have certainly been buoyed up by Dorothy Livesay's and Northrop Frye's positive remarks about him in their respective commentaries on A.J.M. Smith's *Book of Canadian Poetry*.[18] The first manuscript CB sent to Edith Frye (no relation to the Canadian critic) did not include "Grey Ship Moving," perhaps because he was still working on the poem, but by March 1945 she had agreed to the book's new title and told CB that 500 copies would be published by the Press.

CB wondered if Ryerson might be approached "about a possible Canadian edition, but learned from Edith Frye that Lorne Pierce felt "it quite out of the question for them to publish anything outside their own lists."[19] Yet two weeks later Pierce wrote to CB about the manuscript, calling it "splendid" and saying that he wanted to bring it out with Birney's *David* and Smith's *News of the Phoenix*.[20] CB decided to go with Ryerson, whom he obviously saw in his publishing future, and the company estimated it could produce 500 copies for the Canadian market and 500 for export provided the British Authors' Association would import them at 60 cents a copy. Edith Frye agreed to transfer the Canadian rights to Ryerson if she could get "reasonable terms" for a British edition. Apparently she must have, though whether the 60-cent figure was deemed "reasonable" is not known.

After one person had declined the writing of a preface for *Grey Ship Moving*, British poet Wilfrid Gibson agreed to do so. Gibson, a Georgian poet, had mentioned CB (along with Pratt, Birney, Klein, and Kenneth Leslie) in his *Manchester Guardian* review of A.J.M. Smith's 1943 anthology. Just where CB was perceived to stand in the field of modern poetry (and where he perceived himself to be) is revealed by Gibson's remark to CB that he did not like the "prentice-work of some younger writers which are no more than exercises in the cheap smartness which has become the vogue .... "[21] In his preface to *Grey Ship Moving*, Gibson states his admiration for CB's work because it "is uncontaminated by the contagion of cosmopolitan obscurantism" that has sullied the verse of younger writers. Fortunately Gibson has more to say about CB's poetry being "securely rooted in its native soil .... vital with the very stuff of life" and makes favourable comparisons of CB to Whitman and Frost.

Grey Ship Moving appeared in November 1945 at $2.00 per copy in bookstores. The British edition came out several months later. By the end of 1946 CB had received 1.4 British pounds for thirty-two copies sold in Britain, and by May 1947 Ryerson reported 310 copies sold in Canada. Canadian reviews of the book were mixed. The Montreal *Gazette* liked "the trenchant bite of cold salt-water" in his lyrics, but was not so fond of his "mystical Anglophilism with overtones of sentimental humanism" (undoubtedly a reference to "Personal Note," the final poem of the volume).[22] The Halifax *Daily Star* found the title poem weak and "more strength and salt water in such things as 'An Ear to the Ground' or 'Fisherman's Son.'"[23] The *Canadian Forum* reviewer, Alan Creighton, at best, damned with faint praise:

It ["Grey Ship Moving"] is written in clear-cut, readable style, fragments of characterization alternating with poetic commentary. While it has significance as a wartime poem ... there is an absence of climax which leaves one with the impression of a highly elaborated news report. Other poems in this book .... are valuable as thoughtful expression enriched by local color and Bliss Carmanish with carefully polished lines and phrases. They do not always suggest life in its wholeness, however, because of a tendency to justify mass sentiments, to say what can be quoted widely without offense. Also they tend to lean rather heavily upon the assumption that there is something especially hallowed about Nova Scotia and Nova Scotians. [24]

While E.K. Brown, in "Letters in Canada" in the *University of Toronto Quarterly*, did the same, saying that the poetry in *Grey Ship Moving* was "extraordinarily attractive without being strongly individualized" and that it was "extremely pleasant to read. It is minor poetry, but the poetry is authentic." [25]

At least seven of the thirteen lyrics in the collection were written in the 1930s; "Personal Note," of course, had been published by itself in 1941. CB was rightfully praised for "Words Are Never Enough" and "Fisherman's Son"; in fact, the latter won a British Poetry Society Prize (announced in the September-October 1945 issue of *The Poetry Review*) for "Its strong simplicity, its economy, the unpretentious adequacy of its expression," but also for its contribution to "the imperishable vitality of the old traditional ways of poetry." His war poetry may have been in the spirit of the times, but CB was in real danger, at the age of thirty-nine, of being perceived as an older poet who had written his best work almost a decade previously, work that was linked to an earlier, pre-modernist era.

Curiously, no one seems to have mentioned the first lyric in the book that immediately follows the title poem; no one seems to have noticed the complexity of its positioning or to have considered some of the possible implications of its content. "1945" is a love poem about the meeting of two people who had put away "understanding and mirth" "Years ago, when the time came to accept/Another time; and the time of our own was done." [26] The poem is about the dichotomies between, and the unity of, yesterday and today, and about the strength of individual gestures, "habits and images," despite "a world's wheeling and striking." There is an implied sexual meeting as well when the poet writes, "And the blood pounds at your touch."

At the end of "Grey Ship Moving," Stephen Clare's wife is described as finally writing to him: "The forthright words of passion she could not say — /The ardent words reborn in a dream rekindled/Out of a pattern sharp with the colour of living;/The years of success and desire, of failure and love." Is then, "1945," the lyric about love lost and rediscovered, her statement to Stephen? After all, he was in newspaper work, and "The rough drone of a press and the wet-sweet smell of ink" are mentioned in the poem. Perhaps. But it is not difficult to view the placement of the poem as a safeguard against too personal an interpretation of what it says. If it is not Margaret Clare's poem, it could be a more personal statement by CB, and it is possible that he wrote the poem between the time of his return to Canada in July 1945 and the date it would have to be inserted in the *Grey Ship Moving* in time for November publication. Nothing can be proved, nor perhaps should it be, but CB must have been aware of the speculative qualities of the poem. It therefore took some personal courage to publish it, and Irving Layton and Louis Dudek, certainly not bound to tradition, must have noticed its undisguised honesty of tone, its fusion of memory's abstraction with the reality of the moment, when they selected it as CB's only contribution to *Canadian Poems 1950-1952*, published by Contact Press.[27]

Whatever the merits of this one recent poem, when CB returned to Canada with *Grey Ship Moving* on the immediate horizon his output as poet had been very small in the thirteen years since *Tomorrow's Tide*, and his reputation rested on only a handful of short poems. A letter to F. W. Watt in October 1946 reveals CB had no illusions about his stature as a *Canadian* poet, but no doubts as to his ability to write poetry:

> I don't know where I fit into the national picture. But I guess there's a hint in the concluding sentence of the paragraph Prof. E. K. Brown devoted to *Grey Ship* in his review of poetry in Canada, 1945: "It is minor poetry, but the poetry is authentic."

What he meant, of course, was "It seems to be authentic poetry, but, if so, the poetry is minor."

I believe a man can write poetry that is simple and stirring and understandable without drifting into banality; using the concrete terms of life; avoiding smart obscurity .... The whole academic approach to poetry in this country has proved an irritant.[28]

On his way to writing some of the best verse of his life (and a great deal of such verse) CB made it clear that however he was classified as a poet, whatever school he would be put into, made no difference to what he was trying to say or to how he was trying to say it. The man who downplayed aspects of his own intellect — "I don't know anything about poetry ... wouldn't know a trochee from a dactyl"[29] — admitted to Watt, "I'm not really under any illusions that the stuff I turn out is particularly important to anyone except myself." Of course, CB was a craftsman who had long known about metrics and other tools of form,[30] and by producing over the next eight years a body of work that reflected primarily the substance and themes of life along the north shore of his home bay, he learned of the significance of his poetry to others.[31]

By the mid 1940s there were reactions against the "tradition" of A.J.M. Smith, just as Smith had led the way in the mid-1920s, especially in *The McGill Fortnightly Review* and *The Canadian Mercury* in denouncing poetasters and the vulgarities of most Victorian poetry. In 1936 Smith, along with the others considered to be "the chief modernists in Canada"[32] — Scott, Pratt, Klein, Kennedy, and Robert Finch — appeared in the anthology *New Provinces*. In his preface to the book, Scott spoke of the employment of "new techniques" and of the "human [and poetic] energies" released by the Depression.[33] In his "A Rejected Preface" Smith called for "good metaphysical verse" and stated bluntly that "The fundamental criticism that must be brought against Canadian poetry as a whole is that it ignores the intelligence. And as a result it is dead."[34] *New Provinces*, which initially sold less than 100 copies, was published by Macmillan, an indication that those who considered themselves to be on the cutting edge of poetic expression in the country had, as Louis Dudek later put it, "no 'little magazine' or 'little press' movement: no magazines of poetry and experiment representing the rebellion of the creative minority …. "[35] The Depression might have released creative energies, but it kept a financial lid on publication except for the occasional book (for example, only Kennedy and Pratt of the six poets in *New Provinces* published books between 1930-1940) and in such mass-appeal organs as *Canadian Poetry Magazine*, which, according to Dudek, printed "the poetry of appeasement, of gullible sentimentality."

The relative prosperity of World War Two and the accompanying sense in younger writers of a Canadian identity, especially vis-à-vis the United States, resulted in new forums of expression. *Preview* (1942-45) fused literary and political aims (in the anti-fascist cause) either in "the cosmopolitan language of the intelligence," or in expression that was essentially unaware "of the need for local literary stimulus, for variety, for native expression."[36] The founders of *First Statement* — John Sutherland, Irving Layton, and Louis Dudek — "believed in a coarser and more militant approach to poetry" and called for a concentration on indigenous forms and subject matter.[37] According to Dudek, contributors to *First Statement* were "working-class poets" with visceral convictions. Desmond Pacey had a more genteel way of putting it: the works Sutherland brought out in the magazine "were less metaphysical and difficult in style than those selected by Patrick Anderson for *Preview*, were more direct reflections of the immediate Canadian scene, spoke a plainer and more colloquial language."[38] Nevertheless, the two magazines merged in 1945 to form *Northern Review*, under the editorship of Sutherland; most of the other writers fell away from this alliance soon after, and he was left to carry on alone.

Although *Northern Review* became "progressively the vehicle for the opinions of one man," it did play the vital role of sponsor of first books by Layton, Anderson, Waddington, Souster, and others. Most important, perhaps, were Sutherland's editorials and his critical essays and reviews. He denounced Robert Finch, who won the Governor-General's Award in 1946 for *Poems*, as an "etherealized academician,"[39] and in his preface to *Other Canadians: An Anthology of the New Poetry in Canada 1940-46*, his answer to Smith's 1943 *Book of Canadian Poetry*, he railled

against the parochialism of Smith's cosmopolitanism, the limitations of the "English colonial poets" of the nineteenth century
and the present Smith school; he praised those poets "concerned
with the individual and the individual's relation to society ....
who followed American literary models rather than English
ones" and condemned those who had not as having succumbed
to "spiritual old age."[40] None of the six modernists of *New
Provinces* were included in *Other Canadians*.

Where was CB while all these poetry wars went on? The tiny
group of *Argosy* writers at Mount Allison in the mid-1920s were
sheltered by Maritime tradition and loyalty to the Confederation poets, especially to the local gods, Carman and G.D.
Roberts; they had heard Roberts and Wilson MacDonald read
their poems, could not (or would not) quote "The Wasteland,"
and would not have understood Smith's demand for a "new
Poetry" that would "be the result of the impingement of modern
conditions upon the personality and temperament of the
poet."[41] CB, at Mount Allison, was not, of course, very far from
that boyhood world where disillusion and protest of form or
content did not have much place. When he lived in Halifax from
1927-33 he fell in with the Song Fishermen and the continuing
influence of the Confederation poets and traditional verse. Encountering the occasional anti-establishment writer, CB kept
essentially to his own code of no political affiliations and the
need to display insights "flashed [only] from his own experience." It was the lives of farmer-fishermen that increasingly
concerned him, rather than socio-political crusades. In the late
1920s and early 1930s this stance was best expressed in
"Tomorrow's Tide."

When CB moved to Toronto he was exposed considerably to
the poetic debates about what one should write and how it
should be written, but he kept to his ground. The exchange with
Leo Kennedy in 1937 over "immediates" revealed that as a poet
CB was willing to promulgate his belief that the experience of
the common man preceded systems and philosophies, that
words by themselves, written in the name of something, were
never enough. His was the basic tenet that "No one ever writes

good poems to convince anyone of anything. We convince by other means. We write good poems to write good poems."[42]

CB was included in Smith's *Book of Canadian Poetry*, but apart from the publication of "Deep Cove" in *New Frontier* in 1937, his work did not appear in any of the "new poetry" magazines. Sutherland does not mention him, but would obviously have considered CB a traditionalist (as in many ways he was). Nothing was quite as simple as Sutherland saw it: he certainly liked and praised some of the work of Dorothy Livesay and Earle Birney, yet the poem "which established ... Livesay's reputation," "Day and Night," appeared in *Canadian Poetry Magazine* in 1936, and Birney edited *CPM* from 1946-48. CB's own comment (in some undated notes) on the poetry of Layton and Dudek suggests that he was, at times, susceptible to a reductive, black and white view: "It lacks the ring of belief. Lead coinage with a fancy design."

His responsibilities at Canadian Press and his involvement with the war as a foreign correspondent kept CB out of the Canadian poetry fray for the first half of the 1940s. "Personal Note" and "Grey Ship Moving" were his respective ventures into expression of anti-fascism and Canadian identity and sense of purpose in the war, but they were not part of any movement; nor did CB give any indication during this period that his creative expression had to do with anything except personal experience and a general belief in mankind's ability as a "warm branch of nature" to make a faith of "goodwill." However, after his return to Toronto to take up the position of General Superintendent of CP, and at the beginning of his most prolific years as a poet, CB seems to have felt some responsibility to articulate a philosophy of poetry (though he would not have approved of such a formal term for his thoughts about creativity). From roughly the mid-1940s to the mid-1950s he wrote essays, gave talks, and engaged in debates by mail on the writing of poetry with Northrop Frye, W.A. Deacon (who as Toronto *Globe and Mail* Book Editor was a powerful force in the writing community), students who were interested in his verse, and many others. His comments underline his strengths and limitations as a poet — how he was able in his major work to strike "sparks from the common and usual," to display "the gleam of truth glimpsed through lived experience"; how his choice or innate need to stay away from new influences and cutting edges in poetry meant that he had sown and reaped his poetic ground by the time he was fifty, or thereabouts.

In 1950 CB made clear the distinction between his early poetry through *Wild Apples* and some of *Tomorrow's Tide* and the type of poem that would prevail in *The Mulgrave Road* (published in the fall of 1951). He complained about the quality of the verse submitted to the *Canadian Poetry Magazine*:

> Most of it was written by people who obviously were seeking to express something, but who wrote of lovely things as Beauty, or terrible things as Horror, who thought of what they had to write about as abstractions, not as earth and rock, flesh and blood, callouses on hands, a child's laughter, tears in the laughter-wrinkles of a man's face. Who called on abstract adjectives to say what they felt, rather than on concrete nouns and moving verbs to recreate the things that woke the feeling.[43]

Two years earlier he had called poetry "the most personal of all arts, the form of writing in which what you say is what you are or nothing at all."[44] Poetry had become for him the person who wrote it, a true representation of what that person was trying to be, as well as trying to say, or else it belonged on Christmas cards or in literary stunts: "Write only of what you know or have seen .... expression is disciplined by sticking to a person's own observation of the way a spike-tooth harrow scrawls across a plowed field, or the way a man's voice sounds, touched with liking or anger."[45] He was contemptuous of writers who did not write from what he called the *inside* of a subject, who depended on relative vision to describe or explain life to readers rather than absolute vision "in which you just say what happened ... it comes from nature, human nature, and needs no explanation."[46] Similes and metaphors could not be based upon startling incongruities nor quality of craftmanship yield strength of feeling (the reverse, he thought, was true). But CB was adamant that he was not simply concerned with producing word-photographs — stark realism — nor in focussing on isolated bits of human experience; as he wrote to a Carleton University student,

> It may not be clear from the stuff itself, but it is a fact that I have never yet written a poem essentially about the sea or any other aspect of nature. The idea is to get across an idea, or a feeling, usually about people. Ideas are probably much the same whether they are held by people pulling herring out of the Atlantic or running a combine in Saskatchewan. But the fisherman is the one whose accent I know .... [47]

There is some fuzzy thinking here, or at least fuzzy presentation of thought, because CB does not explain the connections between, indeed the unity of, ideas *about* people and ideas *held* by people. But he does make it clear that concrete nouns and strong verbs exist in and create contexts of meaning — the poem is animate, a human experience (and experienc*ing*), not a still-life of a rock or a gull. CB's difficulty in avoiding abstraction himself when attempting to explain poetry's universal qualities underlines his central thesis that it is the poem itself rather than the explanation of it that stirs the reader and speaks volumes:

> ... I do not much like the term "Canadian Poetry." Inevitably poetry written in Canada will be distinguished by the scenes and terms, plants and animals, and the idiom of this country. But the inner excitement (and tenacity of craftmanship) which results in this being transferred outward in verbal excitement and realized image must be the same, it seems to me, whether the transference occurs in Prince Rupert or Salonika, now or in the time of Christ. [48]

Part of the weakness of CB's role as a teacher of, or example for, younger poets lies in the implications of "what you say is what you are." People could read his poems based on his Port Shoreham experience, but they obviously could not write them; to a very considerable extent he seems to have been saying that poets are born not made, and this view is reflected in what he told young writers who contacted him for advice so that they might learn to shape what they already possessed in terms of experience and talent. Go to Rupert Brooke, CB told them, go to James Elroy Flecker, Wilfrid Gibson, Walter de la Mare, E.A. Robinson, and Edna Millay, even to "appealing verse" by Theodore Goodridge Roberts. But CB did not write like these people any more (AE was long gone, except as a delightful memory). He had his own voice and subject-matter that left their influence behind precisely because of his own particular heritage and experience that preceded them in time. He had emerged intact as the poet he was almost despite these poets he listed and because, in the years between such early 1930s poems as "Lunenburg" and those that would be in *The Mulgrave Road*, he had not allowed much in the literary world to shake his strong sense of who he was and where he had come from. The young writers he advised would learn very little, if anything at all, from the poets to whom they were referred by CB; the young writers had been born in the heyday of Eliot and Pound, Hart Crane and Wallace Stevens, and they were experiencing now the thunder of Layton and the quieter but equally strong voices of a host of Canadian poets CB did not seem prepared to recommend. Besides, they had to find the personal accent *they* knew.

CB's strength as a teacher came in those rare moments when he talked to younger writers about the words they had put down on a page. In October 1950 the thirty-two-year-old Al Purdy sent CB "The Extroverts," which CB accepted for *Canadian Poetry Magazine*, but not before he had suggested almost complete changes to two lines of the fifth stanza of the poem. Purdy agreed with these proposed changes not, it is clear, because he was desperate to be published, but because he apparently recognized the result was better poetry.[49] CB offered the same kind of tangible advice to the Fredericton poet Robert Cockburn in 1967, and their resultant correspondence over the next four years indicates Cockburn's admiration for CB as a poet and critic of poetry.

It is interesting that the adage "what you say is what you are or nothing at all" could, for CB, be corrupted by certain psychological types who, as poets, allowed their personal vision to exclude all else. This is evident in the devastating opinion CB held of a man and poet he did not count as a creative precursor of his — Ezra Pound. When Pound was awarded the Bollingen Prize for his *Pisan Cantos* in 1948, CB wrote the *Saturday Review of Literature* to condemn the award not on the grounds of Pound's treasons, but because "Being the man he is he was bound to produce corrupt verbal manure. It is not necessary or desirable to go beyond the evidence of the Cantos themselves; all the corruption Pound evidenced as a man is implicit in the failure of his art …. When art and the artist are as inseparable as they are in poetry, it is redundant to go beyond the corruption of the art."[50] As is often the case, such a diatribe reveals more about the critic than the person being criticized. CB seems to insist, in his reductive assessment of Pound, that what is or is not poetry is defined only by the part of "human nature [that] … needs no explanation." By saying in his poetry what he was, Pound, according to CB, produced "nothing at all" of consequence — his silence, despite the admitted connection between his art and life, would have been preferable. The dark and twisted accent (if that, in fact, is what Pound possessed) should never have been articulated. It is ironic that much of Pound's poetry, like nearly all that of CB's, could rest on the adage of another unacknlowledged poetic ancestor — William Carlos Williams: "No ideas but in things."[51]

VII

Homeward Bound II

In 1943 CB and Agnes sent their eldest son, Alan, who was eleven, to Port Shoreham for the summer. Alan recalls his rather stern grandmother who did not seem to have much of a sense of humour, but he also remembers having the run of the field and beach with young Keith MacIntosh, Harold's son.[1] Memories evoked by Alan's experience and aspects of that experience itself seem to have combined to produce a 'might-have-been' scenario in CB's mind. What if Will were still alive, and what if a grandson could discover his heritage through much the same encounter with farm and sea as CB had had?

In July 1946 CB sent a manuscript to Lorne Pierce at Ryerson, a nine-part, blank-verse narrative poem entitled "The Flowing Summer." "The accompanying story in verse [he wrote] is the product of some rather concentrated night work over the past several months." While he was aware, he said, of Pratt's narratives and of Birney's "David" (1942), "What I have here is definitely different — an attempt to catch the spirit of the somewhat muted drama in common living — not for the sake of difference itself, but because I am more fascinated by the day-to-day story than the single incident."[2] That CB was confident of the poem's quality is evident from his suggestions to Pierce of a format for the book, which would include drawings.[3]

In the poem's opening segment, "Journey Alone," Lee Graham is on the train from Toronto to Nova Scotia, his father's boyhood home, because his father Roy has realized "The task of living was a chase that left/No time for living."[4] It is important that Lee is a young "explorer fitted with the charts/Of a man's memory" but simultaneously "free to set a course/Of his own bearings." When Lee meets his grandfather, old Jack Graham, an immediate "kinship" exists between them, and although Lee had once visited the farm by the sea when a tiny boy, something more than memory claims him on his return. CB is concerned with the symbolic aspects of Lee's concrete experiences with his grandfather, so there is no attempt to describe every moment of every day. Thus in "The Nets" the boy helps Jack set the herring nets out on the bay, learning the hard way how to row on the ocean, but his grandfather's hands join his own on the oars to give "direction to a buoyant landing." In "The Herring Run" Lee is aware of his yesterday at the oars ("the driving ache,/ ... his flesh quickened to the sting of salt"), but he is also focussed on the *now* of the nets, "the gleam of chance" of fish that is present and will "gleam again/Tomorrow morning, and the morning after ...." Flowing in time, as well, is Old Jack who has a partner "For the first time in nearly twenty years," and who drifts in the current of then (the past), now, and then (the future): "Fifty years before/Jack Graham's hands had picked a herring net,/And the quick ardour of that far-off morning/Lived in him still and wakened in the boy." When he drifts to sleep later Lee recalls his father's stories of days gone by, and already a pattern of living and response to living is unfolding.

Lee discovers a small island, which Jack names after him, and which he keeps "Along the inward beaches of his mind"; he sees a trout in a river pool — real enough with "tawny back, the speckled flank and side .... / ... a flickering of lazy fins," but so unexpected and evanescent that when it does disappear it becomes a symbol of reality's transformation into memory. The essence of Lee's summer is found in the sight of his grandfather, a figure of and in time as Jack mows the hay-field with a scythe, and in his own hands as he finds a rhythm with the same tool; the essence is discovered too in an attic on a rainy day amongst the items of his father's youth — a punching bag, a fielder's glove, a muskrat trap, a scrapbook — that "recorded here the drift of simple time." The child becomes the father to the man as Lee glimpses his father as a boy and knows him for the first time. Two lines from Kipling pasted in the scrapbook emphasize CB's theme here: "'When d'you think that he'll come back?/Not with this wind blowing and this tide.'" In a way, Roy Graham, who cannot literally return home, has returned, and in a way he has never left. The wind blows, and the tide of human connections ebbs and flows.

At the end of the summer Lee has a chance to stay for another month if he asks, but there is no need to grasp at time this way, nor is there need for his grandfather to press for the question. Their shared experience on the beach, in the boat, and in the field has joined them forever in "That patterned living at the river mouth." If Lee, departing on the channel steamer, looks to the future, his "newly-raised horizons" are marked by the ebb and flow of memory's tide, the waters of heritage that for grandfather Jack thrust against the curving beach sand of all his days.

Reading *The Flowing Summer* one can hear afresh CB's debate with Leo Kennedy about "immediates." The subject-matter of the poem is very far removed from the aftermath of war and the division of the world between emerging superpowers. The collective memory of suffering peoples was not likely to include such peaceful and ordinary detail as the poem contains. CB could perhaps have been accused of shutting himself off intellectually and emotionally from a political and economic world that demanded attention be paid and that was far larger than the north shore of Chedabucto Bay. Old Jack's way of life can be seen as anachronistic under the deadly cloud of atomic weaponry, and Lee's new horizons as circumscribed by an almost unbelievable innocence. However, if CB was firm in his assertion that poetry was about what the poet knew or had seen, his conviction was still, as he had indicated to Leo Kennedy ten years before, that systems of war and peace are distinct from the common experience of men and women who touch and therefore translate the otherwise "insignificant earth."

In the summer of 1946, when he sent Pierce his manuscript of *The Flowing Summer*, CB met Sandy Bruce in Boylston and began his creative investigation into "cross-roads history," which, he felt, was the past that linked Port Shoreham to all (suffering) peoples and which, if lived through and allowed to flow through the heart and mind, could contribute to the prevention of the holocaust to be found in "political immediacies."

The Flowing Summer sentimentalizes the often harsh existence of the farmer-fisherman and never dwells on the psychological complexities of human relationships, but its own complexity is that while it is firmly grounded in aspects of the real, it is a song of praise to human interdependence and connections through time that is ultimately symbolic in its intention and result. Symbolism for CB did not emerge from word-games but rather from strength of feeling that had its origins in definite reality and the impact on the individual of sensual contact with the world. So dependent on particular time and place, the poem transcends the summer of 1943, or any one season of life. It recognizes that generations come and go, that nothing is ever exactly the same again, but over forty years after it was written it reads in some opposition to Dylan Thomas's "Fern Hill": though time may hold us all "green and dying," we pass into one another rather than die alone and bereft, and there are no chains for the individual who sings in harmony with the sea.

A long review in "Letters in Canada"(1947)[5] paid tribute to CB's "Wordsworthian" method in *The Flowing Summer*: "... a situation is chosen from common life and treated with the vocabulary of ordinary men, and yet raised to poetry by the effort of the imagination, in Mr. Bruce's case a moral imagination, a sympathetic insight." While the reviewer also criticized the occasional "thud of prose" in the poem, he felt that, like CB's other published works, this poem "is almost unscarred by fad or oddity" and therefore would be read and appreciated by posterity. The *Queen's Quarterly* compared it to "the quiet simplicity of Evangeline," while closer to home the Halifax *Herald*[6] used a term that CB did not like at all: "nostalgia," he would say on the dust-jacket of his next book "is the silliest word in the English language."[7]

The range of positive commentary from newspapers and journals across the country suggests that CB's notions of "the gleam of truth glimpsed through lived experience" and of "cross-roads history" had some Canadian validity. During the five-year period between 1946 and 1951 CB wrote more poetry than he had since his boyhood or than he would ever write again.[8] He also wrote and published over half a dozen short stories and wrestled with the embryonic form of *The Channel Shore*. His articulation of a philosophy of poetry in several articles and talks coalesced with his intense focus on who he was behind the General Superintendents's necessary mask and on what he knew away from the wire and news story deadlines. Perhaps his struggle with Stan Currie's return to the North Shore had forced him to explore a literary territory without the major image of home restraining while inspiring him. Perhaps the war experience had made him realize the fragility of that "normal" and "usual" in which he had put his faith but had sung about only from time to time in the previous twenty years. Now he would write the majority of poems for *The Mulgrave Road*, the book upon which his too-small reputation as a poet rests and produce short fiction that contains not only convincing setting and memorable descriptions of character and event, but effective dialogue and dramatic action as well.

CB did look back more than once at the war. In "Spring of '46"[9] there is an ambiguity to the natural world imagery that belongs to any rural scene. Swallows build in "the barn's familiar eaves," and in their "flaring" flight suggest, for veterans, "The flash of canon-feathered wings" in other springs and other skies. Or is it that memories of violence are subsumed by an eternal recurrence far older than war? The latter is strongly indicated by the imagery of "Orchard in the Woods," first published in September 1946 in *Maclean's*, a blank-verse poem about an abandoned farm. The natural world has grown over former fence lines and tilled fields; the cellar's stone crumbles, and broken artifacts of habitation are scattered in the grass. But what has passed here is not war's devastation, just life's inevitable cycle of settlement and decay. The apple trees that were planted long ago have become wild, but bring something of their heritage to their altered condition, "a light ironic bloom/Against the green utility of spruce." So the "gunner going home" (a local hunter) will bite of an apple and taste of a unique combination of the natural and human experience, "The taste of ninety seasons, hard and sweet."[10] There is the strong sense here, with the hunter image, of swords turning into ploughshares.

ORCHARD IN THE WOODS

Red spruce and fir have crossed the broken lines
Where ragged fences ran; ground-juniper
Covers the sunny slope where currant bushes
Blackened their hanging clusters in green leaves.
Where oats and timothy moved like leaning water
Under the cloudy sweep of August wind,
The crop is stunted alders and tall ferns.

Above the cellar's crust of falling stone
Where timbered walls endured the treacherous
Traffic of frost and sunlight, nothing stands—
Under the wreckage of the vanished barn
A woodchuck burrows. Where the dooryard was,
The matted grass of years encloses now
Two horseshoes and a rusted wagon-tire.

Only the apple trees recall the dream
That flowered here—in love and sweat and growth,
Anger and longing. Tough and dark and wild,
Grown big of stump, rough in the bark and old,
They still put forth a light ironic bloom
Against the green utility of spruce.

Clearing and field and buildings gone to waste—
But in the fall, a gunner going home
Will halt a moment, lift a hand to reach
One dusky branch above the crooked track,
And, thinking idly of his kitchen fire,
Bite to the small black shining seeds and learn
The taste of ninety seasons, hard and sweet.

TIDEWATER MORNING

Searching the windy strait with narrowed frown,
She finds between the wrinkled rise and fall
Of marching seas, a dory, cruising down
The channel's reach with tubs of running trawl.
His time were better spent, she knows, attending
The careful urging of her common sense:
Breaking the upper field to seed, and mending
The kitchen roof, and bracing flattened fence...

But as he climbs the rutted pasture now,
Hungry from wind and tide, and oar and barrow—
Her heart forgets the sowing and the plow,
Meeting again the strength that never took
Its grace from gardens, and the long clear look
That never learned its blue behind a harrow.

DISAPPROVING WOMAN

The look she gives you is a tightened thread
Between the stitches of her spoken thought.
In the deft warning of her shaken head
A guilt is whispered, and a lesson taught.
The careful shadow of remembering doubt
Lives in her eyes, and with upright mind
She meets affliction: resolute, devout,
Never unkind and never wholly kind.

The years have given her all the years require:
Birch in the woodbox, credit at the store,
Comfort and friendship, work and food and fire;
But life has endless grief to answer for—
Death, and the sins of men and the blood's desire,
And muddy footprints on the kitchen floor.

Just as he had written in 1937 of the limitations of politics and systems on "the roofless beach," so in "North Shore" CB turns the reader away from "The careful nations, in their long pursuits/[that] Amend the treaty and revise the plan" to the essence of those Mulgrave and Boylston men who fought and helped win the war: "Smell of rain-wet stubble and no wind blowing,/Chimney smoke, and glitter of rain in the grass;/ .... /Clattering wheels on the road ... / ... and the far surf curling white;/Grey dusk falling/And the flicker of Queensport Light."[11]

Although CB wrote to a student in 1964, "Geographically there is a dirt-and-gravel road running from Boylston to Mulgrave along the north shore of Chedabucto Bay and the western shore of the strait of Canso,"[12] this road by its very geography meant people to him; the dual experience of farm and sea. To the north are back-road farms set in the strength of the hills, but somehow sheltered, missing a voice, "the far deep rumour of sea on stone."[13] There are also those who plough within sight of the sea yet do not know it; they are a little too careful, "a trifle cold,"[14] not enough acquainted with chance and change. In contrast is the farmer-fisherman's wife who, despite her frown and "common sense" attitude about land tasks, meets her husband's "strength that never took/Its grace from gardens, and the long clear look/That never learned its blue behind a harrow."[15] This is the man whose sharp memory blurs "in something else,/Next year, tomorrow ... / ... /Turning again to now."[16] As for the old fisherman who has only known "the swaying sea/A lifetime marching with the waves of time," he provides CB with one of his clearest portraits (in "Eastern Shore") of what he meant by sparks struck from the common and usual:

> He stands and walks as if his knees were tensed
> To a pitching dory. When he looks far off
> You think of trawl-kegs rolling in the trough
> Of swaying waves. He wears a cap against
> The sun or water, but his face is brown
> As an old mainsail, from the eyebrows down.

He has grown old as something used and known
Grows old with custom; each small fading scar
Engrained by use and wear in plank and spar,
In weathered wood and iron, and flesh and bone.
But youth lurks in the squinting eyes, and in
The laughter wrinkles in the tanbark skin.[17]

If words are never enough, they come very close in this poem to satisfying the reader's sense of a particular reality down Port Shoreham way. There is something here — when the fact himself (the fisherman) is not literally present — of Margaret Laurence's (Morag Gunn's) assertion in *The Diviners* of a fiction more true than fact.

Women are important figures on the Mulgrave Road. The "Disapproving Woman" is tense, perhaps repressed, looking at "you" with "a tightened thread/Between the stitches of her spoken thought."[18] CB does not create uncomplicated life nor suggest that there is only the glory to hook and not the darkness, because for this woman the commonplace is bound up with the complex: "… life has endless grief to answer for — /Death, and the sins of men, and the blood's desire,/And muddy footprints on the kitchen floor." Just as the "dry-footed" farmer is contrasted with his neighbour who "Move[s] in a sea of sense" and whose "waves of thought/March to the shore of the mind,"[19] so the disapproving woman is contrasted to the female spinner whose "body [is] moving still,/Rapt in the wakened youth/Of old and stubborn skill" and who partakes in and is amused by "the long skein of time."[20] She is strong and creative, CB's figure of fate spinning her own present and future out of her own experience and heritage. Even the "Girls in the Parlor," who placed their photographs "against the claims/Of earth and sea and time" and lost, did not lose "the touch of grace" nor, surrounded by other photos, their dual condition of being inheritors and ancestors both.[21]

CB perhaps overstates his case in "Stories" when he draws exact parallels between the ships built on the local beach and those of Jason and other figures of myth and history. The extraordinary in the ordinary, "the wonder and strangeness in the normal," is best revealed in "The Other Shore" when voyagers from the North Shore sail across the bay towards the "Asian darkness" of the other side, "the cobalt blur/Of that dim country under sleeping cloud," to discover reality there of "Earth, rocks, fields, people" and then turn and see "low and far, the cobalt blur of home."[22] Or rather than views from a distance, there is the close-up sight of a fish-hut with its marks of the wind and the woodworm, "Bare as the bare stone of this open shore," yet still after sixty years a meeting place, a habitation for things and for experience.[23]

There are nineteen new poems in the first section of *The Mulgrave Road*; the final one is the title poem, a ten-quatrain, rhymed tale about a wanderer who leaves home not for adventure, but for pay, and returns years later looking for "Something different, something strange," for the satisfaction of "venture" on his home earth. Why? Because

> You can see the rainclouds gather and pass
> Over Hadley's Beach or the Artois plain;
> And dust on the grass is dust on the grass
> In Guysborough County or Port of Spain.[24]

Certainly this book was an appropriate place in which to reprint two of CB's major poems about home and away — "Fisherman's Son" and "Words Are Never Enough." He altered the latter poem only by creating two new stanza divisions, but hinted at some troubling personal experience by substituting in "Fisherman's Son" (line 9 of the first sonnet) "black biting hour" for "dark hour of stress." These two relatively early works about attachment to the Mulgrave Road territory deserve their place at the heart of the collection.

The last section of the book contains six poems. CB had "1945" reprinted under the title "Of This Late Day" and altered one line in the final stanza.[25] "Sketch For A Landscape" is a rather slight, 15-couplet effort about life in a rural landscape, but "Planes of Space and Time" is a more subtle poem, indeed more consciously complex than usual with its comparison of the human mind to a telescope that brings a distant country close:

> So now, in the tiered textures of the brain —
> Deeper than glass, and moving — curling sea

Comes up, and frosty pastures, and dim rain,
And faces, and known gestures.[26]

In a remarkable final stanza in this poem CB reveals that this country of time, these "moving moments" loom large in the mind because of their connection to a very simple yet evocative present moment: "… this breath, this now, this something said/Of space and time … and lamplight on the wall,/And someone slowly going up to bed."

In his 1952 letter to a Carleton University student of journalism CB wrote that he knew a certain part of the country and its people well, but that in Saskatchewan, for example, "as far as the scene and atmosphere go, I am outside, looking on, observing, rather than sharing in the actual ways of living and habits of speech."[27] These were the days before Birney, Purdy, and others travelled back and forth across the nation and put much of its geography and human life into words, writing about Canada from Rocky Mountain and Ameliasburgh, Ontario roots. It is certain that in the early fall of 1951 CB took the train to the West Coast for a CP meeting, but he also appears to have done this earlier, in 1947; "Lake Superior Coast: Train Window" was one of two published responses in verse to landscape he had never before encountered. There is a remarkable tension in the poem as content pushes against form, escaping even the seemingly rigid *abba* rhyme scheme and the essentially iambic/anapestic metre. The first two stanzas appear to be regular, as CB describes the train's movement from the prairie into the Precambrian shield (obviously on his return journey east):

East of the port, the gaunt euclidean town
At the edge of the prairie sky, at the venturous end
Of the sea's last traffic with the climbing land —
You come to the hills. The spruce and rock steep down

To the mountain beach. Inlet and channel and reef
Return, in the slow dance of the land's turning;
Shadowed and clear and dark in the desolate raining
Of lost and shadowy light, and the lost brief

Moment; flashed and repeated in the drumming wheels.[28]

NOVA SCOTIA FISH HUT

Rain, and blown sand, and southwest wind
Have rubbed these shingles crisp and paper-thin.
Come in:
Something has stripped these studding-posts and pinned
Time to the rafters. Where the woodworm ticked
Shick shick shick shick
Steady and secretive, his track is plain:
The fallen bark is dust;the beams are bare.

Bare as the bare stone of this open shore,
This building grey as stone. The filtered sun
Leaks cold and quiet through it. And the rain,
The wind, the whispering sand, return to finger
Its creaking wall, and creak its thuttering door.

Old, as the shore is. But they use the place.
Wait if you like: someone will come to find
A handline or a gutting-knife, or stow
A coiled net in the loft. Or just to smoke
And loaf; and swap tomorrow in slow talk;
And knock his pipe out of a killick-rock
Someone left lying sixty years ago.

Of space and time...and lamplight on the wall,
And someone slowly going up to bed.

PLANES OF SPACE AND TIME

As when, through plated folds of finite space
We peered at distance, and the subtle glass
Brought up the stick and stone of place and place,
Far hillsides, forests, cattle deep in grass,
And drew their fabric—leaf and root and limb,
The rock, the road, the falling stream, the blown
White fringe of vapor on the mountain's rim—
In, to the dooryard's earth and stick and stone:

So now, in the tiered textures of the brain—
Deeper than glass, and moving—curling sea
Comes up, and frosty pastures, and dim rain,
And faces and known gestures.
                    Silently
The moving moments come: and all, all, all
Drawn to this breath, this now, this something said

LAKE SUPERIOR COAST: TRAIN WINDOW

East of the post, the gaunt euclidean town
At the edge of the prairie sky, at the venturous end
Of the sea's last traffic with the climbing land—
You come to the hills. The spruce and rock steep down

To the mountain beach. Inlet and channel and reef
Return, in the slow dance of the land's turning;
Shadowed and clear and dark in the desolate raining
Of lost and showdowy light, and the lost brief

Moment; flashed and repeated in the drumming wheels.
Repeat...repeat...repeat; the flashing earth
Streams in its rhythm; and the moment's breath
Is time's deliberate breath. The wheeling hills

Drift with its tide...The hills and the quilted flock
Of the sky, and a gull, remotely flying
And stilled in flight...

Time, and the granite flowing
Of stonegrey water and precambrian rock.

However, if "town" and "down" rhyme, locking settlement into descent, lines two and three do not exactly rhyme, emphasizing no "end" to the "land." In stanza two as well, the minor stress at the end of lines two and three as well as the end line enjambment suggest first an elusive, intangible quality to the land ("turning," "raining") and then empty space ("brief" is followed by no word where a word is expected). In the second stanza "reef" and "brief" are joined in sound, suggesting the wreck of the seemingly isolated "Moment" at the beginning of the third stanza, but the "Moment" there is "flashed and repeated," part of a larger rhythm:

> Moment; flashed and repeated in the drumming wheels.
> Repeat ... repeat ... repeat; the flashing earth
> Streams in its rhythm; and the moment's breath
> Is time's deliberate breath. The wheeling hills
>
> Drift with its tide ... The hills and the quilted flock
> Of the sky, and a gull remotely flying
> And stilled in flight ...
>   Time, and the granite flowing
> Of stone-grey water and precambrian rock.

The rhythm of the earth that the poet feels can only be articulated inadequately (but purposefully) through repetition and ellipses. "Wheeling hills" move far beyond "drumming wheels," and the earth breathes beyond the moment's intake. Then four lines are broken into five, and the gull's flight is but an instant in Time where rock flows like water. CB was not writing about ways of living and habits of speech here, nor about Saskatchewan, but this poem indicates clearly that he was not caught in a regional trap of language and that the language of his region provided sound and sense for any part of the country.

The one poem in which CB attempted to deal with all of Canada is not in *The Mulgrave Road*. "Memo for Certain Voyagers" was commissioned by the CBC and broadcast nationally on November 11, 1951 as part of a Canadian farewell to Princess Elizabeth and the Duke of Edinburgh after their royal tour.[29] The sheer scope and variety of his subject matter seems to have encouraged CB to let go of the usually effective reins on his poetic expression, and the result is a free verse piece totally unlike anything in his canon. The poem begins with the image of Maritime timber rivers, and there is enough regularity of form to make all seem ordinary: "Boomed timber on the Miramichi;/And arched on rock, etched on its rim of sky./A stone town ringing with the name St. Lawrence .... " But then as the land unfolds westwards, shorter lines interrupt the staid articulation, as do unpredictable line placements:

> The fields slope south;
> Green, bronze, umber and green,
> Measured and gardened,
> Fenced,
> Greenveined with rivers
>
> (Black chimneys breathing smoke, and smoke in folds
> from the black lips of engines;
> And a shout:
> Somewhere a fogbound siren shouting Erie.)

CB takes the reader, his royal "voyagers" too, through the Precambrian shield country ("The word is North"), across the plains ("Ripe with the gold of now on the black depth of time"), and the mountains ("Whitescarved in the sun"), to the Pacific. Then he asks the royal couple "What breath informs," "What long pulse of life/Lives in the veins of," "What is the blend of fear, strength, song, and dream" in "This heaped geography"? The answer for CB lies in the images and dreams of the people who now and in time have met the land and its waters, including "the lap in the dusk" of a specific "Channel":

> A million answers, voyagers; infinite answers.
> Sounds,
> Images,
> Crowding the memory and the memory of memory and the
> dream of tomorrow;

The breadth of vision here and the form of the poem are unusual for CB, but the essential national theme as finally expressed is not surprising, emerging as it does from CB's expansive regional vision: "Hearsay and Hope — /Last night, tomorrow, and the breath of years/Merged in the breathing Now."

The central place of people in time, the links between yester-day, today, and tomorrow, the heritage handed down — these are at the heart of "Cornerstone."[30] If we must leave time cap-sules for 10,000 years hence, we must "avoid editorial comment" while including records of the war, the atomic bomb explosion above Bikini Atoll, and pictures of famous political figures. We must put in "commoner things: a restaurant menu,/A trout fly and a prayerbook. Next to these/A pinch of arsenic and a strip of lace,/A G-string and a pint of blended rye." Also some evidence of popular culture. All facts, all data, the detritus of history. But we should not fool ourselves into thinking that we are explaining ourselves, our *being*, to posterity with such items. How can we show "A stone-drag moving down the slanted field/And a boy's years of learning purchased here/By knuckled fingers dark with harrowed earth?"

> Only by the peculiar logic of accident
> Shall they catch a glimpse of the dreaming blood and the mind,
> The circle of love and anger, of motive and impulse ....
>
> All we can leave in the end, that bears on the question
> Is neither locked in the box nor the layered earth;
> But lives in the blood, in the measure of love and hate
> Their veins inherit from the living now:

Relics are never enough, but CB is hopeful that the quality of *being* human will be passed through 10,000 years to our descen-dants.

The chief critical response to *The Mulgrave Road* was by and large positive, though there were some dissenters. Both the *Globe and Mail* and *The Maritime Advocate and Busy East*[31] were glad that CB had shunned sentimentality in the poems. The lat-ter paper's positive commentary was also based on the absence of nostalgia, while another reviewer enjoyed the book's "rather nostalgic mood."[32] *Canadian Poetry Magazine*, as might be ex-pected, offered only praise, though the review implied that CB wrote a poetry of no complexity whatsoever: "... there is very little flashing of phrase. These poems are made out of a more enduring, homelier cloth .... it will be a sad day for Canada when there are not readers to appreciate these pictures of a simpler Canadian way of life."[33]

The Varsity, more used to the University of Toronto's campus experiments in verse, perhaps, disagreed: "… a casual glance at this group of poems will only re-assure [readers] that they were better off when they left Canadian poetry where it is generally left — on the shelf …. the poet leans too heavily on local color … and trite universals which meet on the fair-weather ground of inadequate but uninspired words."[34] This was strong stuff, but CB saved his public response to such reviews for the Toronto *Telegram* commentator who wrote, "This is a poetry which reaches into the backwaters which the busy world has by-passed …."[35] Not only did he immediately reply to the paper and emphasize the goings and comings of people on the North Shore — their venture into the wide world and their return — but he also, later in the 1950s, based at least two seminal essays on this theme of a "vital homeland" that contributed to the populace of "the far frontiers of this country" and the world and that received a constant enrichment from those who never forgot their roots: "Something like those backwaters they call Times Square and Piccadilly. Without the traffic and the noise."[36]

The Ottawa *Journal* critic complained that CB wrote well enough about the East Coast, but said that he should apply himself to trans-Canada subject matter. In his response CB stated what he had also told the Carleton University journalism student: "… the fisherman is the one whose accent I know: I can write from *inside* a certain scene and atmosphere because I was brought up in it. In Saskatchewan … I am outside." What he also emphasizes, which is interesting in light of his early poetic influence, is that "The Georgians … wrote smooth and pleasant verse but to me they seem observers. When Gibson [who wrote the Preface to *Grey Ship Moving*] wrote about a man driving a cart he missed something because he never drove a cart himself."[37]

What prompted CB's most comprehensive response to a review was Northrop Frye's commentary in "Letters in Canada 1951" in the *University of Toronto Quarterly*.[38] Frye wrote,

Of the more conservative offerings I find Charles Bruce's *The Mulgrave Road* most consistently successful. His material is almost insistently unpretentious, confined to the simplest landscapes of farms and fishing villages. ... One begins, probably by feeling that nobody can make new poetry out of such material, then one reads:

> Slowly the days grow colder, the long nights fall;
> Plows turn the stubble, fires are tended, and apples
> Mellow in cellars, and under the roots of maples
> Mice are burrowing. And the high geese call.

We may say grumpily that anyway this kind of thing has often been done before. But repeating ready-made formulas is one thing; working within a convention quite another.

CB was particularly pleased by this last line of Frye's, and he informed Frye of what he had said to the *Telegram* and *Journal* reviewers. Frye had objected to occasional sentimental blurrings such as CB's insistence that the farm animals always *knew* it was Sunday, but CB assured him from his own experience that this was so; he then expressed doubts about one image Frye had praised: "And the high geese call" — "It's questionable whether anyone gives much thought to them." CB then went on to articulate his credo on the relationship between initial feeling and final expressions in poetry:

> What happens in the creation of poetry is that the poet realizes a certain set of circumstances, involving all sorts of things — people, buildings, landscapes, events — which cause in him a certain excitement. He doesn't say "These things make me feel so-and-so." He tries to re-create imaginatively and suggestively that set of circumstances, in the hope that through his exactitude — emotional exactitude rather than photographic, perhaps — and his unobtrusive suggestiveness he can create something like the same excitement in someone else. That seems to me to be the whole end and method of poetry whether traditional or modern in form.[39]

The awarding of the Governor-General's Award for poetry in 1951 to *The Mulgrave Road* probably suggested to *The Varsity* that its case about "Canadian Poetry" was closed. Even if some generosity is extended to the campus reviewer and it is assumed that Livesay, Birney, Klein and others were not being dismissed, CB was nevertheless being placed in the company of those described in F.R. Scott's "Canadian Authors Meet," and there is little excuse for such ignorance. CB was a conservative poet, but he was, as Frye said, "working within a convention" and was neither predictable nor banal. The voice of the North Shore spoke (as indicated by letters from readers) to a variety of North Americans in such publications as *Maclean's, Saturday Night, Poetry (Chicago), The Saturday Evening Post, Harper's,* and *The Saturday Review of Literature.*[40] A farmer from Runciman, Saskatchewan told CB in response to "The Settler", "My pioneering was done in the bush of northern Saskatchewan but the thoughts expressed in the poem are mine as, indeed, they must be of many others."[41] It seemed that CB was *inside* the scene and atmosphere of a region called Canada.

A certain amount of his material did appear in the *Canadian Poetry Magazine*. The second sonnet of "Fisherman's Son" was published there under the title "Seance" in 1938. It might be significant that of ten poems by CB in this magazine between the summer of 1948 and the summer of 1951 only one, "Coast Farm," was included in *The Mulgrave Road*. This could suggest CB's opinion of his own poetry in particular and of the quality of poems in general that were published in *CPM*. Dorothy Livesay's 1941 comment to CB about "the deplorable standard set by Canadian Poetry Magazine and like ilk" should be recalled, as should the challenge of *Preview, First Statement, Northern Review, Here and Now* (1947-49), *Contemporary Verse,* and others to traditional expression.[42] But CB was poetry editor of *CPM* from September 1946 until the early 1950s, accepting, among others, Al Purdy's work, and reviewing in detail A.M. Klein's *The Rocking Chair,* a collection not for the staid reader.[43]

Both "The Native" and "In the Long Evenings of Long Summers"[44] would have enhanced *The Mulgrave Road*. In fact, the former poem offers a portrait of a farmer who once knew the sea which is as strongly-presented in concrete terms as that of the fisherman in "Eastern Shore"; but this poem is much more a psychological study:

> The hard years touch him. And the touch is kind.
> But a voice troubles him, now at the last.
> Time is a nagging friend, and the mind blurs,

> Wearied with this and then, today and the past.
> And a voice troubles him: it is not hers.

> It is not mountain thunder, nor the creaking
> Of wheels, nor poplars in a windy place ...
> And you can see the long wave slowly breaking,
> Slantwise, along the granite of his face.[45]

There was also "The Ark Refloated," a humorous sequel to the biblical story of Noah with a slightly edged message: "Nothing sighted yet — /But drifting sky and tilted sea ... and fog." The image of "The old bell-weather of the draggled flock," the camel, "tough as desert rock," standing against some larger adversity is in contrast to CB's obvious concern in "Lines for a Copybook" (written in the same period, though not published) that "The pastures of infinity are bare/Of this and then and now and here and there." The old camel will reach shore again one day (an eternal recurrence), but "the x of time" disturbs the poet elsewhere: "There are no stars along that stranger track,/No stars, and no way back ... and no way back ...."[46]

For half a dozen years after the publication of *The Mulgrave Road* in 1951 CB continued to write and publish a considerable amount of poetry. At least seventeen poems appeared in magazines and journals between 1952 and 1957. He continued to focus on people along the "dirt-and-gravel road." There is his usual faith in those like the boatbuilder whose "hard bright story" of heritage lives within his listeners;[47] there is the same faith in a grandfather's words to his grandson as he answers "why some trivial thing — /Why herring school, or moles burrow or tide turns ... " by "Reading the thing behind it ... / ... the question no word can ever shape."[48] There is the familiar insistence that kinship and human contact overcome individual isolation and frailty. Thus the independent man who asks no help nor gives any, who lives his life alone with his pride, is buried by his neighbours. Thus the woman who marries late finds in the face of the man she fearfully loves the resting-place of her girlhood dreams. And the farmer who loses himself six days a week in work slows down enough on Sunday mornings to acknowledge every detail of the room in which his mother bore him. At the heart of human

10954H

Symbols and markings…

Through a thousand screenings
The signs persist. Shards of a primitive
Frail race that lived, and when it ceased to live
Left ashen words. We have not traced the meanings.

Love dream song pain…the archaic characters
Recur: in rock, in much, in borings taken
From primal stone. Charred words and lines and flaken
Fossilate leaves, and veins of ashen verse.

No key to meaning. But the thing is certain.
They lived. Existed. Were. The Sacred Ash
Enfolds a world that was—before the Flash,
The Cloud, the Flame, the Holocaust, the Curtain…

Think, now. They must have seen the Godhead rising!
For one caught shivering breath—
            they must have known—
The singing done. The word made crumbling stone.
And all, all, all the records past revising.

WAVE

Somewhere far out far off under asian cloud
No line no limit but the invisible curve
In a theorem of sea and sky,
And no eye there to see no mind to prove it—
Wind brushed that fluent sleep.

Wind from the planes
The cold euclidean steppes...

Shiver and stir. Ripple and flaw. Clouded stillness
Darkens where the invisible wind curles up
The waking wave.

Ripple and ridge. Curtsy and dip and lop...
Out from the puppet-shift and sway and stir
The quick dancer walks.

The dancers. Walking. Till the stilted walk
Steadies
And rolls
And leagued in rolling seas and the combers come
Wind-driven in a thousand miles of fetch.

Somber and towering now the ridge, the windscrawl—
That slopes and forms and follows and casts back
Self after fluent self.
Only the form eternal (while the wind holds,
The flowing shape through sea and sea and sea—
Until at last self shape one moment one
Break
On the asking granite of the shore.

vision is always the natural world — "The petal's fall of love/On love without intent./And grass unmindful of/The way the blade is bent" together with the fall of "the form eternal," the wave, "on the asking granite of the shore."[49] There is also the remarkable "10954H" (later entitled "The Archeologists", *Saturday Night*, December 25, 1954) in which CB writes of the discovery of a "Frail race that lived, and when it ceased to live/ Left ashen words. We have not traced the meanings." The "We" are looking back from a point in time exactly 9000 years after the first hydrogen bomb explosion.

This outpouring of verse fell off drastically in the late 1950s, indeed almost to nothing. In 1968 CB sent John Gray at Macmillan a manuscript that included an autobiographical essay, "The Back of the Book," and forty-three poems to be brought out under the title *Living and Recall*. The poems were CB's own selected best that he felt represented him as a poet. With the exception of "Fisherman's Son" and "Words Are Never Enough," they are all taken from *The Mulgrave Road* era and the 1950s. There exists the obvious implication that CB considered he had written nothing of lasting value prior to 1946 or between 1958 and 1968. In fact, no poem of CB's written after 1951 appears in any anthology. This is especially ironic in light of CB's comments in a review of the latest edition of *Canadian Poetry in English* (1954), edited by Bliss Carman, Lorne Pierce, and V.B. Rhodenizer:

> Base your collection on the best work of the top 50-60 people …. Take the people who are there for historical reasons only and put them in an appendix. Place the secondary work of the top 50 or 60 (the consciously patriotic or political and a good deal of the religious and philosophical) in a second appendix …. Place the work of those who are there for regional reasons, or simply because they write a lot, in still a third appendix.[50]

In his own lifetime CB would be increasingly viewed as a regional poet himself, but there were no third appendices for him, and the result was exclusion from anthologies.

Between 1946 and 1959 CB was also greatly preoccupied with fiction: ten short stories were published in magazines and newspapers; he wrote and rewrote *The Channel Shore* before it finally appeared in 1954; and he wrote the twenty linked short stories that form *The Township of Time* (1959). The combination of poetry and fiction represented an extraordinary creative accomplishment that obviously took its toll.[51] In the last eleven years of his life (according to his son Alan he was rather seriously ill for nine of them) CB wrote, under contract, a history of the Southam family's newspaper dynasty, and produced a 313-page manuscript of a novel he called *The Drift of Light*.[52] His first and best fictions must be considered so that the evident depletion of his artistic energy can be connected to his having ploughed and fished the North Shore, in creative terms, perhaps as much as was possible by 1959.

Sarah Tory Bruce as a young woman.

Charles Bruce as a baby. "The little prince"

Charles Bruce and
Wilbur Cummings
(circa 1914)

Charles Bruce and
Harold MacIntosh
(circa 1914)

Charles Bruce (Charlie) and "old Dollie" on the farm in Port Shoreham. (circa 1914)

Charles Bruce proudly holding a muskrat he had just caught. (Port Shoreham 1920)

Harold MacIntosh (left) and Charles Bruce on the beach below Port Shoreham. (1924)

The Bruce Family; Bess, Will, Carrie, Charlie, Sarah, Zoe and Anna at home in Port Shoreham during the mid-1920s.

Charles Bruce and his father Will Bruce in Port Shoreham during the mid-1920s.

Charles Bruce and the staff members of the Mount Allison University newspaper — *The Argosy*. Charles Bruce is in the front row on the right. (1925-1926)

Charles Bruce as a member of The Mount Allison University Debating Team during his senior year. (1927)

Charles Bruce as a war correspondent interviewing a Canadian soldier in England. (1942)

Charles Bruce and his sons Alan, Harry, Andrew and Harvey
on Farnham Avenue in Toronto during the mid-1950s.

The gravestones of Charles Bruce's great
grandparents, Richard and Margaret,
United Church Cemetery, Boylston Nova Scotia.

VIII

Second Fictions

In April 1947 CB wrote Elizabeth Lawrence at *Harper's* that he was going to complete his novel about Stan Currie by the summer of that year. However, there are no further references to *Currie Head* in his correspondence or notes. In January 1949 Howard Moorepark, a New York literary agent CB had retained to place his short stories, received the synopsis of a novel called *The Channel Shore*. Based on what CB told him Moorepark wrote, "I see no reason at all why it should not get placed down here."[1] But just as she had discussed the limitations of CB's earlier fiction, Elizabeth Lawrence was straightforward about the proposed book Moorepark submitted to *Harper's* in 1949. In her remarks there is no direct clue as to how different *The Channel Shore* was from *Currie Head*, but the absence of any reference to the latter does suggest that CB had written an entirely new novel. As well, there is the introduction of a new theme:

> ... he evokes most successfully the feeling of a place with its background of religious conflict. But he does this sometimes at the expense of his characters. At least, for us the people remain shadowy and not always convincing. In the early chapters especially it requires intense concentration to keep the various families and relationships in mind and to follow the chronological order of events. I could wish also for a greater variation of mood, more dramatic accent on characters and situations.[2]

Since a manuscript of "On the North Shore" does not exist, there is no way of telling whether, at this stage, CB had incorporated Grant, Anna, Hazel, and Chance from that short story into his novel manuscript. The term "religious conflict" only suggests otherwise, but that the 1949 version of *The Channel Shore* was not the 1954 published version is indicated by another remark of the *Harper's* fiction editor: "... in particular the character of Dan remained shadowy, and his reasons for returning to the town." Dan Graham is a minor character in the final version of the novel, and there is no town or return of any consequence for him.

In March 1949 CB asked Howard Moorepark to return the manuscript to him, saying he wanted to do some rewriting, especially "to sharpen up the distinction between characters .... it may be toward the end of the year before I can get it finished."[3] Over a year later Moorepark wrote to ask how the novel was coming along, but CB apparently now had his sights set on Canadian publication, because in November 1950 he sent Lorne Pierce at Ryerson Press "2/3 of a 3-part novel. Part three is written, but needs some revision and retyping." He wondered what its chances would be in the Ryerson Fiction Award contest. As well he indicated that he had "put in a lot of hard work on this story over a period of 5 years [that is, since his return from England in 1945] .... While it is not primarily a regional tale, it has regional aspects. The local geography is fictitious in detail, but is drawn from an area of Eastern Nova Scotia which so far as I know has never been treated in fiction (I've used it a bit in verse)."[4] Pierce's response, like that of Elizabeth Lawrence in the previous year, gives no clue as to plot and character, but he felt the manuscript needed much work. CB answered this response, saying, "... what you suggest seems to be virtually a complete rewrite job, which is something I shall not likely be able to undertake, my daily work being what it is."[5] His job at Canadian Press was undoubtedly demanding, but CB was during this period writing a great deal of poetry. As well, in 1948-49 alone six of his short stories were published — three of them were directly about characters who would appear in *The Channel Shore* in 1954; one story was set on the Channel Shore; and one, slightly revised, would appear in *The Township of Time* in 1959, part of CB's chronicle of Shore history.

CB wrote "The Talking Tree" while he was still revising *Currie Head*. Published in the *National Home Monthly* in January 1948, it is about the formation of the North Shore Mutual Telephone Company. The place names — Queenston (Mulgrave), The

Corner (Boylston), Riley's Ledge, Little Pond — are the same as those in CB's first fiction manuscript; in other words, the geography is that of *Currie Head*. The story, which is about the summer of 1919, is told in the first-person by a nameless narrator who is Dan Graham's cousin. Frank Graham (Dan's father), Stewart Gordon and Hugh Currie are important figures, though young Stan Currie is not mentioned. John Forbes is the local mail driver, as he is in *Currie Head*. The plot concerns the community effort to put up the necessary eight hundred telephone poles and string the wire so that people can be hooked up to the trunk system at Queenston twenty-five miles away. One "big dour, taciturn old countryman," Buck Langley, opposes it because he doesn't like the courting of his daughter by the young, cocky Halifax engineer brought in to supervise construction. CB moves his plot along through the twists and turns of this opposition, which climaxes with Buck's son being treated for a serious injury by a doctor summoned quickly on the engineer's makeshift phone.

What happens in the end may be formulaic, but the unfolding of events is not. CB's dialogue crackles with authenticity. There is the measured speech of the Shore people with its directness and deference, and there is the young engineer's own way of talking: "Uncle Frank nearly fell over the first time Johnny called him 'young fella' and I remember being sort of shocked when he said, 'No thanks, darlin' to my Aunt Stell, once, when she offered him a third piece of pie." The Shore people are decent folk who appreciate Johnny's honesty and effort on their behalf and accept his city ways. Even Buck, the erstwhile villain, finally recognizes Johnny's abilities and integrity and accedes to the telephone company and the courtship. The essential theme is that of communal cooperation for communal good, and CB easily conveys this because of the gentle humour that pervades and his obvious enjoyment of the place and people he has invented. He may not have known it at the time, but rather than relying on old manuscript territory, CB was forging a permanent literary landscape.

"The Year of the Stella" also appeared in January 1948 (in *Maclean's*) and was about life on the North Shore. It is likely that this story was written after "The Talking Tree" because the first-person narrator in the two tales is the same, but he now has a name — Bill Graham. CB has also explained what Bill is doing at his cousin Dan's house in 1919: "... the year Dad farmed me out at Uncle Frank's." This story focusses on the Graham home and, in particular, on who will win the hand of Frank's daughter Edith — the "dry-footed" wealthy farmer, Parker Marshall, or the struggling fisherman, Larry Kinsman. CB is prepared to portray something of the complexity of human relationships and points of view on the Shore as he did not do in his previous effort. Bill's Aunt Stell is contemptuous of Larry's livelihood and makes her daughter aware of what seems to be a kind of shiftlessness in him. But Uncle Frank, despite the fact that "questions of love and courtship are women's business," begins his own subtle campaign for Larry by involving him in the building of a two-masted sailboat. The community response to this reveals that CB does not present the Shore in idealistic terms as a happy little spot that clings to old ways and values: "The North Shore was strictly functional. An occasional eccentricity gets by without ridicule, but the idea of wasting time and wood on a two-master, years after the mackerel had vanished from the strait, and when gasoline had long supplanted sail, was pushing the eccentric to the point of abberation." Uncle Frank and Larry are looked on as similar to the wealthy summer visitor who collects local antiques, "junk ... from half the attics on the North Shore." But for Bill Graham (and CB) the boat-building represents a significant aspect of Shore experience and heritage that should not be forgotten: "... no one seemed to understand the sheer satisfaction in the joy of doing something well, the achievement in creating a strong and lovely thing without worrying too much about the practical, in the sure knowledge that strength and grace are their own master." Nor is there a conscious insistence on connections to the past, even though the boat's plans are based on forty-year molds. When the wealthy summer visitor spouts off about "the survival of ancient craftmanship ... the significance of keeping old things alive" he is told by Uncle Frank, "We're just building a boat."

If place names along the Queenston (Mulgrave) Road elucidate local geography in "The Talking Tree," here CB in some detail establishes part of the Shore in the reader's mind through his descriptions of Currie Head, the natural harbour there, and the configurations of the coastline. Once again there is a *deus ex machina* method of resolution to the story's human conflicts. A dramatic rescue at sea, with the two-masted *Stella* proving her worth, results in the always-expected marriage of Edith and Larry. But, as before, CB's delineation of character through dialogue, his commitment to the essential integrity of place and people, and his gentle use of humour combine to reveal a community relaxed and flexible enough to overcome its internal differences. This time, however, particularly through the conflict between Uncle Frank and Aunt Stell over what is best for Edith, CB emphasizes the distinction between male and female values and perceptions on the Shore and indicates that individual behaviour is not always quickly nor entirely accepted by community standards. Some of the themes of *The Channel Shore* emerge; as well, the focus on Bill Graham and the summer of 1919 is further developed. Hugh Currie is not mentioned in "The Year of the Stella"; CB was moving away from autobiographical fiction to fiction based on what he had seen, simply told.

The transition story between *Currie Head* and the shorter fiction that was helping to lead CB toward *The Channel Shore* was not published until May 1949. In "The Red Wing Feud"(*Chambers's Journal*), Bill Graham is spending his "second summer" at his Uncle Frank's farm; although the year is not given, it must be 1919 as there is evidence the war has not been long over. CB has not yet imagined Edith Graham's relationship with Larry Kinsman, because at one point she is described washing up the supper dishes before a church service: "You never could tell what might happen to keep a good-looking girl from getting home in time to do them afterward." As in "The Talking Tree" the focus is not so much on the Graham clan as on events in the community — in this case the dispute between a "zealous" minister and an independently-minded farmer over the loud playing on record of a popular song called "Red Wing" just as the local church service begins and ends. CB throws in a love story concerning the minister's brother and the farmer's daughter to heighten the community response to the conflict. The *deus ex machina*, rather obviously superimposed on the plot, is a forest fire that conveniently unites the opponents as they struggle to save the church. Here CB does not dramatize comfortably through the use of dialogue or let action speak for itself. There is too much description of events and character by the narrator, partly because there is no effective balance between Bill Graham, the man looking back at his time at Currie Head, and Bill Graham, the boy experiencing the summer of 1919. There are also too many minor characters with very little to do, including John Marshall and Stan Currie, as if CB could not let go of his larger scheme in *Currie Head*.

These three stories about the Grahams were written between the fall of 1945 and the fall of 1947, though in the first part of that period CB did give much of his time to "The Flowing Summer" manuscript. After the Graham trilogy came "Inheritance" (*Chambers's Journal*, May 1948) the story of Archie Findlay of Findlay's Bridge; this is fairly certain because various place names exist that have not existed before in CB's fiction, the most important of which is "The Channel Shore." This is the first short story by CB in which the theme of heritage dominates, and the result is a rougher narrative than is present later on. The first-person narrator is not a Shore native, but spent three years there as a boy when his minister-father had the circuit. He knew the story of Archie Findlay's once-prosperous ancestors, and he was witness to Archie's unambitious nature and acceptance of his lowly lot in life. When the narrator returns to Findlay's Bridge years later he finds that Archie is Slats Findlay, the retired, legendary bush pilot and wartime flight instructor who has pulled himself up by his own bootstraps and who long ago made the effort to win the girl he loved. How did such an ascent come out of family decline, the narrator wonders, until he discovers in Archie's background great-great-granduncle Francis, "lost at sea, June 1802" having "met galant [sic] death" in war. The twist of heritage is that Francis Findlay was hung as a pirate in Trinidad; but in CB's scheme of things such an ancestor fits perfectly with Archie's life on the edge — a man cannot escape who he is because of those in his family who came before him. Such a theme is vital to *The Channel Shore* and pervades every story of *The Township of Time*.

From Will Bruce's expressed concern in 1918 or so that CB would not spend his life on the farm "at this kind of work" came Hugh Currie's anguished statement in *Currie Head* about Stan: "I'll never see him tied down to the kind of work I'm doing for a living." In "The Road to Town" (*Saturday Night*, February 1948) CB developed this theme of a father wanting something better in life for his son, but revealed the limitations imposed by an overly-protective attitude and how, despite these limitations, a boy moves towards independence. On their farm at The Head, Jim prevents his son, Lee, from gaining any sense of responsibility in work or play, that is, from growing up in a healthy fashion. This means that Lee cannot take a summer job at the local mill, drive the buggy into town, or sail on the open strait. When Lee's mother protests, there is an outburst from Jim: "He's not going to stay on this land and slave a living out of it. He's going away, when the time comes; and not coming back like I did." But fate intervenes (as it so often does in these early stories and, indeed, in *The Channel Shore*) when Jim falls from the barn gable while shingling and is seriously injured. Lee, who has been feeling a "vague resentment" and then is afraid of what has happened to his father, realizes it is time for him to act; he hitches the horse to the buggy and goes to town for the doctor. The strength that allows him to act comes from memory, from a sense that his experiences with Jim — fishing, trapping, or just sitting around the kitchen fire — are deeper than resentment. He comes closer to his father than he has ever been, even as, through his newly-felt independence, he begins to leave home through time.

In his revision of this story for *The Township of Time* (called "The Road 1918") CB has the father, Lloyd Somers, express his feelings, perhaps even more vehemently: "Even if *we* don't get out of here, *he* will."[6] We learn in later stories in the volume that Lloyd did get out when he took his family back to Massachusetts where he had worked as a young man. The son, Bart, becomes a newspaper man in New York, marries and divorces a rich socialite, and one day twenty-one years after leaving he returns to the Channel Shore looking for something. What he discovers is "the weaving of act and word"[7] still intact through time and the new experience of sailing a sloop on the open strait; he also meets Prim Sinclair who knew him slightly when they were kids, but who links them strongly through a story she tells of her father being rescued from freezing water by a relative of Bart's thirty-two years previously. Bart is home; he stays on the Shore and eventually marries Primrose, and his journey through time is complete at last until his children start to grow. Of course, by the time of "The Road 1918," CB had already dealt considerably with the over-protective father and the "son" who embraces his true heritage in *The Channel Shore* with Grant Marshall and Alan.

All of this had its basis in the depth of CB's relationship with Will, but now CB was using fiction to move beyond autobiographical considerations and creating fiction that contained much more than the chronological unfolding of a life. In November of 1951 he published "The Letters" (*The Montrealer*) which is the single most complex and layered evocation of a father-son relationship in CB's short story canon. The narrator's father died before he was born in a fall from a carpenter's scaffold. When he was young the son felt a complicated "absence of that sense [of loss]. An empty feeling of never having had." Growing older, he read books and placed his missing father in a pantheon of fictional heroes along with Nostromo, Queequeg, and the Sea Wolf. There the father, Dave McKee, remains, until his son, with boys of his own in school, begins to visit the family farm to see his mother. She realizes that he hungers for paternal knowledge and gives him some old love letters between herself and her husband, warning her son at the same time that "Words aren't the same thing as living." Perhaps not, but the son learns that words are intimately connected in these letters with living, and it is only on the farm where they can be translated through time. The farm where "Simple practices of life occupy the body .... [but] so much of life is out of your hands.

A thing of tide, weather, seasons, stronger than yourself .... You learn acceptance, and a larger sensitivity of another kind."

The first two letters are descriptions by his father of the carpentry work he has found on Cape Breton around the mines, but the third is a plea to his wife to come down for a short visit even though it would mean she would leave her schoolteacher's job for a time. The son finds himself "stirred as [he] had never been by literature." Why? "It was no synthetic suspense that held me. This was a gentle and fun-loving man, away from home, among the coke-ovens and open-hearth furnaces and shaft houses; lonely for sloping country and the bay grumbling at night and the winsome flesh he loved." The fourth letter suggests that despite the "impulse and inclination in their blood" his mother and father overcome "the sweet wild wish to be together" in the face of "prudence ... a day's railway fare." But he discovers, through questioning his mother, that she did go to Cape Breton and that he was conceived on that weekend. The result is a profound response by the son to the place of words in life and the presence of life in words:

> A character had vanished from the shadowy country of the mind, the dream country of Lord Jim and Starbuck, of Brete Harte and Stephen Crane. And with the identification of this as the only thing that bothered me, it ceased to bother. It didn't matter at all.
>
> For after 40 years I had something else. I had the real, the active, sense of loss that comes from known things vanished, and a loved person dead.

CB takes a chance in this story because the way in which he presents it contradicts the important tenet offered by the narrator's mother — "Words aren't the same as living." The story's life, the quiet drama of discovery, is dependent on the narrator's thoughts about his father and the farm and on quotations from the four letters. There is very little dialogue and nothing *happens* except in the narrator's mind and in his father's writing. When words and living go together, as they do in the letters and the weekend visit, enriched life and language are the result years later.

There is in "The Letters" just enough of Will Bruce to suggest that on one perhaps not so subliminal level CB had come to terms through his fiction with *his* father. Ed, the narrator, was born late after older sisters who became school-teachers. Dave McKee, like Will, worked at carpentry to make extra money, and Ed's mother, like Sarah Bruce, taught school for the same reason. While a young man Dave had worked in a Boston desk-factory, and like Will he had "quite a sense of humor." The quotations from the four letters may be entirely fictional, but there is an exactitude to them, a completeness that goes beyond fictional necessity, that suggests CB might well have relied on letters from Will to Sarah.[8] Almost ten years after Will's death CB tried to find words to reveal Will's life in *Currie Head*; he did succeed, through the initial portrait of Hugh Currie, in saying much about his father, but if he was to write fiction in which words evoked life rather than merely described it, he would have to let Will rest while portraying aspects of him in the Hugh Currie of *The Channel Shore* and even in Richard McKee and Josie Gordon. What "The Letters" of 1951 suggests, at least partially, is the vanishing of Will Bruce himself as a figure in CB's fiction, the acceptance of his father as "a loved person dead," and the subsequent use of life to enhance words about life with universal rather than personal implications.

IX

Yesterday, Today, and Tomorrow

In November 1950 CB felt that what Lorne Pierce at Ryerson had to say about the manuscript of *The Channel Shore* (as it was then) meant "a complete rewrite job." Pierce had written, "… while it was all plausible enough it seemed to lack drive and the final logic of character …. it needs bold handling, real passion, real suffering by people who are real and not symbols."[1] Pierce also mentions the three parts of the novel, but in the rewrite job CB certainly went back to the beginning, because in February 1952 he wrote to John Gray at Macmillan (Pierce had obviously backed out) telling him that he would like to send Macmillan the first 40,000 words of a proposed 135,000-word novel that was not yet complete. Gray replied that so many words made "my already chilled blood begin to crystallize."[2] However, when he had read the first section of the manuscript Gray wrote CB that Macmillan was "eager to publish this book whenever it is ready."[3] Along with the changes he made CB also wrote much more than he had originally intended — the published novel is close to 185,000 words in length.

In his notes CB explains what happened with his novel between 1951 and 1954:

> *The Channel Shore* was written in two-and three-and four-hour spurts. Any evening when I thought, around eight o'clock, that I could see three or four reasonably uninterrupted hours ahead of me, I would get to work on it. Nothing was ever done before eight because a good deal of TCS coincided with the growth of a small boy [Harvey Bruce] …. I would assemble the tools and stretch out on the chesterfield. None [of the novel] was written in any position except the horizontal.[4]

Harry Bruce reports that one night in the early 1950s, when he and his brothers were playing rather loudly in the house, their mother called them aside and asked them to play more quietly as she thought their father was writing a novel. CB spoke to no one about his creative efforts during the course of writing.[5]

> Then the checking began .... During those sessions on the chesterfield, I would visualize and hear a scene in the mind's eye and mind's ear and go ahead and write it, without worrying too much whether the small externals incidental to it were accurate.
> The book is a three-part novel .... In 1919 I was a boy on the particular part of the coast I had in mind, and I have been back a good deal since. So I could go ahead with a certain amount of confidence that as far as atmosphere and manners and speech were concerned, I was all right.[6]

But there were details of fact that CB wanted just right — the date for a moonlit night in the novel in 1946 had to correspond with the information in the *Canadian Almanac*; the news stories that Adam Falt peruses as he delivers his mail on Tuesday, July 16, 1919 in the novel are those stories that were in the actual Halifax *Herald* on that date.

CB also explains the basis for the opening scene of the novel in which Bill Graham meets Anse Gordon in the gardens of Buckingham Palace in 1945. In late May of that year CB covered, for Canadian Press, a garden party at the Palace for liberated prisoners of war. There he met a North Nova Scotia Highlander named Pat Diggens who was from St. Francis Harbour, "8 miles down the road from the house I was born in." In 1955, in his article for the IODE that he entitled "The Township of Time," CB spoke of his meeting with Pat Diggens:

> It sharpened to something like purpose in my mind a feeling that had been nagging me vaguely for years. I had always been fascinated by the vitality that exists in my own part of the country. In any of those long-settled parts of the country where living is hard and·where one of the principal crops they raise is flesh and blood, largely for export.[7]

In his notes CB explains that the meeting caused him "to remember all kinds of things" that he had forgotten. For instance, there was the conversation he had heard as a boy about a girl perhaps a little older than him — "one of those hushed conversations that make you prick up your ears." The girl had discovered that the woman she had always called 'Mother' was really her grandmother: "Trouble in a family. Trouble of an unusual kind in that strict neighbourhood. Strict. Yet the protectiveness, neighbourliness, kindliness, had been so great that the child had reached the age of thirteen or fourteen without knowing the story of her birth. Might never have known it, except for accident."

CB would draw on life in the creation of his novel, but he was right when he said, "The story is not autobiographical, nor are the people in it intended to represent actual individuals." What happened instead in *The Channel Shore* is that life flowed into art and then art flowed into life, so that, as CB said, various characters reminded him of people he knew, and he became attached to such characters: "I'm particularly fond of Richard McKee. And of Renie Fraser; she reminds me of a rusty red-head I once knew, who is living now, I believe, in Nigeria." Similarly Currie Head is the setting, or the chief one, in *The Channel Shore*, but it is not the Port Shoreham of CB's youth; The Head is in the "country of the mind," of which Port Shoreham, for CB by this point, was a part:

> You will not find the Channel Shore, so named or in exact geography, on any map or chart. But there is a province of Nova Scotia. Two provinces perhaps. A land of hills and fields and woods and moving water. And the image of that land, sensuous with the sound of seas and voices, in those who live or have lived there: a country of the mind, the remembering blood. If it is necessary to locate the Shore, consider these twin lands: and take the edge of any county, on the coast of either one.[8]

The essential difference between *Currie Head* and *The Channel Shore* is that in the latter CB has a story to tell — actually, quite a number of integrated stories. In his earlier attempt at a novel, the entire focus on one main character, together with so much dependence on the unfolding of CB's own life, resulted in a narrative with little variety; few, if any, internal oppositions; a straightforward, undeviating movement of plot; and static characters — in other words, no dynamics. Writing short fiction between 1945 and 1951 obviously helped CB; particularly in the stories about the Grahams and concentrated events in and around the summer of 1919 on the shore. CB learned to pace his narrative, developing it through to-the-point dialogue and descriptive passages in which action rose and fell, took sudden turns, and did not remain staid and predictable for the reader. In just a few pages several different things were happening at once in this short fiction — in "The Year of the Stella," the boat-building, the domestic feud between Uncle Frank and Aunt Stella, the competition for Edith between Parker and Larry, the community response to all this — but the central themes of individual strength within the community and of the pattern of Shore life absorbing all potential and actual disarrangements remained clear.

The rejections from *The Atlantic Monthly*, *Harper's* and Lorne Pierce helped because constructive criticism was provided, and CB could not ignore the common complaint that fine writing did not automatically create drama or effective characterization. He did seem to realize that characters based to a large degree on his father and himself could be minor characters in his fiction with significant but brief moments on the stage, and that the drama of his own life, the psychological conflict he had needed to expose and examine, had been dealt with in *Currie Head*. Whatever the writing of that manuscript had done for CB personally, it did not do very much for other people, that is, readers. The strength of his effort did lie in the tangible conveyance of the relationship between Stan and Hugh Currie and, similarly, in the details of Stan's struggle to leave and return to the Shore. It lay as well in the symbolic aspects of this father-son connection and individual quest for a homeland. The problem was with the dichotomy between the actual and the abstract; CB was unable to combine form and content in order to fuse reality and symbol. In *The Channel Shore* there is no such dichotomy, and the fusion occurs.

In 1945 Bill Graham, who spent the summer of 1919 at Currie Head on the Channel Shore, meets Anse Gordon at a royal garden party for Commonwealth prisoners of war. Anse left The Head abruptly in that 1919 summer and, Bill discovers, like himself, has not been back since. What Bill encounters, to his surprise, in this meeting with the self-possessed, arrogant, yet still-fascinating Anse, is not only a powerful memory of the Shore, but a strong sense of what it represented:

> That was the shape of it, the shape of road, fields, woods and water. But more than this the Shore was people. It was flesh and blood in buggies on the road, swinging scythes in side-hill fields, tramping summer woods, braced to the jolt of oars on rolling water that gave it colour … movement … life. It was flesh and blood, moved by its rooted hungers, by hate, fear, love and the branch and bloom of them — by caution, daring, malice, sacrifice, that formed the story with which Anse Gordon's name was forever linked.[9]

This opening section of the novel — slightly over four pages in length — is called "1919-1945," not because it provides a summary of those twenty-six years, but because the summer of 1919 is "forever" in Bill Graham's mind. Time past is time present, and it has not taken very much to make that startlingly clear to Bill. There is, therefore, an irony in Bill's response to Anse — "Time had touched him with indifferent fingers." Anse, at first glance, seems outside time, but if he is relatively unchanged from the young man of 1919, then, in a complex way, he is inextricably a part of time past, even if his concern seems to be only for "today and the immediate tomorrow." This opening frame section is interrupted by what CB calls "Part One" of the novel and is completed as a frame for "Part One" on pages 175-181 after the story has been told of Anse, his sister Anna, Grant Marshall, and Hazel McKee in the fall and summer of 1919. Thus there is no simple unfolding of events, but rather particular events are presented in "Part One" that exist in a pre-established context of the Shore and its people. We are told that the tale of Anse and Hazel and the tale of Grant and Anna, which we are about to encounter separately, will be joined eventually. It is made clear that Bill and Anse, both twenty-six years away from Currie Head, must merge, despite intervening experience, with "The shape of the land, the colour of moving water. The words, the gestures, and the feel of people."

In 1919 Hazel McKee and Anse Gordon are linked by a mutual dissatisfaction with life on the Shore. Hazel feels trapped: "You stayed on the Channel Shore to work and marry. Or you got away from it to go into household service …. Or to do stenography or teach school." For Anse, there are the limitations of his father "and all the rest of them …. Foolish, because they couldn't see beyond the Shore," and because they are always involved in the same monotonous activity.

CB indicates from the outset the flaws in the characters of Hazel and Anse, so that while each is unwilling to move with the rhythms of land and water, flesh and blood, both depend on such rhythms for their sense of independence and have no alternative to what they would escape. Hazel, with her "spasmodic irritation," is the more pitiful of the two because she has no strong sense of her own experience or that of others, except as "physical fact; important for what you found in it for the moment of its passing." Anse, on the other hand, finds strength in the mastery of the moment, which he would impose on what he sees as the unrelenting sameness of hours, years, and entire lives. Both depend on their furtive sexual union to make the moment stay, but Hazel finds in this union only a "meaningless message," a "sense of something missed," and Anse finds no "lasting sense of triumph" from a woman he cannot dominate and then abandon. Ironically, what keeps Anse alive is his contempt for the pattern of life on the Shore as exemplified especially by the seasonal rituals of the various farmer-fishermen. The energy and life-force of these people at their tasks and the results of their efforts are in strong contrast to Hazel and Anse's view of them:

> Off the beach at Currie Head small sounds stirred and drifted in morning dusk: the Channel's slow and even breathing, the soft thump of rowlocks, the slight hollow sound of an oar hauled inboard, the whispered echo of a voice.
>
> There in the shadowed calm before sunrise men leaned across the gunnels of flats, grasped the tail-buoys of herring-nets; peered downward, while they hauled on dripping head-ropes, to glimpse the shifting flash of silver; and hauled out of tidal darkness the black wet mesh, studded with twitching fish.
>
> …. By then the Shore itself would be alive …. the sunlight blew on hayfields patched with oats …. Potatoes in drilled rows along the brows of hills were coming into blossom. On the branches of ancient apple trees where a seething foam of petals had bloomed and faded … the tiny knobs of small hard fruit were forming, lost in a sea of leaves.

CB's prose belies Anse's scorn and Hazel's sense of emptiness. The long description of the men at their separate work is summarized by the term "desultory activity." That is precisely how Anse and Hazel would refer to it in the sense of random, inconsistent activity; but it is obvious from CB's tribute to the individuals within the community that "desultory" means that there is no *visible* order to what is going on — the interconnectedness is emphasized by the Channel's "slow and even breathing" and by CB's explanation of the sameness as "a pattern," that is, as a design and as a model or guide.

Since Anse and his sister Anna are not the same, either in their reaction to the Shore or to its people, CB emphasizes the role of individual psychology in the pattern. He does so similarly in the differences between Hazel and her father, Richard. It is not so much blood as a sense of self in a larger scheme of things that is important, a sense of that self as part of a long chain of being in which individual wishes and needs merge with what has been and what is to come. Anna loves Grant Marshall (still in the Canadian Army in England) and feels herself favoured by him; therefore, to Hazel, she possesses a visible self-confidence and is in tune with the natural and settled aspects of the Shore: "The low insistent grumbling of the Channel, never entirely still, was pleasant to her ears, too familiar to be noticed. A faint smell of barns and fields and gardens hung in the warm, almost windless, air." CB leaves it vague whether Anna's human relationships are so positive because of her response to what goes on around or whether she sees the Shore as she does because of her individual love for Grant. There is a mixture that cannot be measured, and CB does not encourage a slide-rule interpretation.

Hazel encounters the depth of this mixture in Anna in a simple exchange about the absent Grant and, in her resultant "sorrowful certainty" of what can exist on the Shore, she finds the strength to break off from Anse. Later, when she knows she is pregnant, she senses there is only one person — her father — who will be able to absorb what she has to say and whom she recognizes as such at precisely the moment she gains her clearest view of the blending of fields and beach and water she has not noted before. Anse, however, has an ego impervious to the influence of others or to a world outside himself. When Hazel turns away from him he can only turn to leave the place where his powerlessness has become evident. He walks away from everything he has ever known because he has never *known* it. Like his sister, he is conscious of the Channel's grumbling, "too familiar to be noticed," but it provides no sustenance for the failure of his private power.

CB makes it plain that Anse's dramatic gesture of abandoning the Shore without a word of notice or farewell may snap some threads but will not destroy the web of being on the Shore. Neither will such destruction come from Hazel's pregnancy, nor even from the conflict to come, because Anna Gordon, from a Catholic family "born to oilskins," loves Grant Marshall, from a Methodist family "strait-laced and dry-footed":

> ... Things had a way of happening ... sometimes, a way contrary to all the rules of living. And after the first startled talk, a way of being accepted and absorbed into the pattern of the place. Even sin and remorse, heresy and regret and failure, were dark colours in the pattern.

Almost immediately after this emphasis on flexibility, James Marshall is introduced as he prepares "to assault" his field with his mower. James, with his "little sense of power" over the land, certainly has his rules of living, and those who do not rigidly obey them are treated harshly.[10] CB makes it quite clear that the "dry-footed" James is out of touch with natural rhythms and the rhythms of his fellow human beings. The six-strand wire fence around his property with its "clean lines" is in contrast to the "zig-zag" wooden fence of a neighbour, and it becomes obvious that he has built such a border around his perceptions of others and his emotional response to experience. He thinks with "controlled exasperation" both about the past and the present, the figures here and there who impinge on his certainties — figures like his dead brother, Harvey, and his nephew Grant.

In contrast, Richard McKee makes his hay by hand, in touch with the earth rather than in "exalted pride" above it. CB does not make Richard a saint; he is described as possessing "a private stolidity close to fatalism," but conflicts with his wife

Eva disturb him, and he has no ready answers for human difficulties, nor for his uneasy sense that the old ways of the Shore are vanishing. He is, like Will Bruce, most at home on the Channel and the beach where everything "was like an instinct," and it is his experience of shifting swells, the knowledge that life, like a sea voyage, is not a simple, linear and predictable progression from point to point, that allows him to view the interweaving quality of time, the past as "immeasurably far away, and yet close …. old things new again in an intimate strangeness."

Grant, when he returns, exhibits a healthy interest in the past in general and personal ways. First of all, he aligns himself with settlers of a hundred and fifty years ago in wanting to clear and work his land as they did; he listens to Hugh Currie tell the story that links his land to identifiable ancestors on The Head — Rob Currie, who was lost with his three-master on the trip to Africa, and his fiancée, Fanny Graham. He has also wanted to know about this father and has asked James about him as a boy, but Harvey Marshall, with his laughter and relaxed ways, is a part of the past that James knows he cannot categorize, so he refuses to talk about Harvey, refuses to give Grant any part of a heritage he cannot control. Thus Grant is "part of something he didn't try to explain or understand. Something old and continuing, a blend of today and the past and the future"; however, this "blend" is false because it is partial and has been selected by James to mean a vague contact with generations gone, a today and tomorrow of strict Methodist persuasion that does not include any familial ties with the Gordons.

Grant does want to marry Anna, but it is significant that she is almost obliterated from his mind when he is most concerned with his identity and with his roots. Yet the "blend" cannot be forced by anyone. Anna reacts against James's orders that she and Grant not have a relationship of any kind by saying, "What right has an old man got, who's never laughed in his life — or loved anything as far as I can see …. " Grant's response that he does not know what to do because "whatever it is, somebody's bound to get hurt," shows that in this novel CB is not concerned with simple oppositions. Not simple because essentially they are not contained by individual concerns isolated in time. What James does by invoking duty ("another word for life") and forcing Grant to choose between it and a future that is not a mere repetition of what has come before is to cut him off a second time from a past that can nourish and create possibilities: "Always before he had been able to live again in memory the moments he had spent with her .... The quiet sense of something sweet and continuing, the fulfilment and eagerness that had always come to him these small journeys back and forth in time .... They were no longer there."

There is no magic in individuals because of their affinity with the Shore; Anna, when faced with Grant's inability to deny James, cannot recognize that it is the connection with his dead father from which he cannot turn away. When her mother Josie, anxious to protect Anna from what she sees as inevitable negative links between past and present — "if Anse and Hazel ... then Anna and Grant" — suggests Anna get away to Halifax for a while, Anna acquiesces and denies the possibility of a natural and indigenous unfolding of the pattern. Richard can talk sympathetically to Hazel about Anse and her pregnancy, but in the end he can only send her away to Toronto. Richard is extraordinarily self-sufficient, and more than anyone else he is part of the stability and open to the vagaries of human experience; yet ironically and unknowingly he must depend on the development of others before he can be of benefit to them. It is the man whose individuality is lost somewhere between the past and present whom CB has discover a way on; Grant, in Anna's absence and in avoiding James, begins to see "himself as one of many ... on the Shore," to sense "The aloneness in the heart of everyone" that is alleviated by communal effort and associations. He moves closer to the Gordons, Josie and Stewart, who have lost Anse and through whom his relationship with Anna might grow through contact "common, momentary, and slight."

CB is not above the use of pathetic fallacy when Anna dies accidentally in Halifax and life for many is changed as a result. The night before her death, "An air of wind, chilly with something, colder than the breath of late September" is felt by Josie and Stewart, and a storm ensues, battering their house; in the morning there is "the undulant curling roar, the smothered thunder of surf on Katen's Rocks." It is one of the few times in the novel when there seems to be an unnecessary emphasis on, and manipulation of, the fact that "the shape of ... the Shore was people." If Grant, through his new kinship with others, has felt that he has been "one among many who must move and change with time," Anna's death rushes the future toward him, and he chooses between his uncle who has manipulated the present through a denial of the past *and* a commitment to the Gordon household where gradually, over the years, nothing will be denied and future attempts at manipulation will, as a result, fail. Grant, at first, replaces Anse as a son for Josie and Stewart and then as a father to their grandson.

What Grant does by refusing a rigid and egotistical response to what faces him is to reveal James Marshall's inadequacies; what follows is James's decline in CB's scheme of things. When Grant decides that he would like to buy the land he has begun to work on, James cannot refuse him, though his confused thoughts of stern justice, mercy, and anger allow him no clear vision. When Grant now wants tangible images of his father, he asks Richard McKee and sees at last the face and hears the laughter of Harvey Marshall, "The thing that was alive, that was not cold doctrine or property or measured pride, but simple feeling. Life and death and achievement and failure." So when Josie tells him that she can deal with Anna's death, but not with the flesh-and-blood fact that "There's a girl alive ... a child maybe," Grant hears the voice of the Channel Shore and knows what he must do. In bringing Hazel home after he has married her in Toronto, and in effect allowing her child by Anse to be their child with him, Grant is no altruist motivated by a simple concern for Josie's well-being or to mitigate the McKee's shame. In his flesh he feels "a turning tide" of currents that flow between himself and the heritage he has discovered, and he acts accordingly. So many are connected in time: Harvey, himself, Anna and her family, Hazel and hers, Hugh Currie and the other story-tellers of the Shore. No possibility that will promulgate such union can be denied.

The first frame tale is now completed in 1945. But in the meantime CB has developed the place of Bill Graham in the Shore story. In 1919 Bill chummed around with his cousin Dan and with Stan Currie; he heard Hugh's tale of great-uncle Rob and *his* great-aunt Fanny Graham; he was joined to Grant who chopped wood on the land that was given to Rob and Fanny as a wedding present (a wedding that never took place). Perhaps this was the reason Grant could talk to Bill in the midst of his troubles with James, and why it was Bill who told him first that Anna was going away and then that she was dead. Perhaps this was why Grant went to Bill's house in Toronto, after the summer was over, to tell him that he had married Hazel. Thus Bill and Anse are more closely bound than is revealed when they first meet in London and in ways that Anse would not care about if he knew.

The session with Anse takes Bill back in time to when his father spoke of the Shore — Andrew Graham, who left when young and never himself returned, sent his son instead one summer to find "in the shape of an actual hill, the sound of a stream's voice, the lines in a face, the truth and light and colour — the confirmation of a personal hearsay." Thus in his mind's eye, Bill sees a timeless country that includes his father and his boyhood friends and old Hugh Currie, Frank Graham, and Richard McKee, as well as himself, Anse, Grant, and others, even Rob Currie and great-aunt Fanny: "Not merely the simple memory of outward things, but the memory of recognition .... " Bill recognizes that "nothing is ever finished," that if he returns to the Shore he will not be going back but *on*: "Out of the far past he was looking into a nearer past and a present. Both unknown to him. But alive on the Channel Shore." The completion of the frame tale is not so simple. The reader is taken to the "nearer past" of the winter of 1933-34 and the story of Alan, Grant, Renie, and Margaret, and on to the "present" in the summer of 1946 when Bill's perception of things merges in time with the return of Anse to the Shore and his interaction with Alan, Margaret, and Grant.

The frame tale was certainly one of the narrative and structural devices missing from *Currie Head*. In that manuscript CB attempted to bridge the gaps in time with Stan Currie's train journey home, but the problem was with the great part of Stan's life spent away from The Head. Thus his literal journey to place could only correspond with a trip through time that dealt with his boyhood. Something is disjointed, awry, when Stan on the train moves through the memories of Halifax and Toronto, the experiences of his life when Currie Head was in so many ways receding behind him. The focus on Stan as the novel's main protagonist meant that CB was limited as he tried to set up his thematic framework of links between yesterday, today, and tomorrow.

The Channel Shore is not only the story of Bill Graham, though Bill's story is part of the Shore's whole pattern of character and event, and as such transcends its formal role of narrative device. Everything is part of the maine in this novel, and everyone. Ironically, Anse Gordon's egotistical refusal to return for twenty-six years and his equally self-centered appearance on the Shore in 1946 shape the history of place and people as much as Grant's and Alan's more admirable and less selfish decisions to stay. Bill's role is to see things from the outside in, to be in a vital way a foil to Anse as they return within days of one another, each no doubt partially prompted by the mutual discovery that the other had not been back. The apparent contrast between the two men — CB spends considerable time describing Bill's thoughts and feelings about the Shore as he journeys there, but does not give us insight into Anse again until he turns up on Josie's doorstep — allows the reader a larger perspective on a question of some thematic import: is communion with the heritage of experience and blood simply a matter of going home, as it essentially was in *Currie Head*, or is it, as Stan Currie in *The Channel Shore* is allowed to articulate, a complex matter of meeting and embracing "The living past" whether you are home or not? Another question should also be considered — and is through the remainder of *The Channel Shore*: is the tide of heritage local and confined to the lives of a few individuals, or does it turn on the shoreline of a larger world?

Because of the emphasis in "Part One" of the novel on the links between yesterday, today, and tomorrow, and because of Bill Graham's reflections on time and the Shore in "1945," the movement of the narrative into the winter of 1933-34 is a smooth one. Hazel's child by Anse is fourteen-year-old Alan Marshall, and he is immediately associated with the Shore's past (more specifically with the Channel itself) in a personal and general way: he has heard both his grandfather McKee and Hugh Currie talk of the days of sail, of a time when "there'd be hardly a day you wouldn't sight something …. " But there is a disturbing gap between the nearer past, on the one hand, and the present of Alan and the man he knows as his father, Grant, on the other. The latter is over-protective of his son in daily matters and in the special, guarded history of their relationship — what happened in 1919 has been glossed over: while there are McKee grandparents, for Alan there is no familial connection with the Gordons. The result is a fragility to the present, severed as it is in a fearful way from its roots, so that even a schoolboy's taunt about a blood link between Alan and Josie can threaten the structure of entire lives: "This sly hint of the past and its pattern, living in Channel Shore memory … these things that belonged to a time before …. Drawn close, suddenly … made personal … merged with the living images of life." CB has already made it clear that there should be nothing to fear from the past, near or far, because, as Grant discovered through Anna's death, and when he went looking for *his* father, what exists is "the eternal present"; thus in 1933 when Grant tells his second wife, Renie, who has expressed concern about Alan, "… we'll take each day as it comes," his self-defence fragments time.

Grant, of course, has the experience of his Uncle James to remind him of what happens when bonds are based on possession and not on affection or respect. Despite this, and despite the irony that his bond with Alan is "rooted in the time of Anna Gordon and Hazel McKee," Grant is afraid of revealing the truth. Like Anse he has separated himself from others through a psychologically desperate clinging to private power. If Anse roams the periphery of Renie's thought like a fiction because she never knew him, a necessary fiction has been preserved by Grant "Until in his own mind and heart it wore the shape of truth." The tangled web of father figures — Grant, Anse, James — consists of major threads of denial and of the isolated self. The past, which is so directly relevant to his present situation, can teach Grant nothing because he wants to leave it alone, as something over. He stayed on the Shore in 1919 because of a sense of kinship and responsibility, but now he will run away through Alan by sending him away "to preserve the heart of truth [fiction]." Anse, though he would never admit it, ran for the same reason, so ironically Grant is aligning father and son.

Against this stunted growth of Grant is the slow development of Josie Gordon as a figure, like Richard McKee, in and of time. She still has difficulty in dealing with the nearer past, but the children of that period, especially Alan, have softened her self-protective vision to include "… a kind of relationship of place and touch and word as well as kinship." She is fiercely loyal to the fiction of Grant and Alan as father and son, but her insistence that this fiction righted a wrong is less of a barrier to change than Grant's desire that one set of facts be eradicated by another.

While Grant circles around a present dilemma that he will only vaguely connect with what has gone by, Alan, disturbed by Grant's suggestion that he leave the Shore, senses that the way on is connected to the way back. The person who embodies the past in the present is grandfather McKee, with whom Alan has fished the Channel and experienced in the swells there a movement deeper and more inclusive than any current of individual being. Richard's "presence and what he did were more important than anything he had to say …. [His] character was in his hands. His character, his history and his skills …. In all Richard's attitudes, in his body moving or at rest, there was communication." Because Richard, when we meet him for the first time in "Part Two," is coopering (making barrels), "an out-of-date craft that survived on the Shore in [him]," it is obvious that in his hands, in his moving body, there is heritage.

Communication is tangible, words alone are never enough. In his grandfather's attic Alan touches traces of time far beyond his own memory: "A jumble of worn objects, unrelated to one another, but all linked with some aspect of life on the Channel Shore. Linked, most of them, with ways of doing things that had changed and faded and been replaced by tools and methods of the present." This present, Alan realizes, will soon be the past and these objects part of an even more distant time one day — he glimpses an endless chain of connection that includes ways of doing things as yet uninvented: "For the first time, he was conscious of glimpsing yesterday, today, and tomorrow as part of a continuing whole. It put things in balance ...." This balance, achieved over decades, even centuries, as far as the Shore is concerned, includes the nearer past and, above all, people. Alan finds a photograph of Anse, hears Margaret repeat someone else's opinion that "you're the image of him," and is taken through scraps of memory to "unremembered but not forgotten" incidents linking himself and Anse. In CB's scheme, the balancing process can be interfered with but not broken by power. Unknowingly Alan encounters the remnants of James Marshall's power ("I could tell him right now what right he has to the name of Marshall," James thinks), but caught forever by the one moment in time when Grant announced he was staying with the Gordons — as the flow from Harvey to Grant to Alan continues — James is impotent.

Words may never be enough alone, but coupled with the sense of heritage Richard provides, they can, from Josie, offer Alan "the knowledge of a kinship stronger than blood." When he asks her what it is about Grant and himself that creates talk on the Shore, Josie realizes that truth is more than fact, just as it was with Grant and Hazel's union: "Somehow [truth] had to be the way it was ... the way it was now," so she tells him the story of Anse and Hazel, opening out her own perception and acceptance of the way it was — "They thought of themselves like married people do." She tells him that Anse did not know of Hazel's pregnancy before he left, but emphasizes Grant's "kind of love ... stronger than any other kind" that turned him into Alan's father.

Part of the unspoken sub-text here is Grant's heritage from Harvey and his nearer past with Anna; part of the sub-text has to do with what Josie realizes was "the gift of Hazel" — her "strange happiness" and her having kept knowledge of her pregnancy from Anse. Josie articulates something of that "kinship of spirit," and Alan indicates an awareness of this by responding not to the fact that Anse is his blood father but that Josie is his grandmother by blood and much more besides. When he leaves her house Alan hears the Channel grumbling and, like Grant, fourteen years before, knows he will not leave the Shore. As Grant with the Gordons, Alan will affirm his kinship with Grant and others "by action, manner, habit … working, talking, belonging to … life and purpose …. To live according to the story. To hold in the heart, secret and sharp, the knowledge of a kinship stronger than blood."

Alan, in telling Grant that he wants to stay on the Shore, acts out of a sense of all the years of kinship that have been and that will be — the present is a moment in time. But Grant is described as walking toward his son and the decision that must be made with "the past and future slipping from his mind." What Alan does is to take the decision away from Grant and allow the philosophy of taking each day as it comes to stand without assessment. There is an irony presaging troubles to come when CB describes Grant as not "thinking about Alan, or anyone in particular, but about the whole of life as it included himself and his people, his place and the Channel Shore." Grant does not understand what has caused Alan to speak out, to claim his *true* heritage. Separate from Richard's offerings and Josie's placing of words in the pattern, reliant upon Alan's discovery of who he is and where he has come from without being able to deal with such things himself, Grant has left himself open to a fragmented future.

The second frame tale is now put in place, and it clearly emphasizes CB's major theme of the interrelationship of yesterday, today and tomorrow, as well as the subtle complexity of his narrative. When the novel opens we meet Bill Graham and Anse Gordon in the 'present' time of London 1945. Then we are taken back into time past, to the summer and fall of 1919. However, once this 1919 perspective is established Bill and Anse are in the future to its present. As well, the "eternal present" comes into play when Bill asks Anse in 1945, "… and what's going on at The Head?" What is going on *is* 1919 *and* 1933-34, because these two men, whether they know it or not, are a part of continuing experience on the Shore and have been for more than the twenty-six years since they last met there.

The second frame tale, which is, of course, not 'second' at all, but part of time's unfolding pattern, is titled "1946." In it, Bill Graham, travelling by train toward The Head, is no longer in a future relative to other sections of the text. The frame tale merges with the story of The Head itself in the summer of 1946; as Bill has moved through the future he has caught up with time past, and yesterday and tomorrow become today. CB's perception and presentation of time here transcends the significant but linear experience of it by characters like Grant, Alan, Richard, and Josie for whom yesterday and today often become tomorrow, and tomorrow and today often become yesterday. Bill's father, Andrew Graham, wonders if illusion takes Bill back, wonders if it is possible to go back, but Bill is involved in something other than mere return — what Alan recognized when he considered the items in Richard's attic: "If the old thing wasn't there, you could take a look at whatever there was *in its place*"(italics mine). Even "the timeless land of memory" is not outside time but alive on the Channel Shore as Bill gets down from the train and meets Adam Falt, the mail driver, "just as he had been … twenty-seven years ago …. a year ago …. "

There is not exact repetition in time, but there is close association of events and circumstance. Just as Grant returned to the Shore after a war, eager to get on with the life and work he had known there, so Alan comes home to "the tide of well-being" brought about by familiar tasks and behaviour. Just as James Marshall in 1919 was concerned about too much of Harvey in Grant, so Grant years later worries about Anse in his son — the physical resemblance is there, but what of character influence? Hugh Currie is dead, as is James, but everyone else Bill knew in 1919 is around. Margaret Marshall is wrong, though, when she announces to her mother, "Things are always the same here."

Stan Currie has come home to work the family farm after a long absence, and he brings a new voice to the Shore, an articulation of its character and of heritage rediscovered. Alan is no longer a boy, and Grant's "small inner hysteria" at his son's independence presages change. As for Margaret herself, her protest is an attempt to cover developments within, her feelings for Alan that threaten the balance she does not yet understand.

The emerging love of Alan and Margaret for one another as man and woman rather than brother and sister is, ironically, part of the balance of yesterday, today and tomorrow rather than an aberration to destroy it. Driving home from a dance the two enter the garage that is on the ground floor of the old house where Alan lived as a boy. The pattern of the wallpaper impacts on the centre rather than on some corner of his mind, and he realizes this was Grant's and Renie's room; he remembers how he ran here for comfort one night in a fierce storm, and then: "... the repeated pattern, and with it the feel of the mattress, the half-fearful relief of nightmare gone, and the morning sun." Even as he and Margaret are about to admit their love for one another and introduce, they believe, fearful complication into the lives around them, CB supplies images of potential and then places the lovers in a context of possibility, of what has been and is to come: "A moment of truth that flowed imperceptibly into other moments: Richard McKee's attic and the sense of old things useless and rusted, yet having in them the colour of vanished life .... the feel of Margaret's smallness in his arms."

The threat to the balance appears to be Grant because he is still taking each day as it comes, hiding 1919 behind this accumulation of isolated achievement. He will not talk to Bill about their closeness during the summer of Anna; when he avoids the detail of memory one morning the Channel is described as "like glass," a mirror reflecting Grant's stasis, rather than in grumbling motion as it has been when various individuals have refused to stand still. He talks to no one about his doubts and fears, while Alan, who does think about going away so he can avoid contact with Margaret, talks to Josie, gaining sustenance from what Grant would deny: "The self-revelation [Alan and Josie] had shared that day was woven into the background on which the pattern of their everyday relationship was traced .... " That is why he can realize the reality of the Shore that is both old and new; it is why CB has him "make out a tiny, whitish glint, perhaps a sail" on the Channel as Anse walks in the door. Almost immediately Alan senses that this return is a part of the pattern, and by refusing to leave, to run from responsibility, he aligns himself with the one father-figure who, years ago, stayed on the Shore.

On his return, however, Anse must create a fiction in order to sustain the illusion of his private power. He lets people wonder if he knew about Hazel's pregnancy by saying nothing, and he wants them for a while to think of him as well-meaning, to be lulled into a false sense of security about his intentions. CB's irony regarding this is not hidden: Anse feels confident that he recognizes the "pattern" in others' behaviour as they encounter him. But his desire and need for "A drawn-out, continuing victory, climaxed perhaps" by a claiming of Alan, his seeking of control, are contrasted with Alan's feeling of "emotional peace" and "shared freedom" between himself and Margaret, based on the memory of that afternoon in Richard's attic, an experience itself containing no victories or claims or masks to twist the truth of heritage.

Anse's tool for control is the refurbishing of his father's old two-master, but while he has the skill to make this worn object (too big for Richard's attic) useful again, he has no sense of his task or its accomplishment as "part of a continuing whole" (he is not just "building a boat" as Frank Graham and Larry Kinsman do in "The Year of the Stella"). Anse's ego is still the motivating force for action as it was in 1919, and in seeking to bond Alan to him through their working together on the boat he seeks "possession. Fatherhood" and more: a chance to revenge himself on the Shore, to smash the pattern that threatens to include rather than exclude him, something the self-centered Anse cannot endure. Margaret, in her frustration, her desire and need for a climax, thinks that "Anse could break the shell of the past and re-set the pattern of the present." Anse does have a role to play in the balancing process he has already helped to set in motion: if his eventual loss of control is, ironically, the climax he has been seeking, the rising action that brings it about depends on the very kinship through time that he abhors.

Like his mother once did, Alan walks naked into Graham's Lake, but there is no emptiness as he swims forward, and he does not feel "a prisoner," because Hazel broke free from her prison cell shared with Anse, broke away from a trap of sexual union so that her son might one day find guiltless fulfilment in such consummation. As he once talked to Anna about possibilities, Bill now talks with Renie and articulates what others in their way have done over the years: "About all a person can do is stand by." Words alone might never be enough, "but Renie's heart was lighter for having talked with Bill." And, like Hazel and Anse before her, Margaret seeks communication with Richard McKee — still, it is emphasized, "His voice was an accompaniment of what he was doing, of his moving hands." Only Grant and Anse still see themselves in the glass of the Channel; off the beach where Margaret and Richard talk "shore and sea [merge] in a continual splash and grumble of slow sound."

Just as he was coopering in the winter of twelve years past, so now is Richard engaged in a practical craft that comes from years of experience; he mends the nets for the fishing he still does out of time's habit and enjoyment. He has not changed essentially, but he recognizes and accepts change, responding to Margaret's tale of herself and Alan by saying, "You'd be surprised what time does in the way of getting people used to an idea." He also summarizes quite succinctly and accurately not only the lovers' situation, but the pattern as well: "It's natural. Complicated, though." What Richard emphasizes is that it is not time alone, but people in time who will absorb and accept the love between Margaret and Alan. In that love Richard affirms not an end but a "beginning," which is really a continuing.

CB does not idealize Richard or suggest he has all the answers; he was often pained by images of Hazel and Anse, and he cannot control events now any more than he could have in 1919. The Channel is just a channel and Richard just a man who fishes it, but they are joined in symbolic import in CB's vision, representing as they do the respective depths of the natural and human factors in time's balance. Heritage, Bill reminds Grant, cannot be figured on a slide rule: "All kinds of things get scribbled in, from other people, other generations. Or edited out."

CB's irony continues as the two-master is readied for The Holiday, the annual picnic on the beach. Anse, who has tried to cut himself off from the past so that he might control the present, is responsible for putting a sailboat on the Channel, the kind Hugh Currie used to sight. But his crude and unfeeling remark about naming the boat after an unfortunate woman on the Shore, Vangie Murphy, who used and was used by men like himself, bonds the listening Alan to him in a kinship of shame. When Alan thinks of himself as Anse's son for the first time he realizes how thin blood can be; in this moment he is closer to the abused woman than to his blood father. The seed that Anse sowed and that he wants to reap now is connected to the illegitimate seeds sown by others in Vangie Murphy — Tarsh Findlay, for one, whom Anna did not deny — and to life on the Shore in a way Anse cannot allow himself to comprehend: Josie thinks, "The story of the Shore was the story of a strange fertility. A fertility of flesh and blood that sent its seed blowing across continents of space on the winds of time, and yet was rooted here in home soil, renewed and re-renewed." The Channel that he will sail on is no symbol for Anse; it is another body to be used.

It is no surprise that Josie, who once told Grant, "There's a girl alive ... a child, maybe," should now tell him that Alan knows who he is and even put into his mind the idea of Alan and Margaret's love. Grant's heart, because he has protected it "each day," is "seared [by] images out of time past." He is afraid of yesterday and, as a result, of everything else, but his shared heritage with Josie strengthens him and allows him to see how "The past had subtly changed the present." His individual attempts to fragment time then fall away: "The weight was lifted, the pressure lessened, as if others now walked beside him to share a burden he had considered his alone." He does not know what will happen, but he knows where it will come from, and he is content to watch and wait. What Josie actually says to him is not what matters — the voice of the Shore is more than words

It was not clear to her. She merely felt the truth. No good telling Grant that whatever it was these two had shared, it was finer than any tie of blood. No good telling him that this, also, was something Alan knew. No good trying to convince Grant that doubts were useless. There were things you couldn't be told [or say] that you had to see for yourself.

But all Anse has are words; they are his weapons, divorced from a sense of time: "he had been plagued by impulse. To say his say, or have it said; to break the shell round the Marshalls, round the McKees, and look at the wreckage, and go …. " Thus his spoken attempt to bind Alan (as with the boat-naming) when he suggests, indirectly, a fishing partnership, fails doubly — because there is no shell to break and because Anse speaks of an old craft in a manipulative and possessive way. Another afternoon Alan has a "sense of time in precarious balance" as he watches from the boat Richard on the beach with his nets. Anse is beside Alan "on the point of speech, on the verge of words for which there could be no reply," but it is his egocentric attempts to balance on moments of his own devising that are threatened. He makes no sound, while Alan recalls days with Richard on the Channel.

Everyone descends to the beach for The Holiday, the community gathering held every August for eighty years, a picnic in the eternal present. Grant remembers finding Harvey on the beach when he spoke with Richard about his father; this connects with images of Rob Currie and Fanny Graham, of Uncle James and Anna, as he explains the history of the picnic, the past beyond his own memory, to Renie. He feels the nearer past constantly well up in the waters before his time, and then Alan helps the outsider, the cripple Skip Wilmot, just as Anna at a picnic in 1916 had reached out to Tarsh: "Anna … Anna's careless confidence, Anna's casual good nature and lightheartedness … alive again in Alan." Grant can let Alan go to Margaret, not worry about a competition between himself and Anse for their son, because the blood-line of the Shore is more than that in individuals, and it is more than a seed sown in sexual union. Now Grant moves beyond himself, beyond the personal fiction of silence. He will talk to Margaret; there is nothing he *has* to say to Alan Gordon.

Margaret, in her impatience, is like Hazel, though different because she has a purpose, a goal: "Now and then … it angered her that what she wanted must be brought about by the slow steps of time, of life unfolding in an unhurried slowly-changing pattern of days and nights and common acts and ordinary words." CB's ironic view of connections through time is found in the fact that Margaret depends on some dramatic action taken by Anse to set her on her life course, a dramatic action that will involve Anse leaving again; and ironically, Margaret's love is for the person who is the result of Hazel's desperate attempt at freedom and Anse's calculated attempt at control.

The ironies continue as Alan is "linked … through the boat" to Anse; they both ride the Channel, with Alan alive in the feel of the wind, the curve of the sail, "the march of rolling water," while Anse *uses* the Channel for his private sense of power by letting the boat fall off so that several female passengers are drenched, not once but twice. The Channel is never personified by CB, but it is a life force, animate and part of the balance, that serves as a natural chorus to the human action. When Alan and Anse bring the boat inshore, "The Channel's blue-green had darkened, its roll was longer and more leisurely, the sound of sea on gravel deliberate and long-drawn." On the boat "swinging to the lift and fall of the Channel," Anse tries his manipulation of human affairs for the last time. He cannot expose himself by asking Alan openly to join him in a fishing venture — the element of chance in change is not allowed — but he does talk about himself and Alan in the third person as if the partnership were formed. This is Anse's empty hook that he throws into the channel of human experience and heritage that he would deny. Alan does not take the hook, and the result is that Anse feels "powerless," as he did in 1919 when Hazel walked away from him. All he is left with are words and a public grab at power.

By summarizing the history of the Shore as gutless and the present as "Sheep manure and sawdust" (a snide reference to farmers who no longer fish), Anse divorces himself utterly from the very thing he would possess, and his twisted metaphor of possession reveals the ugliness and inadequacy of language outside time, when there is no flow between words and life: "If I'd known I'd planted a crop here, I'd have stayed to watch it grow." When Alan answers with an open hand against his father's face, "There [is] no other sound except the long sighing grumble of the Channel." Flesh and blood are not the *sine qua non* of human relationship, which is why Alan has no compunction in levelling a man who has spit upon the interweaving of people and place — the Shore is the repository of faith, not a receptacle for the only sound Anse has left: obscenity. When Anse leaves that night, sneaking away (ironically, the Channel bears him), CB focusses on Richard, who realizes that Anse has finally "established the emptiness of fact in the face of warm and living truth. Established the link between Grant and Alan, and perhaps Hazel, as a thing deeper and more telling than the accident of blood." Richard falls asleep, thinking of Hazel in the eternal present when she was/is untouched by Anse.

The final chapter of the novel is entitled "1946" to remind the reader that there is no frame tale and really never was. A sequence of events does not have to be strictly chronological to be a sequence, and events flow both ways in time. Before he leaves the Shore (the start of his return journey the next summer, or the following year, or …), Bill Graham learns from Grant that Alan, as Grant did in 1919, has moved to the Gordons to continue (not begin) his life: "'A start,' Grant said. But it was neither. It was past and present and future, eddying here in the flow of time." Bill realizes that the tale of Alan and Margaret and the others is already becoming part of the pattern, like the story of Rob Currie and Fanny Graham, "linked through tenuous blood-lines to the moving Now."

Here CB allows Stan Currie to articulate his feelings about the Shore, to speak for himself in a way that he did not in *Currie Head*; there is no better indication of CB's sense of time and place in 1954:

> "It's the fashion now to rule out … to forget the past. The *living* past, I mean. A virtue not to know who your grandfather was or where he came from or what he was like. Not to care. That comes, I guess, from living in rented places. No one gets identified with a stretch of land …. Nothing but themselves. They don't know

they're a part of the last generation or that their kids are a piece of *them*.... Look, I can go down on the Head and see the ridges in the ground where Ed Currie made bricks about eighteen-ten. I can show you where Sandy Currie found a spring and walled it with rocks. Maybe I got the same kind of kick out of putting in running water and a new foundation that Ed did when he dug his first well. Or Sandy, finding a spring to save lugging water to the beach ... I can go and take a look at Rob's cellar if I want to bother. In the parlour closet there's a tin-type of Hugh .... Taken when he went away to Boston. Every bit of it adventure. On the Shore they don't think about those things. But it's *in* them. If they go away they know where they come from. They come back to have a look, or they look back. They look back sometimes ... Some of them stick to the hard living, because, whatever else, there's still the independence ... Some of them leave, try to get comfort, ease ... Or just for the sake of going. The best of them, now and then, take a look back ... "

CB agrees, no doubt, with what his character is saying, but Stan is no longer CB; rather CB is one of those whom Stan perceives as having gone away but knowing where he came from. As one of the many emigrants from the Channel Shore, contained within the mind of his own creation, CB demonstrates quite consciously how life has flowed into art and now art flows on into life.

Stan says these words to Bill Graham who has a clear vision of yesterday, today and tomorrow in balance. He will return and bring *his* son, perhaps even his father. If Richard McKee is not there on the beach to greet them, then others will be, not because of what you could predict in the future, but because "All you could see were the following waves of time."

Critical response to *The Channel Shore* was generally positive, though even those inclined to high praise had reservations and contradicted one another. While the reviewer in the *Montreal Star* said the book was "not a poet's novel," his counterpart in the Montreal *Gazette* stated that "At times this book seems to have more of the qualities of a descriptive poem than of prose."[11] There was complaint in the Saskatoon *Star-Phoenix* that "It's a long poem, with many quiet and slow passages; otherwise, it's a long novel too slow-paced for its action"; this reviewer also thinks there are too many characters, but it is significant that throughout his commentary he refers to Alan as "Andrew."[12] In his "Letters in Canada" response to fiction in 1954 Claude Bissell called *The Channel Shore* "the best ... of this group of serious realistic novels," but was critical of CB's narrative method and the novel's tone. He paid tribute to the source experiences of the novel, to its unifying idea, and its disciplined use of words, but then asserted "... even this book cannot escape the stylistic blight that settles on so much Canadian fiction":

> Effects are built up by the slow accumulation of detail, by constant repetition; the freshness soon wears off, and a monotonous flatness descends upon the prose. Mr. Bruce's frequent espousal of a journalistic, breathless style — as if he were pausing to say, 'Look now, all of this is really very quaint and mysterious' — is no deterrent to the final effect. *The Channel Shore* is certainly good enough to invite comparison with Ernest Buckler's *The Mountain and the Valley*, another study of Nova Scotia community, but Buckler's book still remains our finest example of regional realism.[13]

It is not surprising that *The Channel Shore* could not measure up to Bissell's glowing report of the Buckler novel;[14] however, the accumulation of detail on the Shore is varied because of the constant shift in point of view, while in *The Mountain and the Valley*, the dominance of David Canaan's perspective often results in repetition and accumulation of material that is maddeningly slow. The accusation of "breathless style" is hardly substantiated and seems to stem from Bissell's own "quaint and mysterious" reader response. Bissell did not attempt to see as deeply into the intentions and implications of *The Channel Shore* as did Fred Cogswell: "Charles Bruce sees in acts of sympathy and understanding, roots that creep through community life .... If the roots are not sufficiently strong to justify optimism, they are at least enough to justify faith."[15] Kay Rowe in the Brandon *Sun* felt that optimism was in the novel because of "a tide-like rhythm through [the] book" — the presence of the living past, something more than creeping roots.[16]

The United Church Observer reaction to the novel is very defensive and fails utterly to deal with it as literature, preferring instead to cavil about the presentation of church life and to accuse CB of not knowing about the unification of Methodists and Presbyterians: "Mr. Bruce's aim, apparently, is to draw out the hum-drum, monotonous character of Nova Scotia rural existence. He endeavours to show that life in such communities is very restricted in both purpose and achievement .... but tells us even more ... of ... himself."[17] CB wrote Thomas Raddall that he had heard about this review "from home," that is, where Sarah Bruce was now living in the renovated farmhouse. He replied to *The Observer* that the novel contained references to Methodists only in the "1919" section and denied any discrimination against the United Church "... or any other, including the altars of God that may be lighted without organized human ministry, in the searching hearts of men."[18]

The 1954 Governor-General's Award for fiction went to Igor Gouzenko's *The Fall of a Titan*, but on the short list along with *The Channel Shore* were Robertson Davies's *Leaven of Malice* and Ethel Wilson's *Swamp Angel*. W. A. Deacon, book editor of *The Globe and Mail*, wrote that "the greater popularity of the Gouzenko book was in part the result of considerations outside literary art," while CB's effort was a "Canadian classic"[19] that thankfully lacked "the latest fashionable gambits in psychology" of most modern fiction.[20] Deacon was one of the three judges on the Canadian Authors' Association panel that chose the fiction winner (along with Bissell and M.E. Nichols, a former president and board director of Canadian Press). He and CB were friends and colleagues at the CAA, which probably explains why CB did not object to Deacon's remark that his novel "is of plain people in a backwater." At least he did not reply directly, but since the remark was redolent of what the Toronto *Telegram* reviewer had said of *The Mulgrave Road* in 1951, it obviously strengthened CB's resolve to straighten out this matter of backwaters.[21] Perhaps more interesting is that both positive and negative reviews emphasized the "background" of the landscape and seascape of the Shore, as if blind to the integration of the natural and human worlds in Richard McKee, the shared rhythms of the sea and blood, the heritage intrinsic to the Shore territory, and CB's use of the Channel in particular, his *fore*grounding of it, as a chorus for human voices and individual experience. There were many letters of appreciation from ordinary Nova Scotians who felt the novel portrayed a familiar and time-honoured way of life. The United Church notwithstanding, a woman from North Queen's County in Nova Scotia wrote CB that "there was a Vangie Murphy some miles up [our] road" just like the one in the book.[22] One hopes this correspondent recognized CB's complex and sympathetic portrait of Vangie and her situation in the novel.

The debate about "regional realism" must be concerned with the question of whether a particular fiction is confined by region or is defined by it in ways that add to, rather than detract from, its universal significance. CB addressed this question in a series of remarks he made about *The Township of Time* after its 1959 publication, but they are certainly relevant to the place of *The Channel Shore* in Canadian literature. They also emphasize CB's own perception of himself as a writer of realism. He speaks of the three main elements in any story — character, action, and environment — and stresses the influence of time and place on fictional people and events. In the United States, he writes, "Areas and events and traditions that are of interest in themselves [are] recognizable parts of a larger whole, and thus produce a sort of built-in reader appeal. In Canada we haven't got these traditions or areas of reference."[23] Our growth has not been, he continues, like the manifest destiny movement westward in the United States, but rather "through the development of a series of small frontiers, circling out from many centres. Our background seems almost aimless, our tradition complicated by anomalies." So all a realist writer can do "if he has this twin urge to tell stories illuminating the continuity of human nature and feeling, and people's problems, and to tell them in a setting recognizably Canadian, is to do his work in one of the many areas of reference, the many small frontiers, the many centres of a smaller metropolitanism, that go together to make up this country and its people." All this has to do, perhaps, with the debate about melting pots versus cultural mosaics; however, there is a possible explanation, in CB's brief historical description of the origins of Canadian regionalism, for the attitudes of critics and academics (in particular before the paradoxically unifying explosion of Canadian culture in the 1960s) that novels such as *The Channel Shore, The Mountain and the Valley, Swamp Angel, The Double Hook, Who Has Seen the Wind*, those of Grove and many others, were bound to certain parts of the country by virtue of their settings and their place in the unfolding and development not so much of the nation, but parts of it.

CB also offered some opinions of his contemporaries in the novel-writing field that illuminate somewhat his view of his own fiction. In a 1949 letter to a Mount Allison student writing a thesis on the Canadian novel, CB said of those Canadian novels he had read, "I think their greatest virtues are sincerity and attention to accuracy of atmosphere, the details of setting and so on .... the *accoutrements* of life .... " But he did not like the lack of humour, a lack he defined in the following way: "By this I don't mean wit, but [a] kind of underlying warmth [where] themes may be essentially tragic, but whose people [sic] leave you warm with a feeling for humanity, even though you have an ache at the back of your throat."[24] He felt emotionally unmoved, therefore, by Gabrielle Roi's *The Tin Flute*, "the most impressive Canadian novel," because "There is not a laugh in it." As for Hugh MacLennan, "... at times he is ponderous, obsessed with the problem he sets up to deal with, and not always in touch with his characters." Morley Callaghan, who perhaps more than any other novelist of the pre-1960s era could not be defined in terms of region, was annoying to CB because of his "conscious understatement. He seems to be saying to you: 'See how simply I say this? I could be lush if I liked' No one wants him to be lush, but I'd like to see him human."

From 1955 through 1958 CB was a judge for the Beta Sigma Phi Award for first novels (part of the Governor-General's Awards). He agreed to serve for a second year in 1956 "with some reluctance" because he was afraid a friend's manuscript might turn up, but mainly because "last year I think there were thirteen entries and at least ten of them were almost incredible trash."[25] That his judgement of fiction was certainly sound and perceptive is indicated by his first choice for 1956 — Adele Wiseman's *The Sacrifice* — and for 1957 — John Marlyn's *Under the Ribs of Death* (though this title he considered "silly and melodramatic").[26] These novels apparently lived up to CB's adage that "Good writing is a joint crop with life, like the clover and timothy you sow together."[27] Such writing was not something CB could easily define as "creative": "I don't think the working practice of producing even the greatest fiction and drama and poetry is essentially creative, in the precise sense of the word":

> It is really re-creation; the taking of dreams and emotions and physical facts that already exist and merging them in a pattern, an arrangement, that satisfies and excites — and perhaps changes — the personality of the writer and of his audience.
>
> There is something like creation, of course, in that element of change. But what I mean is that any writing that really matters is concerned with life, with people, with emotions you can recognize. That when pure creation is attempted, out of stuff that isn't already flowing in your veins, the result is fantasy; a fantasy that isn't useful or living, or even understandable in human terms ....
> No novel ... can hold you unless it has the ring of reality and unless it is true to the customs and habits and emotions and the idiom of its age. These are not obtainable in the imagination. They are obtainable only in the life of the period itself.[28]

In July 1955 CB received $450.00 from the Canadian Broadcasting Corporation for the airing on the Trans-Canada Radio Network of "Marshall and Son."[29] He had written and had had broadcast several drama scripts on CBC before this — two of which were based on stories he later incorporated in *The Township of Time* manuscript.[30] "Marshall and Son" grew "from the central theme of *The Channel Shore*: the father-and-son relationship between a man and a boy who are not in fact related."[31] The drama, with its cast of nine characters, its Narrator, and three Voices, is about the winter of 1933-34 when Alan learns of his heritage from Josie, and Grant clings to his philosophy that "We'll take each day as it comes." The play is narrated by Renie, who also plays her role as wife and mother. The Voices provide the various responses of the Shore to Grant's marriage with Hazel and his raising of Alan ("It was wonderful, you know — what he did for Hazel McKee — .... Must be queer, though, raising another man's ... ").

The scene in Richard's loft with the objects and photos that help to provide the balance of yesterday, today and tomorrow is presented through the dialogue of Alan and Margaret, with Renie looking back through twenty years (that is, from the mid-fifties) to provide details and perspective. She does the same thing when Josie and Alan speak of Anse, with dialogue lifted straight from the novel, and there is even an exchange between the Narrator and the adult Alan about his motivations and actions regarding Grant at that time. What is curious about all this is that Renie from her vantage-point does not mention the return of Anse in the mid-forties nor the struggles that resulted then. She summarizes the state of things after Alan has decided that he wants to stay with Grant on the Shore by saying that "Separate and alone, two minds would keep and guard the long illusion. While in their hearts the other thing — the warmth of work and love and long companionship, the thing that was not illusion — worked out its shining truth. Two, now, living by words Grant said to me so long ago. 'We'll take each day as it comes.'"

Obviously the complexities of the novel cannot be conveyed in a radio broadcast probably an hour in length, but CB so reduces the intricacies of Alan's and Grant's relationship that the listener who has not read *The Channel Shore* is lulled into thinking all is well that ends well. The philosophy that "We'll take each day as it comes," the last line of the play, seems capable of overcoming any obstacle, whereas in the novel its fragility is revealed. The irony in the novel lies in "as it comes" because days arrive replete with yesterday and tomorrow. The reader of the novel is bound to feel slightly cheated no matter how well this extraction from the text is presented. Surely CB could have dramatized the return of Anse in a second part of the play, which would, of course, have demanded a greater examination in the first part of what occurred in the summer and fall of 1919. Josie and Richard are Voices, not characters; their human involvement in the story of Grant and Alan is missing. CB presents in "Marshall and Son" the heart of the matter in the 1933-34 section of *The Channel Shore*, but does not, by choice, convey "the balance" at the heart of the novel.

X

Hearsay History

What is rather remarkable is that while he was producing the final version of *The Channel Shore*, CB drew up elaborate plans for a seven-part novel he called *No Left-Handed Reaping Hook*. Twenty manuscript pages exist of the first section of the proposed book and are about the boyhood of Wes Davis, who lives on a farm by the sea in eastern Nova Scotia. A pencilled map accompanying these pages[1] shows that the farm is not in Channel Shore territory, and since Wes is born in 1874 much of the tale is meant to take place before the 1919-1946 period on the shore. CB describes this novel-to-be as "concerned with time."

When Wes is a boy, time is very nearly all in the present and therefore almost limitless (1880); when he is in his late teens, time is going faster because it's all a looking ahead, a reaching out (1892); in middle age Wes wants to put time behind him because he finds his present disagreeable; when he is in his late sixties he looks back at his life, sensing it is over; but even later he lives each precious moment much as he did as a boy, not because time is limitless, but because it is almost over for him — yet there is still some compulsion toward tomorrow. This, at least, as found in CB's notes, is the scenario, and CB had various characters and individual scenes arranged for the different sections of the novel; he seemed to have a strong sense of direction and of what he wanted to say. He describes young Wes gazing into a stream's pool on his father's farm, "A tide of private wonder, light and quiet, rising in all the inlets of his being ...." The pool was Now." But when Wes discovers his great-grandmother's left-handed reaping hook (a sickle) "Something about the graceful curve of it touched him with a curious joy. It was unlike any of the tools they used," and he is taken both back and on into time: "The storybook closeness of earlier times, the comfortable closeness, was gone — they were far away in time, but time itself had been brought close, reality was nearer .... And now also the future was something to be reached."

The life of Wes Davis was not at all based on CB's life; for one thing Wes was descended from Florida loyalists, not an immigrant from Aberdeen. There are connections between author and main character as Wes's father came back from away to run the farm, and Wes attends a small New Brunswick college, but essentially CB's concern with human experience in and through time seems to have resulted in plans for a convincing fiction.

What happened, then, to this novel? Perhaps the effort required to complete *The Channel Shore* (which, after all, he had been working on in one way or another for almost a decade) undermined CB's incentive for another long work. This does seem likely, because in the mid-1950s he was preoccupied with what he called "communication through TIME .... continuity in human affairs .... Cross-roads history."[2] Instead of another novel, though, he concentrated on short fiction and on articles and talks. In 1932 he had written "Land of Home-Loving Wanderers" for *Port and Province* in which he described the emigration of restless Nova Scotians to other parts of the country, but he wondered then if these men and women viewed their province with "their closest attention of mind as well as heart" that it merited. In the summer of 1956 CB spoke on CBC Radio of the connections between Port Shoreham and all parts of North America, but especially the rest of Canada, of his "sense of a country-wide community" that has grown from interprovincial movement for generations:

> So it seems to me that the community I come from — and there are scores and hundreds like it — has two sets of boundaries. There's the one that sets it off from South Manchester, a mile or so up the road, and from Manasette Lake, a couple of miles down. And there's that other boundary, vague and elastic and endless, that sweeps out and around the borders of the land, wherever men and women from Rural Route One have taken up the job of life.[3]

Venture and adaptability send people away, but memory and the unchanged atmosphere of home bring them back. CB was no romantic looking for a home frozen in the time of his boyhood; he lauded external changes that would make life easier on the farm, but he insisted that "behind the externals there is something else." Perhaps his most seminal point made on his two national radio broadcasts was the following:

> ... there's no conflict between regional affection, consciousness of a local environment, and recognition of a common nationality. Regional affection and nationality are not opposed characteristics, but complementary. It will be a sad day for Canada when the imprint of the Rockies and Selkirks on the soul of a British Columbian, the sweep of the high plains in the mind of the man from Saskatchewan, the salt in the blood of the Nova Scotian, are erased by some fanatical effort to label such things as heresy toward a national ideal.[4]

For CB such continuity in terms of space and distance could not be separated from continuity, and therefore community, in time.

In his article written for the IODE *Echoes* magazine and published in the autumn of 1955, CB began with the community of space by describing his 1946 meeting with Pat Diggens at the Buckingham Palace garden party, but moved quickly into "The Township of Time" as he examined the journeys across the United States border of his mother and father and then his talk with Sandy Bruce in Boylston about great-great grandfather James and his descendants. This latter conversation, CB says, led him to the Nova Scotia Archives in search of history and of facts. He discovered facts about James Bruce, great-grandfather Richard Bruce, and his grandfather Charles Bruce. He also found out what there was to know about great-uncle James Bruce, who vanished in his three-master on the way to Sierra Leone. But what fascinated CB were the gaps between the facts that were filled with what he called "hearsay history" — stories "alive in human memory":

> They left no writing, these pioneers. The wave of local history and hearsay and laughter, rolls up from the memory of a man's grandparents, perhaps from a little beyond, but the waves behind roll through a mist of time .... Occasionally the mist lifts .... Glimpses only. You take them, and look at the land and sea, and

the faces of the people and the images roll up out of the mist beyond those nearer waves of life .... And what you have is continuity .... limits and boundaries in another dimension, forever opening out a township in time .... Through a sense of relationship to past generations, a feeling of kinship to generations still to come.[5]

CB stresses that he is not speaking here of old documents or textual evidence that provides "the doings of the Major-Generals, but rarely the heartbeat of the settler"; rather he is referring to the companionship in time found in stories handed down orally through generations. He is speaking of things "Remembered, somehow, on a common and personal and community basis. Remembered, if not in the records, in something that continues in the blood and breath and bone, passed on .... "[6] *This* was nationality, traced back through people to particular spots of earth, and the national/regional writer of stories had a responsibility to be as authentic as possible in his use of historical material while attempting to convey the truths of human connections through time by fiction: "To do otherwise is to commit a crime against the future."

What CB had begun to have in mind was a chronicle, an unfolding of the pattern of human experience in time in the form of linked short stories. In the late 1940s he had written "The Wind in the Juniper"[7] about a physicist from the Channel Shore (Forester's Pond, to be specific), John Forester. This man has lost his sense of tomorrow because he is dying, but there is still time for him to explore the past. He was raised by an aunt he called "Mam" and a great-uncle he called "the Captain." In his description of John's family experience, CB employs material from *Currie Head*. The Captain and John pick stones from the field, tend the herring nets on the Channel, and John learns to trap for muskrat. Just as Hugh Currie and Stan had a misunderstanding about the money earned from muskrat fur, so John hears the Captain explain to his aunt that he does not want John "tied to the kind of work we do for a living,"[8] and so the money will be used to send him to college. Like Stan, John has a vision of "the road," and like Stan, he carries the North Shore with him despite the distance he travels. His capacity for work, for stamina, comes from the fact that "Dr. John Forester was the boy from The Pond, his aching arms keeping the stemmer headed up in a sou'est wind."

There is a troubling ambiguity to John's choices about work over personal happiness, particularly the one that takes him to the American southwest to work on the atomic bomb project. Avoidance of personal contact at crucial moments in his life seems rationalized by his perception of those who have mattered to him, "not as individuals but as people whose qualities were woven into the fabric of himself," and in his movement from A-bomb work to nuclear medicine. It seems finally, though, when medical studies are on the immediate horizon — when the personal application of knowledge might occur — that he considers a visit to the Shore for the first time in years and is aware in his thoughts that "There were times when past, present, and future were all part of the same thing." There is a link between his moving away from compromise toward his heritage and his imposing his body between pieces of radioactive material when a machine malfunctions in a laboratory experiment and individual lives are threatened. He never saw Hiroshima, cannot imagine it, but this particular human destruction he cannot allow in the name of physics. The result is cancer, and the result is memory of the Captain and Mam, of his boyhood, and of the juniper tree outside his bedroom window at the farm; the tree symbolizes something "more than yesterday's harrowing and the birch logs and the sawhorse," something that poses an eternal question physics cannot answer: "Where does space end and when did time begin?" Strangely, through the identification of the present with the past John gains a sense of tomorrow, of what others will do even if he will not. Others he once knew and will never know, linked because their "work was the fabric of their living [on] ... the gleaming road of time."

Taken by itself, "The Wind in the Juniper" is a more philosophical (because of the meditative quality of its narration) and a more serious consideration of the Shore than most of CB's other short fiction to this point. While the humour of "The Talking Tree," "The Year of the Stella," and "The Red Wing Feud" capture something of the quality of life on the Shore, the story of John Forester is closer to that of Lee in "The Road to Town" and of Ed McKee in "The Letters" because of the emphasis in each on the open-endedness of human experience and companionship in time. The spark for the chronicle was certainly struck in the late 1940s because a few years later CB worked backwards from John Forester's tale with three stories, two of which fill in something of the Captain's early life and the other a day in John's boyhood. CB was, by 1956, envisioning his collection of linked short stories and so was able to see the place of "The Road to Town" in his scheme: he changed the name of Lee to Bart Somers, either before or after he had written "The Pattern of Surrender" about Bart in 1954 and certainly before he produced "The Sloop" (about Bart's return to the Shore) in 1958. But with all of these stories he had only ventured a few years back into the past; he had not yet, in any of his fiction, built upon tales handed down from long ago, he had not yet tried to look through the mist of time. The story in which he first so built and looked was called "Tidewater Morning," which he wrote in the early 1950s,[9] and which, because it involved him with that responsibility to be as authentic as possible and to go beyond his *own* historical experience of the Shore, is the true cornerstone of *The Township of Time*: however, he did not finally decide on this title and indicate that he could see the chronicle entirely in the terms he had laid down in his IODE article and in the two talks on the CBC until May 1958.[10]

Apparently the mist lifted once when CB heard "the story of one who lost his wife, and sick with sorrow, started for Halifax on foot, and called in to see a friend on the way, and found his friend was dead; and stayed to marry the widow."[11] Out of this brief vignette and the investigations he had made in the late 1940s and early 1950s into the history of settlements at the head of Chedabucto Bay,[12] CB created the fiction of Richard McKee, former member of the 71st Scots Regiment who fought at the battle of the Brandywine during the Revolution. Richard comes to settle in 1784 with his friend John Cameron (whom CB has as the author of a verse stanza straight out of "The Standing Woods"), but they are granted land far apart. Each marries and makes a go of his respective plot, with Richard mackerel fishing in the Channel as well. While Prim Cameron bears a son, Mary McKee dies soon after of consumption, and Richard in his grief decides to leave the Shore, but not without saying a goodbye to the Camerons. He learns on arrival at their farm that John died two weeks previously under a falling tree and that their son is named Richard McKee Cameron. What Richard realizes and accepts is that there is no escape from whom he has been and what he has known. Indeed, his memory of Mary provides him with the strength to deal with the present, as do his past links with John. He will stay on the Shore, and although CB does not spell it out here, Richard and Primrose will marry.

This simple tale is given substance by CB's attention to the details of loyalist immigration — facts that he culled from history books and his correspondence with A.C. Jost and Thomas Raddall (among others) — and to the daily lives of farmer-fishermen: the wood they chopped, the crops they planted, the nets they knitted, and the tools they used.[13] CB knew that homespun shirts were coloured brown "with dye brewed from maple moss" and that "the raw hide round the hocks" of slaughtered cows was used to fashion "shanks" (the narrow part of the sole of a shoe); he knew the woods trails a man would follow walking west along the North Shore towards Guysborough; and he had heard the story of young William Campbell, later Chief Justice of Upper Canada, who supposedly stood on the beach at Guysborough in 1784 and announced to the father of a young woman he had just seen for the first time, "There stands Mrs. William Campbell!" Not just fact, then, but hearsay makes its way into "Tidewater Morning" as CB simply changes Campbell's name and has John Cameron as a witness to the event. By having John write the four lines from *his* poem (arguably the most beautiful and moving lines in "The Standing Woods"[14]), CB emphasizes in a unique way factual connections between the future and the past. Or did the entire long poem about the facts of the Bruce family on the shores of Chedabucto Bay grow from this poetic fiction that is, for Richard McKee, not convincing as proper verse because it does not rhyme? Certainly life other than CB's own was flowing into his art, and it is tempting to believe the latter explanation for the poem as an apt illustration of the reverse flow. CB did not know it yet, but the "life" he created in "Tidewater Morning," as it would continue through the union of Richard McKee and Primrose Cameron, would both people the Shore (the large group of characters in *The Channel Shore* seems small by comparison) and yield artistic descendants in time.

Certainly the actual construction of the chronicle is testimony to CB's view of a community in time in which continuity in human affairs stems from an interweaving of future, past, and present. "People From Away 1917," for example, was very probably written in late 1955 or early 1956 as it stands in *The Township of Time*,[15] but much of it was lifted, sometimes verbatim, from the first part of *Currie Head*; the adult Hugh Currie has an important role to play as Stan learns how and why his father returned with him to Nova Scotia. "Reprieve 1881," a story of Hugh's boyhood, of the past that contributed to Stan's future, was undoubtedly written after that future had unfolded. There were apparently straightforward chronological progressions, as with the three-part saga of Bart Somers (1918 — 1933 — 1939) in which CB built upon past fictions. But the story of the middle-aged Colin Forester in "Voyage Home 1910" and the teenaged Colin in "The Fiddlers of Point M'sieu 1873" depended greatly on John Forester's recollections in 1945 and on CB's already having explored those memories. The textual dynamics in *The Township of Time*, in which stories in the text precede those that follow them in time, yet are about days of future past once their successors have been read, are reflected in the way in which CB, moving chronologically through his own years, produced individual tales — as part of a logical pattern in time, but where the future that he had already written often presaged the past that he had not yet conceived.

After "Tidewater Morning 1787," CB went back a year in order to provide a solid ancestral base (along with Camerons and McKees) for the generations to come on the Shore. Colin Forester had fought with Tarleton's Legion and met Richard on the boat heading up the bay in 1784. "The Sloop" is set two years later as Colin runs his crippled boat with the swell down to the St. Augustine settlement rather than take half a day fiercely tacking home. There he encounters Lydia Willoughby, whose temperament matches his own, and determines to make her his wife. The sense of time and place is conveyed sharply through details of dress and habitation:

> Feet bare — he'd stowed his shoes in the cuddy ... — sailcloth breeches that ended in rags-and-tags half-way between knees and ankles, a dirty woolen singlet under an old blue sea-jacket .... He and the sloop, they were both home-made.
> It wasn't a bad hut, but nothing to brag on, either. Two rooms by the look of it, with a cat-and-clay chimney and two windows, one of glass and one of scraped hide, and a door a bit off-line .... two generations lay ahead before the rags and homespun would again be satin, and the log walls white clapboard, the parlor panelled oak.

As well there is the special nature of Colin — attendant with frontier practicality to tasks at hand, but pushing at restrictions, both natural-world and human, with stubborness, compassion, and hope. As with Richard and Primrose, the intimacy of Colin and Lydia is governed by fate — a falling tree, a damaged mast — and fate stays its course on the Shore, but in these two tales of progenitors CB makes clear the individual strength of character and vision beyond present necessities in the mists of time.

One of CB's major themes in *The Township of Time* is that single years, months, days, and indeed moments, are part of a collective human experience that has its rhythm in decades and even centuries. The flash of a narrative light at any particular point of this experience will reveal, however, that this larger rhythm depends for its very being on individual aspects of character and event, each related to another, much as a reef is built up over time through the life and death of tiny creatures that adhere together in coralled pattern. Thus we next encounter Richard McKee in a story essentially about his two boys — Richard McKee Cameron and John Cameron McKee — in "The Pond Place 1800-1." Nothing much happens here except the boys get briefly lost in the woods, but running constantly through young Richard's mind is a sense of the Shore, its human history and growth, paralleled by his sense of family and self: "Slight and elusive, a thing felt but unconsidered, the thought ... of Richard and Ma and John and the young ones, and his own place in it, and the first John, buried on the hill at Tidewater, ran like fleck-ed sunlight in the back of [his] mind." The direction out of the woods is taken because young Richard recognizes an individual marker tree, but also because he can range comfortably back and forth on trails of time, even at fourteen responsive to heritage and life to come.

When Colin Forester next appears, over a quarter of a cen-tury has passed since he met Lydia. They have, in "Juniper 1813," five daughters and a son, and Colin's favorite is his third girl, Willoughby. She is courted by the self-satisfied merchant and farmer Ben Farren, who looks, to Colin, "like a man standing in the stern of a flat, rowing face first." But her love is reserved for Angus Neill, who has apparently deserted the Shore for a life of privateering. The plot centres around Farren's deceit in the mat-ter of Angus's disappearance and is resolved when the young man returns with a story of forced impressment on a British frigate; but CB really focusses on the unity of the Forester fami-ly that rests upon Colin and Lydia's shared memories of earlier times on the Shore. Only with an openness to "memory's unbid-dable way" can "the slope of the land, the look of the Channel bec[o]me the familiar soul of life." Only then can "The flow and beat and essence of this life [be] in today, tomorrow .... not in talk but doing." Colin plants two small junipers, transplanted from the woods, in front of his house to represent himself and Lydia, but then, because of "the drama and color and passion" that lie behind their shared experience and because of "the drawn-out quiet part of living" as well, the trees come to repre-sent Willoughby and Angus and all the pairings that will result from his children, who are beginning, like the trees, "their long growth into Time." It is only towards the end of the short story collection, with John Forester's memory of the juniper outside the gate of his boyhood home, that the lasting quality of the natural and symbolic essence of Colin's action and vision is evi-dent: "That was what it was, a curved and feathery treetop seen in sleep, that had caused the union of past and present in his waking mind. All the years were there — the juniper the one small thing, wavering to the conscious surface, to bring the whole alive." As Colin sees the future in his trees, John Forester begins to explore his coniferous past.

Of all the characters in *The Channel Shore* between 1919 and 1946 only Hugh Currie receives prominent mention in *The Township of Time*. But one character who was born at The Head and spent his boyhood there is Andrew Graham, father of Bill Graham (not mentioned at all in the short stories), and Andrew is the protagonist of "Duke Street 1896." Sixty-two years before Andrew's meeting with his "ancient cousin" Naomi Harvey on Duke Street in Toronto, seventeen-year-old Naomi Neill, daughter of Willoughby and Angus, encounters her school-teacher and future husband, Francis Harvey, in "Cadence 1834." Naomi and Francis are trapped together in the schoolhouse by a blizzard, and to avoid speculations about their overnight activity Francis decides that Naomi should practice her spelling. She is rather rough-edged and free-spirited, much like her mother when young, but CB emphasizes her involvement in the natural-symbolic scheme of things when she identifies an apple she is eating as a "Primrose": "Grandfather Colin used to plant an apple tree whenever grandmother had a baby. The first one was Mary Primrose." CB employs Edenic imagery here as Naomi tempts Francis with her combination of ignorance and wisdom, but the wisdom is the result of ties and rhythms beyond the original garden as it is represented in *Paradise Lost*. CB has Francis quote Milton in order to define the word "cadence," which Naomi does not understand. Thus Milton, who would keep Eve in her place: "... the sound of blustering winds which ... now with hoarse cadence lull sea-faring men." And Naomi: "Or waves, I guess. Waves on the shore."

Francis is an outsider on the North Shore, studying for the law. He knows of Sir William Baillie, justice of the King's Bench of Upper Canada, but CB's portrait of the human community in space as well as time continues as Naomi tells Francis of Sir William's first-settler friendship with grandfather Colin and old Richard McKee (Baillie was the young man on the beach in 1784 who spied his future wife and announced it bravely to her father). Later, reflecting on all this and the accompanying history of the Shore, Francis gazes ahead into time and wonders "How it will be when Naomi Neill is eighty [Sir William Baillie's age in 1834]? That would be — when? Sixty-three years from now. Well, sixty-two and something over .... You couldn't see that far."

Beating on, sceptical and confident, boats against the current, Andrew Graham, in 1896, is borne back ceaselessly into the past by his "duty-bound" meeting with Naomi. She teaches him, much as she taught Francis (though there is no ignorance, only wisdom, now) about time's cadence. Listening to her tales of the Shore — one of the junipers blown down in the August gale of 1873, the legend of Colin's first meeting with Lydia, her own night in the schoolhouse with Francis — Andrew recalls that "Somewhere he had heard that to the Hebrews time is a unity. Past, present, and future merged and continuing .... [Now] it was as if the walls of time were down." Andrew senses Naomi's need to have her own tale "live in memory," so he too looks ahead, as Francis did, "fifty, eighty, a hundred years from now" to someone else looking back "to form in words the tenuous cadence of that story." This *someone* is Bill Graham's father, old and retired in Toronto exactly fifty years later, but in *The Channel Shore*, who fingers "the tarnished silver stag" paperweight (made for Francis when he left the Shore) given to him by Naomi in 1896. Speaking "with more gentleness" than Bill can remember him using before, Andrew allows that a return to the Shore might be more than living an illusion. Andrew has, since he last saw Naomi, given himself over to a life of books and academic ambition, but her influence must have lingered, because he sent Bill to the Shore for the summer of 1919, "To see the country he had sprung from."[16] The simultaneous movement through time and from book to book of Andrew Graham and the paperweight, and the relationship between Andrew, his ancestors, and his inheritors, suggests that the essential theme of a collective human experience in time not only binds together CB's individual stories and distinct prose fictions, but transcends and contains them as well.

In an undated and unpublished talk about the writing of *The Township of Time* CB stated that the two stories for which the most research was required were "Cadence" and "Duke Street."[17] He relates how an old school-return of 1834, giving the school-teacher's name and the names of the children in attendance (one of them was great-uncle James Bruce), started him thinking. He read a book about a teacher in early 19th-century Nova Scotia, discovered a box in the attic of Province House in Halifax that contained a list of the law books Francis Harvey would have studied, found out the coinage of the period, and read a lot of issues of Joseph Howe's newspaper *The Nova Scotian*: "This must seem to you like a considerable amount of work to put on a 4000-word story — without even getting to the writing part yet — and it is. I just haven't found any other way of doing it." As for "Duke Street," CB chose to locate Naomi there because she and Francis lived in the house that once belonged to Sir William Baillie, and Baillie was based on Sir William Campbell who built Number 56 Duke Street in 1822. The owners of the house in the 1950s allowed CB to tour it; then he walked the route Andrew Graham would have taken from University College and consulted 1896 issues of *The Varsity* to see what students were wearing and talking about then. All this research had not to do with an obsession with exactitude: "… none of these stories is a catalogue of customs for its own sake. There is — I hope — no antiquarianism in them. What I've tried to do is tell each story naturally in the idiom and setting of its own time, and to suggest that these times are fluid, not static, that time is not a succession of fixed points, but a flow. I hope the digging doesn't show in the tales." The digging does not show, but in the story structure that rests on such excavated ground there is that attention to "truth of behaviour and circumstance" that CB deemed necessary to any mimetic fiction worthy of its name.

The extraordinary intertextual connections, in which time's unity contains all, continue with "Morgan's Woods 1851." Homer Graham married Colin's second daughter, Melody. One son, Saul, went off to sea, abandoning his heritage almost completely, while the other, Long George, resented the son of his first marriage to a girl he had made pregnant as "the symbol of entrapment." Homer, watching the ugly behaviour of his son and his grandson's unhappiness, is not "comforted by kinship, one generation fading and merging in the next." But around him he is aware of a larger kinship:

> Axe and fire, sickle and flail. Fields, fences, buildings, widening back from the water, flailed out of the woods. He could remember when you couldn't see a house. And how, just now and then, after days of pulling stumps, building fence, working a strip with a wooden plow, there'd be that feeling of excitement. A glimpse ahead, of how the land would be ... Well, here it was. And now he was looking back.

Associations abound. His land. The land Homer bought for George and Saul because of something old Richard McKee had said at a Shore gathering for Colin and Lydia twenty years ago.

Now as Homer's grandson, young Dan, prepares to leave home under the pressure of his father's insults and provocations, Homer senses something "come out of the mist, to take on the angles of possibility, of probability." Since Saul left it was understood that Long George would get "the home place" when Homer died, and now against that Homer will persuade George to let Dan live and work with him on those hundred acres of woods he bought two decades previously. It will be Dan's Place eventually, a future growing out of a somewhat disjointed, but nevertheless integral, past: "Waves of memory ... Boulders crowbarred out, on this place here, fifty years and more ago. Could he do it now? ... For a moment he felt the old strength .... That was nonsense .... Show Dan the tricks. Be as useful as you could." And the final irony: "He was almost grateful to Long George for making it come to pass." Not links in the chain, but vital threads in the web of being. This is where the intertextual leap occurs — not to *The Channel Shore* this time, but to *The Flowing Summer*.

Dan Graham's son, who inherits The Place, is Old Jack, Lee Graham's grandfather, whom Lee visits to discover where he has come from, "the patterned living at the river mouth." The relationship of a skipped generation between Homer and Dan comes up again between Old Jack and *his* grandson. As Homer thought to show Dan the tricks of the past, so Jack ponders "... a wondering voice/And a boy's hands to guide and train again/For common living. Just the wakened pulse/Of his own blood beating in the veins of youth."[18] The journeys on and back, to and from the Shore, continue in ever-widening circles, washing over other families and back on themselves — one of Old Jack's cousins is Andrew Graham; one of his nephews (his half-brother's boy) is Dan Graham of *Currie Head* and *The Channel Shore*. Even Stan Currie, in the flush of his own return to the Shore, his constant awareness of heritage, can trace his bloodlines, and more besides, back to Colin Forester, who, on his father's side, is Stan's great-great grandfather.

There are two stories about the Curries in the collection. The first, "Reprieve 1881," about young Hugh, was based on a short tale about Stan as a boy that appeared under the title "Suspense" in the *The Dalhousie Review*.[19] The changes CB made in the few years between the stories indicated how his vision of the Shore had expanded beyond the immediate and personal, beyond the biographical. In "Suspense" Stan finds a swallow nestling on the ground below the barn eaves and resolves to keep it. It is a Sunday morning, and Aunt Christine, preoccupied with church matters, does not approve. But Hugh, who declines the invitation to church, encourages his son, and while Stan frets through the hymn, the sermon, and the benediction, his father gives the bird its needed water. There is not much else to the story; it appears to be an understated portrait of a father-son relationship and a tribute to Hugh's more than merely Christian behaviour. There needs to be a fleshing out of the Curries, something to make it more than just another short tale of boy and father and pet.

"Reprieve 1881" is much more complex, both in intention and result. Eleven-year-old Hugh Currie discovers the swallow nestling beneath the eaves; his mother, "a harried woman trying to get her work done by church time," disapproves, but here the father-figure plays no part. Instead, it is Hugh's grandmother Jen (Colin's youngest daughter) who volunteers to help. The bird is placed in a home-made nest constructed from a wooden box Uncle Rob Currie (lost at sea) brought back from the West Indies; at church, having viewed the Channel "blue and calm, with the two-masters anchored off the Head," Hugh remembers Uncle Rob and "something about Grandmother Jen, the surrounding occasion all mist but the central image clear ...." These thoughts of the past have to do with Hugh's knowledge that he cannot keep the swallow forever; just as he senses that it must fly south and then return changed and beyond him, he senses "that Mother, Father, Grandmother Jen lived and moved in circles wider than the ones he knew them in, the circle of kitchen, pantry, chip-yard, pasture, beach. And that these wider regions extended into time as well as space." Having raced home to preserve the swallow, Hugh finds that his grandmother has already given it water and that "frail, unquestionable life" is in the wooden nest. But such frailty hits him for the first time, threatens to overwhelm him completely. He recalls *Young Richard McKee*, "a white-haired old man" come to visit Jen; how Richard, Jen's father Colin, and her son Rob are all dead — living men and women of the Shore "Rushed without chance or choice" toward death. What Hugh does not realize yet, as he feels regret for these ancestors and himself ("that he must watch them go"), is that he is involved in a community of life of which death is only a part. Then he observes his mother's simple act as she helps his younger sister down from the buggy back from church, watches his mother break off a spray of lilacs and speak softly to her daughter, listens to his grandmother sing American Civil War songs, and is astonished "to find that something in him, slight as a bird's breath, had stirred with laughter." The "reprieve" of the story's title is ironic, because this response to the strength of life's frailty involves more than a temporary respite from death's fearful claim. Hugh is shaped by a sense of himself as inheritor and ancestor both in this community of time and space, and years later he will attempt to pass such heritage on to Stan.

"People From Away 1917" is based on seventeen pages of the *Currie Head* manuscript in which the Curries are visited by former Shore inhabitants who moved to New England where they knew Hugh as a young man and still live themselves. The first two visitors, a man and his wife, the Frasers, chatter on about past experience with Hugh and Christine; listening to their exchange, Stan is described, rather blandly, as excited by this expanded world. Then two locals drop in, and Stan's sense of "newness" is heightened when he is included with all the men in a ride in the Fraser car. Finally, Brad Johnson (who was present when young Hugh found the swallow) arrives after a ten-year absence from the States. Stan learns of his father as a youth, as more than a farmer-fisherman, and "The continuity of time and circumstance began to form." He overhears an exchange between Brad and Aunt Christine, of Christine's sacrifice of their serious relationship when Hugh brought Stan back from Boston to raise him "among his own people." At the end of this section of *Currie Head* Stan is aware that his own life, like his father's, will reach beyond the Shore.

The important aspect of "People From Away" is the narrative frame provided by Stan Currie's looking back on this day of visitors, the clarity of his vision "lighted by an understanding and warm with love. And touched by one regret." All this has to do with detailed memories of a great deal of talk by Hugh and the Falts (brother and sister-in-law of Adam Falt, the mailman in *The Channel Shore*) about their shared past. Stan is much more than simply excited here by an expanded world:

> These had always seemed … like things that happened in a story finished, a book read. For the boyhood of Hugh … was far-off and unimaginable …. The tale was finished …. [But] what was coming to him now, felt rather than formed in thought, was that it was not a story, it was not finished. It was life going on and on ….

Then Brad Johnson arrives and talks to Stan about *his* boyhood on the Shore. Essentially Stan hears the same exchange between Brad and Aunt Christine as occurred in *Currie Head*; however, afterward his awareness is not that, like his father, he will eventually become one of the people from away, but that, like Hugh, he belongs to all the sacrifices on the Shore, all the movements of leaving and return, all the individual experience "implicit in the shape [pattern] of life." His one regret is that he never got the chance to let Brad Johnson know how much he too belonged.

The three stories that relate Bart Somers's twenty-year voyage away from and back to the Shore have their roots in "Sand 1907," a seemingly slight tale that nevertheless reveals the twistings and turnings of what is an unfinished story as far as plot is concerned, but the undeviating integrity of character and theme. Mel Somers, a forty-two-year-old bachelor lives on the beach, fishing when he wants to, willing to give up his own chores to help others with theirs, "not always a thing to respect." When his friend Cam Sinclair wants a mate for winter trawling, though, Mel does not think the meagre rewards are worth the effort and so declines. Cam asks him, "When're you going to walk that bridge-rail?" a reference to Mel's refusal years ago to try a balancing act with the other boys thirty feet above a river: "Well, what's the use of it?" Mel recalls a later time when another local did not think that he had much "sand" in him, meaning that in a tight spot Mel was likely to back off. The morning after his exchange with Cam, Mel watches his friend's dory on the cold Channel and the ice starting to form along the curve of the beach — open salt water freezing for the first time before his eyes. Anticipating that Cam will recklessly try to smash his way to Shore or walk it, Mel is warmly dressed and out the door with his nets in his hand as the fisherman slips from the dory and then hangs on to the edge of the ice "feet dangling over sand and gravel seven fathoms down." At the core of the situation, CB writes, "was Time." Mel has been the subject of tales of the past, frozen in a sense in time as the boy/man without sand, and this is potentially just another such tale for the telling. If he does not get Cam Sinclair out alive will the story of his failure become yet another example of Mel Somers backing off in a tight spot? CB does not answer this question until thirty-two years have passed on the Shore and another six stories intervene in the text before "The Sloop 1939."

In 1939 Bart Somers, third cousin of Mel, and who has not even heard of him, returns to the Shore that he left with his family at fourteen. In the collection of stories Bart already appeared in "The Road 1918," (out of "The Road to Town") where he began to grow up quickly through fetching the doctor for his injured father, and in "The Pattern of Surrender 1933," where as a New York newspaperman he became involved with the cool and wealthy woman who was to become his first wife. Bart does not know why he has come back or what he is looking for, but there are "small sharp images in the misty generalized recollection of [the past]" that haunt him. His father Lloyd, who left the Shore, came back, and left again, has been dead for a year, and for much of the story Bart seems to be repeating the comings and goings. When he discovers his family home has been replaced by a bungalow he feels "Surprise, in a context of emptiness," and although sharp images of the house appear, "They [seem] like things from a story half-remembered, not something known and touched." He meets the man who was his boyhood chum and gains a sense, through memory, of "The weaving of act and word" in human experience, but tells himself there is "nearly nothing" to gain for having come back so far. Yet something does pull him to action that is tied to the past, to working with his hands on a sloop he buys, and anticipating, again through memory, the lift and sway of the Channel where he and his father had tended herring nets. The weaving comes from action and words that by themselves are never enough, but which together have always been part, the main part, of the township of time. The words in this case, come from Prim Sinclair, daughter of Cam, whom Mel Somers did save from the icy water back in 1907. She rows out to Bart on the sloop and tells him the story of "sand" after he has complained to her that he should not have tried to come home again — the past is gone and the future is not here, Bart attempts to insist. But realizing that he is only talking to her in 1939 because of an action taken by the only other surviving Somers, Bart is opened to the future through the past: "This was the spoken beginning of thought, of the mind's opening toward a prospect just then surprised, new and engaging; a delicate excitement." Mel's act in a tight spot meant that Cam would live, and therefore Prim too, and that Somers's will again people the Shore. The weaving here is visibly part of the pattern of heritage — literally a life for lives; and in this Bart is truly Mel's descendant.

The final story but one in *The Township of Time* is "The Wind in the Juniper" that closes with John Forester's death in 1945 and with the end, apparently, of the Forester name on the Shore. But Colin and Lydia are much more than a name, and as CB says in his note on Shore genealogies at the back of the book: "One can only hope that Colin and Lydia, themselves perhaps a little shaken by the extent and variety of the thing they began, would consider this [partial chronicle of the heritage they handed down] reasonably fair and representative." If the suggestion here is that the fiction of the Shore has become real (as CB addresses his readers directly about the genealogies and apologizes for their incompleteness), then Hugh and Stan Currie also appear to be in their Forester ancestry distinct from Will and Charles Bruce. That this is finally so, that CB has laid to rest at this point the biographical identification with the Curries, however much their lives are similar to his own, is revealed in the last story of the book, "Schoolhouse Hill 1950".

Here a man named Jack Cameron, son of Will, and great-great grandson of the first Cameron on the Shore who died under a falling tree, opens up the old family farmhouse on a brief visit from "central Canada" one October. He has been back before, but never in the autumn has he been home since he was a boy, so there is a "newness of things forgotten and again remembered." Things like winter evenings with his father in the kitchen, listening to stories of the August gale of 1873 and of Boston, and memories of memories before his father's era. The reader is addressed directly here as well, and the words provided are enough because of the chronicle that has preceded them: "If you can forget conventional sentiment and your fear of it; your fear of disillusionment and that other more cynical convention that the past is dead, it can be a very rare thing. Old as time and as new as the moment's breath."

Jack talks with Angus Dunn, an old fisherman who, like Sandy Bruce with CB in Boylston in 1946, begins to talk of the history of the Shore.[20] Until he spoke with Sandy, CB had kept his distance from Port Shoreham and related experience beyond his father's generation — there is only brief mention of great-uncle James in the character of Rob Currie in *Currie Head*. Sandy's story of Lipsett's pasture where the first James was buried opened up extraordinary emotional and intellectual — creative — territory for CB that is perhaps best summarized by Jack Cameron when Angus Dunn takes him to the pasture where John Cameron (whom we never actually meet in the chronicle, but who provides, along with Primrose, the first child born in it — Richard McKee Cameron) is buried:

> This was discovery. This strange new thing in the heart of things at one time so familiar. The puzzlement I had felt, the elusive nagging, began to vanish in a light pulsing elation. I knew now what it was. It was the fact that the idea I had never quite accepted, the idea of my birthplace as a region backward and static and bounded in space and fixed in time was false. It was something quite different I had caught a glimpse of here. What I was seeing was continuity. The continuity of birth and death and venture.

CB wrote "Schoolhouse Hill" (or a version of it) before May 1950, because he sold it to the CBC for broadcast on Robert Weaver's "Canadian Short Stories" at that time.[21] It might be argued that then CB was simply creating another persona for himself and was molding the Shore out of Bruce family history, even if in the story the history stretches far beyond Will's day. However, seen in the light of the chronicle and placed where he is in the collection, Jack Cameron, it is clear, is not the voice of CB; rather by 1959 CB has become the voice behind *all* the voices (not only of Stan or of Jack).

Angus Dunn, looking back at the pioneers, says, "They didn't leave no writing." When the chronicle was published in 1959, CB had already stated similar words himself in his article for the IODE, written four years previously and called "The Township of Time." The radio script of "Schoolhouse Hill" is no longer extant, and therefore it is impossible to know whether CB was giving Angus Dunn new words for the chronicle that he had not uttered in the original version of the story, or old words, "completed and yet continuing," which had moved from art into life and back into art again. The fictions were gathered together under the same title as the factual article, but that article was definitely influenced by fictional explorations already completed or under way; this suggests a strong awareness on CB's part of how, as Malcolm Lowry said, "… life flowed into art: how art gives life a form and meaning and flows on into life, yet life has not stood still … how life transformed by art sought further meaning through art transformed by life …. "[22] Nowhere in CB's writing is this *flow* better articulated or more profoundly conveyed as having to do with the cycle of life and death through time and space than in the last lines of the chronicle:

> And I was touched by a gentle fancy. That oblong patch of cradle-hills [the graves of John Cameron and others] among the scattered spruce — it looked for a moment like something written there. Not runes on ancient stone, left for the speculation and conjecture of later learning. Not precise records in the stilted language of antiquarians, between the covers of books. But cramped lines in a scribbler, the slow labor of a childish hand, a signature in the earth.

By the end of October 1958 John Gray at Macmillan had the complete manuscript of the chronicle and had sent CB an advance against royalties of $150.00. Gray also sent a copy of the manuscript to a literary agent in New York, who within a month had sent back Harper Brothers' response. It was redolent of their reaction to his earlier prose: "Mr. Bruce writes well, with a strong touch of the poet. But I think he hasn't yet the skill to handle effectively a complex narrative with a large case [sic] of characters such as this."[23] However, undaunted, Macmillan provided CB with a further advance of $200.00 in January 1959 and brought out *The Township of Time* in the fall of that year. Critical response was, as usual with CB's work, mixed. The newspaper reviewers objected to the number of characters ("we have to use the family tree all the time"[24]) as did *Time* magazine: *"Township* suffers from Bruce's failure to humanize many of his laconic heroes ... almost as hard to separate as relatives in a 19th-century novel."[25] The term "nostalgic,"[26] not one of CB's favourites, was applied again. The Winnipeg *Tribune* felt that CB was now a "major talent in this country, if not internationally," but at the same time emphasized his regional importance;[27] another reviewer did not like the regional bias that seemed to suggest "that virtue lives on the Channel Shore and dies everywhere else."[28]

In-depth responses to the book were provided by Sally Creighton on CBC Radio's "Critically Speaking"[29] and by F.W. Watt in "Letters in Canada" in the *University of Toronto Quarterly*.[30] They are somewhat contradictory views. Creighton feels the shifting from character to character and from period to period "engenders the touch of irritation which is apt to be aroused by a volume of letters." This is an interesting analogy, but a limited one; like single letters in a volume of letters, each of the stories contributes to the whole text, but unlike letters each of the stories can stand on its own — there are no arcane references in individual tales, and above all there is no simple focus on subject matter isolated in time. Creighton accuses CB of only "good reporting" because readers do not see "behind the chosen details ... the whole .... " There is, apparently, no "pattern" or "final authority of vision" in what Creighton calls "the whirling kaleidescope of incident," despite the presence of "deeply known and loved material." Such remarks must be measured against Watt's view that indeed the "genealogies become more and more complex, and the threads connecting episode with episode, generation with generation, either tangle or break," but that "the essential vision remains, vivifying and giving great power and pregnancy to the life of the soil and sea":

> Like Bruce's poetry, the book catches the freshness of life waxing and the sadness of its waning, offering no intellectual pattern or justification of its cycle. If philosophy there be, it is only that of naturalism as Santayana describes it. The chief problem is one of perspective, to be distant enough to get a sense of the sadness of things, of the constant *flow* of youth and life into age and death, but to be close enough to share at least for the *moment* in the individual's happiness or grief.(my italics)

Watt grasps CB's intentions for the 'gap' structure of the chronicle — that what is left out is no less important than what is included — even if he cannot always approve of its results. There is a great deal of difference between a "whirling kaleidescope of incident," which suggests formlessness, and a spinning of threads that do not always join together successfully to form the perfect web. The "final authority of vision" that Creighton finds missing, Watt defines in terms of a purposeful absence of intellectual pattern; but the presence of a vision that may or may not include Santayanian naturalism cannot be denied and is perhaps best articulated by Fred Cogswell in his already-mentioned comments on *The Channel Shore*: "... acts of sympathy and understanding [exist], roots that creep through community life .... If roots are not sufficiently strong to justify optimism, they are at least enough to justify faith."[31]

The faith Cogswell refers to arises fom tangible acts that are rooted in the physical world of the Channel Shore, such things as the harrowed field and the objects in Richard McKee's loft that have been handed down through time. On the Channel Shore time is not an abstraction but an extension of that physical world, and both time and the world are knowable in terms of people and the material and *'mistical'* reality they pass on. Watt's reference to the "chief problem … of perspective" does contain a perhaps unconscious irony because the struggle of writer *and* reader to be "distant enough" and "close enough" is a reflection of part of the same struggle for the characters in the book. For CB such perspective, or lack of it, would be a problem only if thought and language in the chronicle were not rooted in the material world. This is not the case, however, and thus the struggle for perspective within the text and in reader-response to the text is an article of that faith that Cogswell emphasizes. What Watt fails to appreciate is that *the moment is the flow.*

XI

World Enough and Time

As early as 1952 when he had been General Superintendent of Canadian Press for seven years CB spoke of leaving the organization. When he wrote Gil Purcell that he had developed "parallel interests in other things"[1] he was not referring to another job, but to his creative writing — he was at the half-way point of what must be considered as his peak years as writer of poetry and fiction: 1945-59. He told Purcell that he was hoping to resign from CP by 1960. In fact the irony was that Canadian Press did not interfere with those "parallel interests" nearly as much as might be assumed because of its rather inflexible demands and CB's many responsibilities. When he wrote to a friend in 1958 that he hoped to leave CP within three years to "get out of my system the writing I want to get out," he also spoke of the effect on himself of his organizational and staff relations work: "... it's a thinking and figuring and 'feeling' job rather than a writing job. The result is that when I go home at night I am not 'written out' .... It's a paradox, but precisely because I don't write much in CP I *can* write in the other vein."[2] He was not so positive in what he had to say to fellow-artist Thomas Raddall two years later: "For the last few years, under the onset of the ills of middle age and the wear and tear of this peculiar business I'm in, I've been feeling increasingly dragged down and lifeless." He told Raddall that he wanted "to see what kind of deal I can make to get out of CP early in 1963" and not wait until the normal retirement age of sixty-five.[3]

Most of the time as General Superintendent CB was in the office, where Gillis Purcell reports that he was really an Assistant General Manager who hated administrative work but liked dealing with the staff (he considered, among other things, staff budget increases and made specific recommendations and decisions in regard to staff-management relations and individual positions within the organization).[4] Normally CB would not attend to the news desk, but, as has been said, if something major came over the wire he would advise the local bureau chief how to handle the news-gathering. Both Purcell and Jack Brayley attest to the admiration of CB by his colleagues. Brayley describes him as "understanding, quiet, and kind as a boss"; his opinions counted especially because of respect for him as a man and as a writer.[5] Canadian Press staffers certainly knew of the Captain Cluett story, but as late as March of 1959 they had a chance to see CB-as-reporter in action when he went to Newfoundland to cover the tenth anniversary of the province's entry into Confederation and the controversy and violence surrounding the strike of IWA members against the newspaper industry.[6] Those at CP were also very aware and proud of CB's accomplishments as a poet and fiction writer, despite his extreme reticence on the matter.

Although he did not have much opportunity to write within the news organization, CB played a strong role in the supervision of those who submitted copy. One of his basic tenets about journalistic prose came from his belief that "what's hard to say is hard to read."[7] In his desire for "clear and crisp copy" CB was always ready with advice on grammar and punctuation, the use of "synthetic" words ("reportage," for example), unrelated facts, unjustified or accidental implications, and hasty conclusions. He wrote to his London Bureau Chief about "the hyphenation of adjectival phrases compounded with adjectives"[8] and to the *Globe and Mail* criticizing its misuse of "that" and "which." Along with Gillis Purcell he founded *Copy Talk,* an internal CP newsletter that was essentially concerned with the proper use of language by staffers. An article written by CB in November 1948 on "Plain Writing (Know Your Subject, Pick the Central Fact, Translate Special Jargon, Trim Your Sentences)" was followed by over forty issues of *Copy Talk* during the next twenty-two years. CB was also responsible for the CP *Style Book,* which, according to Harry Bruce and others, is still a measuring stick for journalists and news organizations today.

CB's creative energies were enormous during his time as General Superintendent, as if he were driven into poetry, fiction, and radio drama in order to survive the "rat-race" of the news agency. While completing *The Channel Shore* and planning out the seven parts of *No Left-Handed Reaping Hook*, CB accepted an offer from the CBC to write a 45-minute script for the "Lives of the Poets" series, for which he would be paid $300.00. CB chose Andrew Marvell as his subject because he "possessed ... a capacity for tolerant (almost 'modern') thought which characterized some of the heirs of the Elizabethans," he criticized corruption and dissolution of court and government (refusing a place at the palace), and he defended the principle of the liberty of conscience.[9] More than these things perhaps CB sensed a personal affinity with Marvell. Not an autobiographical letter writer, Marvell did "make brief and affectionate reference to his father"; he was "a solitary" who liked his privacy and at the same time he had a "Friendship, enthusiasm for people," but he was "homesick" for Hull most of his life in the big city. Also, CB wrote, with Marvell life "went further than friendship, deeper than art. Behind these there existed a cool objective view of things. Almost a detachment from causes, contrasting with a contempt, or an admiration, or an enthusiasm, for men. And a touch of something else, a kind of higher fatalism, almost."[10] The script begins in November 1660 with Cromwell dead two years, James II on the throne, and Marvell member of Parliament for Kingston-upon-Hull. Great use is made of quotations from Marvell's letters and poems, the defence of Milton and Lovelace, and his powerful last pamphlet, "An Account of the growth of Popery and arbitrary government in England." CB also focussed on Marvell's look back from "busy and dangerous years ... to earlier times." The script was broadcast on the CBC's Trans-Canada Network in 1954.[11]

It is extraordinary, given his output and the quality of his best poems and fiction, that the reputation of the author of *The Mulgrave Road* and *The Channel Shore* was starting to fade in critical circles even as he reached his peak as a creative writer. If it is difficult to understand why some piece of his prose was not excerpted for Klinck and Watter's *Canadian Anthology* in 1955,

or why along with Layton he was excluded from Earle Birney's
Twentieth Century Canadian Poetry in 1953, there is no excuse
whatsoever for the failure to cite his fiction in the definitive
Literary History of Canada, first released in 1965.[12] While Desmond Pacey in his *Creative Writing in Canada* (1961) calls
attention to the "quiet contemplative dignity, an unspectacular
strength, a steady accumulation of exact and telling small
details" in CB's poetry (after rather smugly referring to him as
"a pleasant if not particularly forceful poet"), he merely notes
that in the mid-fifties CB "gave up poetry for fiction."[13] Ralph
Gustafson included "Eastern Shore" and "Biography" in his
Penguin Book of Canadian Verse in 1958, but it is difficult if not impossible to find CB in any new poetry anthology after that
date.[14]

All this must have been somewhat discouraging to the man
whose work had not only been widely published, but also greatly appreciated by a variety of Canadians, ranging from a
Saskatchewan farmer to students of literature and fellow writers
such as Dorothy Livesay, Al Purdy, and Thomas Raddall. It must
have played a part, along with those "ills of middle age" (increasing high blood pressure, chiefly), in CB's decision to leave
Canadian Press in 1963. In the previous year he had been offered
a post at the University of British Columbia "equivalent [to] a
full professor" with a generous salary and pension if he would
give courses to students in the Departments of English, Education, and Extension. The idea was that CB would provide
students with the benefits of his expertise as a poet, novelist, and
newspaperman. The offer came from Norman Mackenzie, an
old friend, who was about to retire as President of UBC. According to Agnes Bruce, CB considered Vancouver a "dead end" as
all the news went east from there, but what he actually wrote to
Mackenzie as he declined the offer with thanks is revealing:

> After thirty-five years of servitude to the clock and telephone
> am getting out of my present job with CP sometime in 1963 and
> hope to work at my own pace on some writing I want to do. The
> truth is I'm damn tired; and since most of my family now are self-
> supporting, this looks like the time to cut loose. There's an
> element of gamble in it, but I've built up some pension equity and
> won't starve.[15]

CB had told Thomas Raddall in 1960 that he was "fooling with a story based on personal relationships that will have to be issued under a pen name if it ever is …. It's utterly different in the main from anything I ever tried …. Haven't got very far with it, anyway."[16] That this "story" represented the beginnings of the manuscript to be called *The Drift of Light*, which would preoccupy CB during the last few years of his life, is indicated by a letter he sent to his London Bureau Chief in 1960. He asked Alan Harvey about the workings of the theatre in wartime London and something of "the flavour of the period" because "I am being nagged by a kind of idea for a novel that requires some war-time [London] atmosphere …."[17] A considerable amount of *The Drift of Light* manuscript is set in London between 1942-1945.

Retirement came on May 11, 1963, CB's fifty-seventh birthday. Along with many plaudits for his contribution to Canadian journalism, CB received a Fred Varley water colour at the dinner given in his honour; in return he presented the CP library with copies of two versions of the Bible, and copies of the Talmud and Koran. What he was giving up were two very important factors in his life — the profession that had governed his daily existence stretching through four decades, and at least $17,000 a year. Alan Bruce emphasizes how "very conscientious" his father was about his CP job,[18] and Harry Bruce writes that "It's his poetry and fiction that preserve his memory, but it was to Canadian Press … that he sold his days and sweat …. Six-day weeks at CP were routine for him, and often he reported to the office on Sundays as well."[19] What CB would have trouble doing without was a regimen of work that especially involved deadlines. The recognition of this, despite his plans for fiction writing, and the careful assessment of his pension equity must have been what led him to accept an offer in mid-1963 from Southam News to write a history of that organization.

Ross Munro, publisher of the Winnipeg *Tribune*, made mention of the "Southam project" at the retirement dinner in May 1963, but the earliest extant correspondence with a member of the company is a July 1963 letter from CB to St. Clair Balfour, the President and Managing Director of the Southam Company, in which he says, "After a couple of weeks concentration on a small part of The Southam Company's records, I believe an interesting story can be put together."[20] He then outlined a tentative format, indicating that he had given a great deal of time to the project almost as soon as he walked out CP's door for the last time as General Superintendent. By the fall of 1966 he had, working seven to eight hours (or more) a day on the book, produced a first-draft of 700 typewritten pages, "probably close to 200,000 words."[21] There was obviously little, if any, time for any other writing in his life during this period, and it was the spring of 1968 before *News and the Southams* actually appeared. CB was essentially under contract to the Southam Company as he had negotiated a $150.00 per week payment; more must have been provided, because in May 1967 St. Clair Balfour wrote to CB that he had been paid, thus far, "approximately $30,700."[22] The important point was that when CB had told Norman Smith, Raddall, and others of the writing he had in mind when he retired from CP, being "wrapped up in [the Southam project] for 3 1/2 years on a full-time basis"[23] was certainly not what he consciously intended.

As far as the book itself was concerned CB had two main aims. First he wanted to tell the corporation history — the factual record of dates and events, such as the takeover in 1877 of the Hamilton *Spectator* by a young printer named William Southam; the growth of the company's printing business in Toronto and Montreal in the last part of the 19th century and the first decade of the 20th century; the establishment of Southam Limited in 1904; the formation of the Southam Publishing Company Limited in 1927 as a holding company for six newspapers (the *Spectator*, the Ottawa *Citizen*, the Winnipeg *Tribune*, the Calgary *Herald*, the Edmonton *Journal*, and the Vancouver *Province*); open ownership via stocks in 1945; the issue of centralized power as the company continued to grow; and so on. Second, recognizing that there was a general reading public beyond those who were in the company and the Southam family and beyond the newspaper crowd in general, CB wanted "a finished book that will be more human than the usual corporation history, and will (incidentally) tell something of the story of Canada through the history of the newspapers concerned (stories they carried, editorial stands they took, etc.) and the personalities of the men who owned and ran them."[24] He indicated that the only way he knew to accomplish all this was "through proliferation of incident." For example, he did not think it enough to mention that one Edward Bancroft Whipple Morrison, who became commander of Canada's artillery in World War One as major-general, was at one time city editor of the *Spectator* and later edited the *Citizen* from 1897-1913. Therefore, we learn that Morrison — whose nickname was "Dinky" — set up Sunday afternoon classes for young reporters in which he spoke on such matters as how to get a story, how to write about it, and the ethics of journalism. He once told a reporter who insisted on using the royal 'we' in his copy, "There are only two people in this business entitled to use 'we' — an editorial writer and a man with a tapeworm."[25] We also learn of Morrison's service as a lieutenant in the Boer War and his letters about the war sent to the *Citizen*, one of which "raised an international furore" when it was severely edited by the New York *Sun* and the Manchester *Guardian* and used as an anti-war missive.

CB follows strikes, political crises, and natural disasters such as the Winnipeg flood in 1950 through editorials and stories in the various newspapers; he discusses political leanings on editorial pages and competition among city dailies. He does all this with a view to presenting history as objectively as possible. His personal opinion of individuals is expressed only in the sense that he believes their professional lives are illuminated by things they did or said outside the daily routine and the business world. Thus Harry Southam's conversion to Christian Science in 1907-08 and his subsequent influence on his older brother Wilson resulted in journalistic "idealism" in the *Citizen*. The brothers let their staff know they wanted *"reliability"* and *"absolute fairness"* in every story, meaning that the "'other side' of every story should *invariably* be given."[26] However, Harry and Wilson both became teetotallers, and the *Citizen* "campaigned against liquor traffic." CB comments simply that "This went considerably further than care in handling news,"[27] and leaves moral response entirely up to his readers. Both Jack

Brayley and Gillis Purcell emphasize that such personal reticence was entirely in keeping with the Canadian Press tradition that reporters and editors did not attempt to shape stories through their subjective interpretation of facts.

CB reveals no political prejudice of his own in *News and the Southams*, but reports that "Neither of the two aspects of independence asserted by Southam newspapers [in the 1960s] — local editorial autonomy and freedom from party ties — precludes tradition."[28] As governments came and went, federally and provincially, around the various papers "certain political traditions gathered: the *Spectator*, Conservative from the first; the *Citizen*, radical and variable but in modern times consistently Liberal at election time; the *Tribune*, the *Journal*, the *Herald*, and the *Province*, generally conservative but with varying degrees of emphasis and a habit of knocking or commending according to circumstance."[29] Perhaps the most evident example of CB's objective commentary on the Canadian political scene is his chapter "The Urgent West" in which he deals with William Aberhart's rise to power in Alberta as Social Credit leader and then as premier in 1935. On the way up Aberhart attacked the *Herald* as a tool of big business and once elected regarded it, the *Journal*, and any other "dissenting" paper, as "mad dogs in our midst." CB obviously believed in a press free from political control of the news and felt that the Southam chain, whatever its internal leanings, did not provide a predictable voice of either government or opposition policies throughout its history. Aberhart's insistence that Social Credit was "an economic movement from God himself"[30] and that newspapers must therefore serve as the voice of the Social Credit god, or not at all, must have been anathema to CB, but he compiles the details of Aberhart's attempts to control the press in a dispassionate manner. Events surrounding the introduction in September 1937 of the "Act to Ensure the Publication of Accurate News and Information" are made clear through the words and actions of government officials and newspaper stories and editorials. CB indicates that the press reaction was vindicated by the March 1938 decision of the Supreme Court of Canada that ruled the substance of the Act beyond provincial powers and by the awarding of a Pulitzer Prize by Columbia University to the *Journal* "'for its leadership in defense of the freedom of the press in the province of Alberta.'"[31] These are presented as facts, and no special pleading on CB's part surrounds them.

In the end there was not much cutting of material in the manuscript by either CB or Macmillan. The published version of *News and the Southams* runs over 400 pages (at least 185,000 words). CB had read countless editions of old newspapers, assessed a tremendous amount of material in the company archives and elsewhere, interviewed many people, and corresponded with a great many more (well over a hundred individuals, with numerous letters to and from more than a few of them — thirty-six exchanges with St. Clair Balfour alone). The total effort, including, of course, the writing, was prodigious. When it was all over CB told Balfour, "What kept me reasonably happy was that I got fascinated. The whole thing is dullish in spots because of what I felt I had to go in [sic] for the record, but I am hopeful there are enough more colorful areas to rouse a bit of interest — at least among the newspaper crowd."[32] But he told his wife Agnes, "… if I were you I wouldn't bother reading it,"[33] and he informed Thomas Raddall that his efforts to reduce the size of the manuscript were "Almost as hard as editing it in the first place."[34]

On July 17, 1968, the Southam Company Board of Directors passed a motion of "appreciation of the high quality of research and writing" by CB. Reviewer response in Southam and other newspapers was enthusiastic. The Calgary *Herald* said the book was "no dry-as-dust chronicle …. [but] abounds in memorable sketches and incidents";[35] the Edmonton *Journal* and the Hamilton *Spectator* followed suit with huge spreads of their own. If the Southam-influenced (minority shares) London *Free Press* lauded CB's objectivity, the independent Ottawa *Journal*'s commentator wrote the following:

> … as newspaper groups are coming in for some criticism these days, it is interesting that Bruce refrains altogether from comment as to whether groups are good things or bad …. But … the nature of his narration lets us assume he feels the root question is not whether a paper is in a group or in enviable isolation, but whether

it is a good newspaper, native to its community in thought, conduct, and personality.[36]

There were dissenting voices, chiefly from individuals who objected to aspects of CB's descriptions of their characters and actions — one former Southam bureau chief in London during World War Two, and later editor of the *Citizen*, did not like being called "a crusty little correspondent" who was at times "cranky" and "opinionated," but those who had known him backed up CB's assessment.[37]

No appropriate comparison can be made between *News and the Southams* and CB's prose fiction. Obviously his interest in individual behaviour within a community on the Channel Shore attracted him to the story of the five surviving Southam brothers (the sixth and youngest died in World War One) within their corporate empire and to the host of minor but vital characters who worked for or were in some way affected by that giant business community. The companionship through time of the Southam family is examined, but CB's natural reliance on anecdote and incident, as far as elucidation of personalities was concerned, emphasized his distance from the 'inner' men. He re-created events first and character second, because the story of the Southams is essentially a public one that CB told, not from *inside* where he felt comfortable with accent, scene, and atmosphere, but from an unusual combination (for him) of inside-outside: CB knew the newspaper profession well — the terms, the language, the relationship between management and staff, the way in which news was gathered and reported — but he had never worked for the Southams, so much of his source material lay in archives and in the selective memories of men who were not his fictional characters. By sticking to his Canadian Press code of being "factual and objective" so that while one's own "personality may show in turn of phrase or crispness of style ... the copy must be 'straight down the line,'"[38] in other words, by not being able to combine authenticity with both hearsay history and creative insight into human behaviour, CB found his vision of time and place was very much restricted. *News and the Southams* certainly deserves its high place as an accurate and accessible account of a significant part of the history of the press in this country. However, as a testimony to what CB could do with language when he had the freedom and the inspiration to deal with what truly mattered to him — mattered to his heart and soul, as ultimately his professional life did not — the book is incidental.

What was not incidental was the effort and time required to produce *News and the Southams*. When his obligations to Southam Press Limited were finally over CB was a tired man. He seemed to realize that he should not again tie himself down to contracts and deadline writing. In late 1966 he had been offered a job for a year in Ottawa as protocol officer for forty to fifty heads-of-state visits.[39] Despite the considerable salary involved, he declined. When Eric Dennis, Vice-President of the Parliamentary Press Gallery, wrote in June 1967, asking CB to prepare "an appropriate history of the Gallery to help mark the Canadian Centennial," CB replied that he was just finishing with the Southam book and wanted "to get back to some personal writing this summer and fall."[40] However, he did tell Dennis what it would take as far as money was concerned for him to write the 70,000-90,000-word book — $7,000 plus expenses — and if Dennis had not replied that the Gallery could not afford such costs, CB might have been locked into such a project. At the same time he apparently turned down the opportunity to be a Visiting Lecturer at Brandon University; the Alumni Association there was inviting to the campus "prominent men in various fields for the purpose of lecture and discussion with our students and at least one public lecture." CB replied that he was "a little puzzled" as to the kind of contribution he could make: "Any English literature student could stump me on modern poetry .... Perhaps I could work in something somewhere on my favourite obsession: plain talking and clear writing."[41] There is no record of any further negotiations.

In February 1966, while he was in the midst of condensing his Southam manuscript, he indicated that while he might not have the time to work on any other large project (or even small creative ones, as there are no poems or short stories extant between mid-1957 and 1968), he did want to keep his hand in at journalism. Interestingly enough, he wanted to write about facts and history, as if he could not move too far beyond the shadow of the Southam material. He suggested to Ross Munro, publisher of the weekly magazine *The Canadian*, that in the weeks leading up to the Centennial year of 1967 the magazine "might run a feature ... a series of brief pieces that would be centered on specific years [in Canadian history], within the memory of readers," tentatively titled "The Memorable Years."[42] He suggested, for example, 1926 with its customs scandal and the constitutional-issue election; 1928, the great Olympic year (combined with 1929 when the North began to be opened up by plane); 1932 with the Depression unfolding, the organization of the CCF, the Mad Trapper; 1935 when King defeated Bennett and Social Credit rose up in Alberta; and other years. Munro agreed that the series would be worthwhile, and CB ended up writing copy for at least five different years (1919, 1923, 1929, 1932, and 1935). In a relatively minor way that nevertheless reflected aspects of his Southam effort, CB paid an emotional price for his involvement with this series. In a letter to the editor of *The Canadian* he objected strongly to the "butchering" of his first piece on 1919. A seventy-word paragraph had been completely removed in addition to other changes made. CB stated that if his other copy (for the remaining years) was "to be hacked as extensively ... I want my name removed." It could not have done his high blood pressure any good to have to write the editor, "*The Canadian*... has broken a record. This is the first time in forty years in the business I have complained of anything that happened to my copy between the typewriter and the printed page."[43] Less traumatic involvements with journalism included his serving as advisor for the Toronto *Telegram Style Book* in 1969 (that, unfortunately, did not help prevent this newspaper's demise in the following year), covering the Special Senate Committee on Mass Media (chaired by Senator Keith Davey) in December 1969 for Southam Press, and judging, with others, the National Newspaper Awards as late as 1970.

His resignation from Canadian Press was to get out from under a daily grind; the Southam book occupied him for almost four years on "a full-time basis," and after that it was obvious that CB was not especially suited to a life dedicated wholly to creative writing. Ironically, as he himself said, he had been able to write his poetry and fiction because, as demanding as CP work was, it was not primarily a writing job; however, something of the routine, the slog work at the news agency, must have helped to carry CB through the drafts of *The Channel Shore* and to lie down night after night on the couch after a hard day at the office to work on the manuscript. Similarly, the inspiration behind his poetry must have, at least in part, been a mental, emotional, and spiritual reaction to the "rat-race" that Port Shoreham experience never was. When he was actually writing the Southam book and revising it, he was not capable of developing that "story based on personal relationships" that he had mentioned to Thomas Raddall and another friend in 1960. Not until late 1966 and early 1967 does his correspondence indicate that he is again thinking about fiction, but he does not seem to have begun to write his final, full-length prose work until late 1969 or early the next year. As far as his poetry was concerned, CB had stopped writing poems for publication; he seemed content to organize the best of what he had written for a selected poems volume and to review his own poetic history in an accompanying essay, "The Back of the Book."

In February 1968 CB wrote John Gray at Macmillan that he was working on a long essay that he hoped to put "in the back of a book entitled simply verse [sic], the front of which would be devoted to a rerun of most of the stuff from *The Mulgrave Road* (a couple a bit revised, and a dozen or so pieces written since, which constitute all that I think is worth preserving in the *front* of a book). Probably about 90 manuscript pages only, front plus back."[44] Gray replied that while the project sounded attractive "The Back of the Book" as a selling title did not. In his essay CB seemed to be happy as he considered his early verse from Port Shoreham days, took himself to task for his early pantheism, recalled the Song Fishermen with great fondness, and spoke sometimes ironically but always perceptively of his poetic inspirations and results: "The back of the book would be open, I guess, to criticisms that it is either an expression of egotism or an unnecessary exposure of juvenile scribblings. So what the hell? I'm having some fun with it."[45] If CB is somewhat defensive here, perhaps it is because he sensed that perceptions of poetry in Canada had passed him by.

Over the next year or so CB chose forty-three poems for the proposed volume, which, poems and essays together, would be called *Living and Recall*. The manuscript, which he sent to Macmillan on May 25, 1969, contained every poem from *The Mulgrave Road*, with the exception of "Note for a Textbook"; there were also "An Ear to the Ground" from *Grey Ship Moving* and fifteen "new" poems written between 1951 and 1956. CB does quote in full in "The Back of the Book" (the essay accompanying the poems) those earlier poems that might be considered to be among his best — "Tomorrow's Tide" and "Lunenburg" from *Tomorrow's Tide*, and "Immediates," "Alternative," and "Return and Introduction" from *Grey Ship Moving*. What is disappointing about the essay, at least as it seemed to have been presented to Macmillan, is that it peters out with very brief references to his best poetry of the late 1940s and the first half of the 1950s. CB offers several fine comments on this verse and then seems content to let the poems in the front of the book stand or fall on their own:

> ... everything in *The Mulgrave Road* [and presumably later poems] ... grew from a sense unconsciously developed that Poetry (for me) is the art of striking sparks from the common and usual, the discovery of wonder and strangeness in the normal and the skill to pass the news along. The flying sparks have often seemed to be happy accidents that occurred in the midst of infinite labor with ideas, dreams, and words, the trick being to work like hell and let yourself be accident-prone."[46]

Two months after receiving the manuscript John Gray wrote to CB that Macmillan could not publish it. His remarks are a sad comment on the lack of a sense of tradition in the publishing market-place. The remarks of Gray also emphasize, in an unconsciously ironic way, CB's poetic silence, which was over a decade long:

> I am sorry to tell you that the verdict of readers of *Living and Recall* is that it is attractive material but in the world of today's poetry would probably pass unnoticed. However, you will be interested and, I hope, cheered to know that one reader, who is a

modern poet of some standing, found the recent poems the most interesting and impressive of all, which is a great tribute at this stage of your career.[47]

CB took the direct implication that while he was a poet he was not a *modern* one in a way that emphasized clearly that his poetic fires had gone out, if not his thoughts about poetry:

> I can't say I am particularly surprised at the decision on *Living and Recall*. I am not naive enough to feel that any reader who regards a particular fashion (present or past) in poetry as the last word would have much feeling for verse written within a tradition and a discipline. Personally, as a reader, I am not much conscious of fashion as long as the stuff moves …. I rather doubt that I'll be writing any more verse, as what energies I have left now are spent in other directions.[48]

This is fairly mild stuff from one who has been told that he is a poetic anachronism. We look in vain for a vibrant and lasting riposte like "Immediates."

Some of the encouragement for those "other directions" came from a young New Brunswick poet and teacher, Robert Cockburn. In July 1967 he had sent CB some of his poems, and CB did offer various suggestions for improvement, but more important was the praise Cockburn gave to CB's fiction. He told CB that *The Channel Shore* "puts Ernest Buckler to shame …. But I feel that *The Township of Time*, in its own way, is even more of a success."[49] Their correspondence continued over the next four years, with Cockburn telling CB that his students at UNB were very interested in *The Channel Shore* and CB responding to Cockburn's book on the novels of Hugh MacLennan (based on his M.A. thesis) in a way that suggested he was tackling some new subject matter of his own: "MacLennan's inability to write realistically about physical love stems, I guess, from — well, inexperience isn't quite the word I'm after; perhaps a lack of *deeply felt* experience in the physical sense. Even at that, I think I prefer his way of going about things to some of pseudo realism that gets perpetrated."[50] He went on in the same letter to criticize Margaret Laurence for her euphemistic use of the word "sex" to indicate "hardened penis" and "crotch" in *The Fire-Dwellers*; he was not, he said, advocating the use of "four-letter equivalents,"

but he did not like the twisting of words. In March 1971 he told
Cockburn about his own novel-in-progress: "... I'm not slug-
ging at it overly hard, and will probably put in another year or
so on it before I see the end down on paper (It's clear enough in
my mind)."[51] He also mentioned *Living and Recall*, but called it
"a collection that is outdated in form at least."[52]

In these exchanges with Cockburn CB does not refer to any
new poems of his own because there do not appear to have been
any, with the exception of the unfinished "The Explorer." Here
CB, who had never liked to sing against war, seems to be writing about the Vietnam conflict: "Yes/Beyond the towers, the
pavement, the dialled eye of computers/Beyond the flame in
the village, beyond/the screams at the consulate war and death
in the rice [fields]/There are outlying lands in the kingdom." As
he had almost forty years previously in "Tomorrow's Tide," CB
placed against destruction and exploitation the territory of earth
and sea and heritage that he still knew best: "The field. Timothy.
Stubble. Rockpile rimmed with ragwort and sheep
laurel/ridged and stiff to the plow where the horsetrack
ran/before the road./And in the shop/strung on nails and
strapless over the work bench/rusted stirrups." There was too
"the bay marching" and the gull crying "from the crest of the
windwave."[53]

It was his novel, however, that concerned him, and in his May
1969 application for a Canada Council Grant CB revealed that
he was well along in the planning stage: "It will have as background theme the influence of city living on a young man born
and brought up in the country a generation or more ago. The
localities concerned are a farm in Nova Scotia in the 1920s, Toronto in the 1930s, wartime England, and Toronto just after the war."
He stated that he was "already doing some preliminary work
on this and see it as probably a two-year job."[54] It is ironic that
CB, who had never received any financial support (beyond
meagre royalties and the occasional prize) for his work as an artist should finally apply in the 1969-70 financial year when
apparently the Awards Competition of the Canada Council was
suspended "owing to austerity measures."[55] Two years later,
using Gillis Purcell and John Gray as references, and enclosing

fifty pages of his novel-in-progress (though the Council would have been happy with a copy of the Southam book), CB applied for a short-term grant and in July 1971 received $1536.00. In a progress report to the Council written in September of that year CB stated that he had "spent most of August in the Provincial Archives" of Nova Scotia and in the eastern part of the province. He planned to visit New York during the winter and had earlier indicated that he wanted to get over to the United Kingdom "early next spring" (that is, 1972). He felt that the novel "should be finished around mid-1972 or possibly a bit later."[56]

CB had been slowed considerably by health problems. In the late summer of 1970 he had some "prostatic repair work" that subsequently resulted in the wonderfully euphemistic but not particularly pleasant "stress incontinence" (or "seepage in motion," as CB called it). Then in the summer of 1971 he underwent six days of testing that involved "cardiograms, skull films, encephalogram, [and] blood tests."[57] According to his son Alan, CB's left ventricle or auricle was not functioning properly, and he had been "in quite poor health" since 1962. In the last year of his life his weakening condition was very obvious.[58] Harold MacIntosh reports seeing CB in that last summer in Port Shoreham and felt that "he must have had a little stroke then, because his face was slightly sideways."[59]

Although his strength was ebbing and he wrote to a friend early in 1971 that he was working on a novel "on and off (mostly off)," CB did complete a draft of *The Drift of Light* that is 313 manuscript pages in length. While it is obviously a work that he planned to revise considerably, the novel as it stands does provide clear evidence of CB's greatest abilities as a writer of fiction and indicates as well that his best writing lay far in the past. Indeed, it was his abilities that limited him.

XII

Another Shore

Part One of *The Drift of Light*[1] is set in a place called the Devon Shore in eastern Nova Scotia, with not the Channel but "the Reach" as its local body of ocean. Young Chris Harris and his family live about a mile and a half from the town of Wynefield, inland at a place called Foxberry Hill. With Chris about to move into town to begin Grade 11 at the Academy there and planning to return to his father's farm every other weekend, CB's reliance on his own life is suggested early on. But CB is not writing about The Head or about some facsimile of the Bruces. The first-person narration does not focus on the Harris family and Chris's home, but rather on the family of his close boyhood friend Cav Ackerman, and particularly on the father, Harley.

It is to the Ackerman house that Chris goes more often than not every other Sunday. Vignettes are provided (unfortunately, nearly entirely in descriptive terms as they were in *Currie Head*) to emphasize the special relationship between Chris and Cav — they sail and sled together and share a "bit of freak geography," an absolutely flat acre of land at the bottom of a steep, three-sided slope, called "the hollah field." Harley Ackerman is meant to be bigger than life, a farmer-fisherman who is stronger, wiser, and more independent than his fellow-men. CB certainly intended to provide more substance to the legend, because what Harley comes to represent for Chris after he has left the Devon Shore resides too much in a memory that is kept apart from the reader. There is one vivid incident in which Harley picks up a 196-pound flour barrel "without clumsiness and without strain" and puts it down an inch or so from the toes of a young storekeeper who has questioned his integrity, but this is not enough.

The weak link in the Ackerman chain is the recalcitrant older son, Garnet, who skips bail after a rum-running charge and is eventually killed during an attempted bank robbery. Despite only a brief appearance together in the novel's opening section, Harley and Garnet are supposed to have something profound in their father-son connection, because 300 pages later CB has another character recall Garnet's death-bed words to his father, and the symbolism of the family reunited is meant to be paramount. Garnet's pained effort to say "Hi — Harley" should resound, for the reader, through thirty-five years of Chris Harris's life and memory of the Ackermans, but does not.

What do stand out are CB's brief portraits of Wynefield residents and his creation of that fictional town that for the reader as well as Chris is "full of color and life, a glimpse of tomorrow and a sharpened and heightened present." "Mostly," as always in the best CB fiction, "it came back to people" who keep the town alive although the days of sail are over and the railroad has never come. If he was drawing on his own life, CB was certainly not dependent on it in the portrait of Wynefield, for he had written long ago to Thomas Raddall that Guysborough "has a certain decadence, slightly Faulknerish, enhanced by the fact that no one who lives there sees this. That atmosphere is quite different from that of the surrounding country, which I think is alive, essentially vital."[2] Present, too, are evocative images in which something of life's *being* is contained in simple, everyday experience: "… the headlights [of the car] bringing up first one stretch of road and then another, from turn to turn through the woods of night … a dreamlike fascination, the feel of the old car's throbbing rattle over packed dirt and gravel, and through the massed darkness, the drift of light."

Meanwhile, characters drift apart without any sense of inevitability provided by CB. Cav Ackerman goes west on the harvest excursion after failing grade 11, but even after the emphasis on the deep quality of his friendship with Chris, CB is either unwilling or unable to suggest an eventual melding of distinct life patterns; indeed Chris and Cav never meet again, although the reader certainly believes they should, and although Chris's focal point on the Devon Shore will always be the Ackerman family. It is, throughout the rest of the manuscript, as if CB wants to emphasize his old theme of companionship through time, but wants to avoid the obvious — the inevitable reunion of the older and wiser chums (like the reunion of Stan Currie and Dan Graham in *Currie Head*). The tension between plot and theme ceases to be creative as Cav's name is brought up again and again as a talisman (along with that of Harley) by Chris, a symbol increasingly without substance and, finally, a word only. CB was normally too good a writer to let such things stand in a revision, but there is no way of knowing whether he had the energy and vision left to lift the Devon Shore experience to its intended place at the heart of narrative perceptions in his novel. Neither does he successfully present such narrative perceptions themselves, because the third-person intrudes more than once, and awkwardly, in the midst of Chris's articulations in the first section, then takes over completely until the last three pages of the manuscript.

CB's attention to Stan Currie's years at Royal University does not amount to half a dozen pages in *Currie Head*. Despite the autobiographical nature of the novel, it was as if sixteen years away from Mount Allison was not enough for CB even to select from his experiences there and present them in terms of Stan. But after four decades there were not the same hesitations, and Chris Harris's time at Marshlands Academy in the small New Brunswick town of Carmanville is based heavily on CB's own college days. Unlike Stan Currie, Chris is an aspiring writer, so his contributions to the campus newspaper, *The Caravan*, are emphasized. Unfortunately, CB handles awkwardly the integration of fact and fiction: lines are quoted verbatim from his own *Argosy* pieces "October" and "The Nature of Gayety" in order to make Chris's creative struggles *real*, but they sit amidst the narration of his thoughts and feelings and the more distanced commentary on his talent as a writer like fragmented and unleavened lumps of undergraduate prose. There is no imaginative portrait of Chris Harris as budding artist, but rather a curious clash between life and art that CB hardly intended and was not prepared to explain.

   Chris's contributions to the paper (which also include essays on Carman, Pickthall, and Brooke, not surprisingly), while they gain him a reputation on campus, appear to be a recipe for future failure. After college he spends much of his adult life trying to write fiction, or worrying about his not possessing the gift to create convincing plot and character; however, there is no satisfying explanation as to why this undergraduate prodigy — who becomes in his senior year editor of the *Caravan*, and who is contacted before that (much as CB was contacted by Andrew Merkel) by a journalist intrigued by his writing, and is subsequently hired by a Halifax newspaper to report on campus activities — fails to live up to his potential. The question as to why he fails to live up to CB's potential might be considered irrelevant, because, after all, CB makes it clear in the first part of the novel that the story of Wynefield and the Ackermans is not based on his own early days. What shows, however, in *The Drift of Light*, is that CB, having said all he could say about the Channel Shore territory, could not construct another commensurate fictional region, nor even sustain a fiction without falling back on what he had seemingly laid to rest over twenty years previously — his own history. The clash between his own art and life is evident because there is really no place for Wynefield and the Ackermans in the Marshlands section of the novel; indeed CB has trouble reasserting the thematic influence of the Devon Shore through the last three-quarters of his story. It is as if CB is split: one part of him is still concerned with the pervasive influence of rural heritage, while the other wants to write of the here-and-now heat of personal relationships in a larger world shaped by economic and political forces.

   Chris has a romance in his last year at Marshlands with a gifted young musician who is "One more gleaming thread in the drift of light" as they hover in balance between where they have come from and where they are going; suddenly, Chris is snapped up by *Business News*, a Toronto-based trade journal, and into a world of passion, ideas, and eventually war. The past, in the form of the Ackermans and brief visits home by Chris, is unintentionally fragmented and interruptive for the reader, though CB intends the past to jar the Chris Harris whose present is spiritually hollow while filled with intellectual exchanges and sexual encounters. Thus we are meant to focus on the Ackermans and Chris's own family, who are both summarized in a paragraph that also provides us with the information that people in 1928 were reading Huxley's *Point Counterpoint* and Callaghan's *Strange Fugitive*, that there were signs of a serious market slump, and that the Canadian North, for better or worse, was being opened up. We are meant to remember where Chris has come from as he moves in a few pages from the bed of a solid, older editor at his publishing house into the arms of the young, beautiful, wealthy, and artistically-talented Stephanie Riggs.

Stephanie is an interesting character because she can write and successfully sells her stories to such eminent magazines as *Harper's*, but she remains curiously removed from life, not living it as much as observing it from verbalized distances. It is obvious that CB places her in the "words are never enough" school of creative writing, in the sense that all Stephanie has are words. When her short story — which we learn nothing about directly — is accepted by *Harper's*, CB mentions virtually on the same manuscript page, in a summary of events in January 1931, the death of a Canadian liquor-runner at the hands of the U.S. Coast Guard in lower New York Bay. It is a comforting reminder to himself, and a stronger sign to those readers who recall his Captain Cluett article, that quality writing comes from some deep connection between author and subject matter.

To emphasize both Stephanie's creative talents and inadequacies CB has her write a story based entirely on one told to her by Chris's father when she meets him on the Devon Shore after she and Chris are married. Stephanie has a wonderful ear for dialogue, but her chief concern is "for not going further than she could help into matters beyond her own experience." There is no connection between the authentic detail of the story and the artist's vision, because Stephanie has no vision, no desire to convey felt experience or to deal with themes that carry her readers beyond the present contained by her impersonal use of language. Small wonder, then, that she does not want children, for whom words are an extension of an immersion in life that is

not self-conscious and who suggest a living and breathing balance between yesterday, today, and tomorrow. CB parodies the kind of writing that could be done about the Devon Shore when Stephanie sees Chris's heritage purely in literary terms: "'That Ackerman story …. Look what Faulkner's doing with his piece of Mississippi' …. Her idea was the development of a kind of saga that would show forth the characteristics of a region, a people, wherever they were. Timothy or cotton, oats or cane … rum-runners from St. Pierre instead of corn-liquor stills in the hills." CB's point is well-made only because we know the ways in which his heritage contributes to *The Channel Shore* and *The Township of Time*; the problem in *The Drift of Light* is that the Ackermans, after page forty-eight in the manuscript, are known to the reader only in literary terms, that is, as too-obvious symbols of a way of life not presented through dialogue and action, but through insistent statements, issued by the author, that such a way of life matters.

A tremendous amount of insistent statement also surrounds this portrait of Stephanie as young artist — talk about the relationship between literature and war, for example, as Chris wonders about the relevance of Rupert Brooke's idealism, the humanity of Wilfred Owen, and the bitterness of Siegfried Sassoon, or, earlier, the rise of fascism — so that when a striking, original image appears (for example, "the bombed group of Ethiopians who seemed to Benito Mussolini like flowers bursting into bloom") it is quickly lost in the shuffle. Lost along with the apparent importance of Chris's 1939 visit to the Devon Shore when he (so briefly on the written page) feels "the thrust of a personal urge, not to get away from these haunted fields, this strange familiar house, but to reach the surroundings he now knew as part of him …. " If Chris feels that the boy he once was is "a stranger" to him, the reader certainly and ironically understands, and if he feels "the blow of time" because he is so divorced from his heritage by the intervening years and experience, the reader, unfortunately, is similarly removed.

Stephanie finally writes a novel about an artist who paints his native western Canada while living in Rosedale in Toronto with a wife whose wealth and social aspirations slowly erode his artistic independence and integrity. CB is caught in the difficult situation of having to convince us that as good as Stephanie is she is ultimately no good at all. Chris has "Respect for the imagination that has conceived this story and the persistence that had brought it forth, had faced the drudgery of shaping sounds and images and conversations into the semblance of life." We are told that Chris feels Stephanie's characters are "more than merely believable. They lived," and that is what, chiefly, his respect is based on. CB attempts to gain *his* readers' respect for Stephanie as writer by quoting extensive passages from her novel, *Alice in Rosedale*. Unfortunately, her world — especially "the social habits of the particular crowd who came to life in her book" — was never CB's world, and this shows in the way he writes Stephanie's writing.

Much earlier in Chris's life, well before he meets Stephanie, his boss at *Business News* describes his dream of a quality Canadian magazine "produced and edited and partly written here in Canada but not so goddamn consciously trying to be Canadian." This man has in mind something along the lines of *Harper's* or *The Atlantic Monthly* and without stories in which "characters called J. Gaston Royce and Julian Thane [go] around saying things like 'it's utter madness' and 'to be sure.'" Despite this strong case made for *Northern View*, the characters and dialogue that CB presents from Stephanie's novel seem as contrived and artificial most of the time as Royce and Thane and their words, and as if they were part of a soap opera:

> Alice tried mockery: "Why sister, *dear*...."
> "Sister dear, hell. I just dropped in to tell you. Don't make yourself obvious any more. It's no use, no use at all, you know, Al."
> "Now what would that be, Jean dear, that's no use?"
> "I don't need to tell you, but I will. No use thinking you're going to mark up Gene Hammond as another notch on your gunbutt. He's not interested. Only embarrassed. You know that now, and I'm letting you know that I know. That make you feel better?"
> Alice's right hand closed on the slim polished mahogany of a curved chair back ....

This kind of fiction weakens considerably CB's important thematic emphasis through Stephanie that art cannot be of any quality if it results from mere observation of life and/or life is manipulated by the writer "to *make* material." Running through Stephanie's novel are scenes and interactions between characters that Chris recalls as having been possibly arranged by her in their life together. He not only senses that her art is craft only, soul-less, without redemptive qualities; there are no roots in her life experience or art that are strong enough to justify optimism or faith in anything at all.

Stephanie leaves Chris and he goes to wartime London for two years as business correspondent on the economies of Allied countries; there, for the first time in years, spurred on by Stephanie's creative limitations, he tries to write about the estrangement between himself and his own roots, and especially about the Ackermans. Once again, our experience of the family is not commensurate with the words about them, words that, it is increasingly obvious, will lead one day to Chris's writing his own novel:

> I could never think of them without a sense of loss, of lighthearted life leached away by grief, by sickness and violence and death. Even in later years as more and more the boy I was became a stranger and as looking back from different points in life the man I came to be began to seem a succession of chance acquaintances outside this present self, I was never to lose the knowledge that for them too (these almost strangers who were, or had been, me) and despite the sense of personal destiny that drives out recognition of a universal fate, the Ackermans and the blight that touched them had been an image of the iron truth of life.

CB is on familiar ground here: the first six lines or so of this passage (with the removal of "grief" and "violence") could belong to John Forester in "The Wind in the Juniper" thinking of Mam and the Captain. Chris is carried back into the past not, like John, by his own dying, but through war-death and his mother's demise. Yet when Henry Harris writes his son from the Devon Shore, telling him of life and of his feelings for his very ill wife, CB has Chris, without any intended irony, think "How little, really, he knew about [his father]." Despite a page of memories on Chris's part, the reader does not know Henry Harris *at all* (the focus on the past, in its fragmented way, has always been centered on the Ackermans).

Curiously enough, yet perhaps appropriately enough, the page-long passage in the manuscript of *The Drift of Light* that describes Chris's reasons for returning to Canada is not the clean copy of the other 312 pages. Sentences have been reworked or crossed out entirely, and CB has obviusly struggled to get clear Chris's "renewed surge of the consciousness of his own country .... [that] was not to be understood through the machinery of reason .... [or] the stylized devotion and drunken passion of public patriotism. This was personal .... " Words, however much revised, are certainly not enough here, nor, as said previously, when Chris learns of Garnet Ackerman's final bonding to his father. We have not seen Cav Ackerman since Chris first left the Devon Shore, nor Harley, except in terms of reminiscences. We leave Chris Harris walking over to see Harley, this seminal and symbolic figure in his life whom he has directly avoided for over twenty years.

At the end of the manuscript CB returns to the first-person narration of Chris and offers a final passage that underlines the unrealized potential of his last fiction, the shadow that fell between the vision and the reality:

> The drift of light that moves for a moment on the dark of life, the moment in which again and without warning the mind is rescued from the baffled dream. Another level. A place beyond all levels, in which a man is conscious of past loves, heroisms, resistances to evil, with no sense of triumph; and of past and present sins without remorse. Aware of failures and successes, loves and angers, hurts given and received and errors irretrievable, blowing wisps in a throbbing wind, foam on the sea .... Something recovered? A tenuous personal continuity .... I walked into neither past nor future but a strange exciting present in which both past and present had their part .... alive in this middle-aged man who walked the Devon Road .... Perhaps, now, sometime soon, we could get the feel of it into words.

Not even the certainty that Chris will write his own version of *The Drift of Light*, or even the veiled suggestion, through the framing of the third-person portion of the manuscript by the first-person narration, that he already *has*, can disguise the fact that CB could no longer say, in sustained fashion, what he wanted to about world enough and time.

Between 1959 and his death on December 19, 1971 CB published no new poetry or fiction. When David Arnason, one of the editors of the *Journal of Canadian Fiction*, wrote to him in October 1971 to ask if he were willing to submit any material, CB responded with a short story entitled "South End Avenue," which was a slightly revised version of the 1948 story "Young Avenue" published in *Saturday Night*.[3] The Channel Shore was still on his mind as he re-emphasized after twenty-three years that perceptions across generations could overcome class barriers, that a girl from the Shore, Marian McKee, was like a breath of fresh wind in the arid fields of upper-class Halifax, and that simple instinct was much stronger than conventional affection. In a note of tribute that followed the story in the Winter 1972 issue of the *Journal of Canadian Fiction*, editor John Moss referred simply and eloquently to CB's "legacy of the past" in the closing lines of *The Channel Shore* and to the influence of CB as a writer: "Nothing is ever finished."[4]

As for the territory that had inspired him from the days of the *Shoreham Searchlight* and the creation of Lingerlong down to his portrait of the Devon Shore, CB returned to it usually once a year in the last decade of his life. When Harold MacIntosh spoke with him in the summer of 1971, they walked down to the beach together and to Bruce's Island (no longer really a peninsula, as it is joined toward its western end by a dirt-and-gravel causeway to the mainland). CB told Harold that he wanted to build a cabin "up on the hill" of the Island where he "might write another book."[5] But he had already written his old Mount Allison friend Charles Blue that he was taking six pills a day for blood pressure, was concerned about a "tiny arterial blockage," and felt "like a personal disaster area."[6] With Harold he insisted on looking to the future, but he also asked about the past. When they were boys together Will Bruce had a play boat, "thirty inches long or so, not a seam in it," that had been carved out of a log, perhaps by CB's grandfather. Every spring it was CB's job to get this little two-master down from the attic, clean, and refit it. In his final summer CB told Harold that he could not find that boat, and Harold remembered that when their sons (Alan and Keith) had played with it in 1943 the boat had no masts. CB and Harold chuckled over the memory of sailing it in the dammed-up pond of the brook.

Certainly CB's need to be near medical expertise, particularly after his operation, prevented any permanent return to Port Shoreham. But he did want some permanence there in the form of Bruces, so he encouraged his son Harry, who in 1969 "wanted his advice on buying land in Nova Scotia," to "consider the homestead" and "Bruce's Island."[7] According to Harry, it was his father's word-portrait of a potential cabin site overlooking the bay that convinced him, and in 1970 he bought ten acres of ocean frontage from CB's sister Bess for $350.00. A Bruce was home on The Head. About twelve years later Harry bought the entire farm property from Bess, and with CB's sisters, son, grandchildren, and even two great grandchildren on the homestead at various times of the year, there is indeed a balance between yesterday, today and tomorrow.

Conclusion

I have written here of a man who published one novel and one collection of short stories in his creative lifetime, as well as perhaps two dozen lyric poems cut, as CB himself might say, from superior cloth. Charles Bruce is hardly a household name or, indeed, one that falls frequently from the lips of academics, even those who specialize in Canadian literature. It seems that between 1959 (the date of the publication of his last book of fiction or poetry) and 1979 no article appeared on his work in any major literary journal in Canada[1]; nor was any restrospective view of his work provided after CB's death in 1971. The only critic of note who has given attention of length to Bruce's fiction has been John Moss.[2] The first edition of *The Canadian Encyclopedia* (1986) made no mention of Bruce the artist or of Bruce the newspaperman who influenced considerably the way in which news was written in this country for almost a quarter of a century. As I have said previously, there is no mention of either *The Channel Shore* or *The Township of Time* in the definitive *Literary History of Canada* (1965, 1976); neither Bruce's fiction nor his poetry are included in any major anthology of Canadian writing designed for use in high schools and universities.[3]

It strikes me that rather than there being a visible insistence by the critical establishment over the past twenty-five years that Bruce is just an unimportant writer, there has been an unspoken but effective reaction against his work, and the result, through silence, has been his virtual elimination from the literary canon. This has occurred despite Moss's efforts and those of several M.A. students who have written theses on Bruce. Gradually things have changed with respect to CB's work, and will continue to change: McClelland and Stewart has reissued *The Channel Shore* and *The Township of Time* in the New Canadian Library Series (though the considerable influence of Malcolm Ross played a significant part here), and Pottersfield Press published an edition of CB's selected poems; in 1988 Formac Publishing released a trade edition in paperback of *The Channel Shore*; these works are now being taught in high school and university programmes and are, of course, accessible to the general reading public. Nevertheless, there remains the distinct impression that those who have been in a position to bring Bruce to the forefront of serious discussion about Canadian literature consider him to be not only as E.K. Brown suggested in 1945, a minor writer, if authentic, but somehow a threatening one as well.

It is clear that CB was a loner as an artist. Though he lived in Toronto, certainly a literary centre in Canada from the 1930s through the 1950s, and was a leading member of the Canadian Authors' Association, he did not need the company of his fellows to produce his poems and fictions, at least not between 1946 and 1959, his most prolific and final period of creative writing. From his Song Fisherman days in Nova Scotia he had made it clear that he had "no political convictions" but "only enthusiasms" for the translation into art of life that he had personally experienced. The need to turn away from the administrative demands at the Canadian Press and the daily grind of supervising the writing that other people wanted written seems to have propelled him creatively as he lay on the couch on Farnham Avenue or scribbled first drafts of poems on the backs of envelopes at various times and in various places.

CB said that he wanted more time to write what he wanted to write and that was why he was retiring early from the Canadian Press. But it is evident that his health was impeding his ability to handle both a full-time job and the rigours of being a consistent producer of quality fiction and poetry. It is clear, too, that CB did need the opposition of the daily "rat-race" and creative expression in order to be effective as an artist. *The Channel Shore* came into being largely out of the crucible of Toronto responsibilities and demands. CB was a newspaperman who could not stop being so just because he had retired from the company version of the profession, and it appears that his agreeing to write *News and the Southams* under contract signalled a strong desire on his part to keep that side of his life in gear. In an important way, the effort of writing and the resultant book were the cap on his career in the news world.

Interesting questions arise. CB was very concerned with his financial responsibility to his family on his retirement. Although three sons had left home by the early 1960s, Harvey Bruce was just entering high school. The book on the Southams meant an income for Farnham Avenue beyond that provided by the CP pension and any savings. Why did CB not turn to the Canada Council for money to allow him time to write a novel or poems? Between 1963 and 1967 he earned approximately $30,000 from the Southam company; in 1972 Margaret Laurence, Al Purdy, and Rudy Wiebe all received major grants from the Canada Council, each worth $7,000! Obviously, if CB felt that he needed financial support over a number of years, the Council could not be of help. But from what I can gather, while money was welcome, CB was not desperate for it. The family would have survived comfortably without the four demanding years of Southam work; indeed, when this work was over CB did not find it necessary to write the history of the Parliamentary Press Gallery or to become Visiting Lecturer at Brandon University (he had also turned down the offer of a full professorship at the University of British Columbia to commence in 1963). It does seem that he was confident he could work on the Southam book and do the "personal writing" that he had always looked forward to doing once he had retired. This would be very much like working at CP and writing creatively, but without the 9-5 (and usually much longer) regime at the office. However, writing about a newspaper company was obviously a kind of creative writing for CB — or at least made similar demands upon him — and he could not, whatever his physical health, sustain two projects at once.

CB did begin work in earnest on *The Drift of Light* after *News and the Southams* was out of the way, but three years (1968-1971) was only enough time to produce a reasonable first draft. Counting the necessary expression of *Currie Head*, *The Channel Shore* was a dozen years in the making. The stories for *The Township of Time* were written over a decade. As far as fiction was concerned,

CB required some time to achieve a draft suitable for publication. He may very well, in another four or five years and with a great deal of rewriting, have turned *The Drift of Light* into a fine novel, but the view does remain that he had already investigated his heritage for fictional purposes as completely as possible.

In terms of poetry CB does seem to have sensed a critical reaction against his material because of the rejection of *Living and Recall* in 1968. His response as expressed in his letter to John Gray at Macmillan is unfortunate because undoubtedly there was still an audience for the poetry written "from inside a certain scene and atmosphere," poetry about the shores of Chedabucto Bay that could speak volumes to a farmer in Saskatchewan. CB had, though, too much personal integrity and an awareness of the extraordinary link between his heritage and his creative expression to stop writing poems as a protest against the lack of Macmillan support for his proposed volume of selected poems. He was fighting with his high blood pressure and other ailments, and, like so many artists before and since, he had said considerably what he had to say, at least in one art form. He can be particularly compared in this regard to Margaret Laurence who, having created a fictional territory about which she wrote almost exclusively (five books in ten years) in her fiction, had one day nothing more to offer in this area of expression.

However, CB's almost complete silence as to the publication of fiction and poetry during the last twelve years of his life does not explain the neglect, since 1959, of his major creative efforts. Margaret Laurence's reputation remained intact, indeed grew, in the ten years without a novel after *The Diviners* (1974); Sinclair Ross maintained a high profile as a writer in the more than twenty-five years between *As for Me and My House* (1941) and his collection of short stories, *The Lamp at Noon* (1968); Sheila Watson received considerable attention during her long silence after *The Double Hook* (1959), as did Adele Wiseman in the almost two decades between *The Sacrifice* (1956) and *The Crackpot* (1974); Ethel Wilson's peak in fiction was reached in the 1950s, yet her work had not faded from critical view at the time of her death in 1980.

As for CB, he was lauded for *The Mulgrave Road* at the time of its publication, though within certain bounds. Northrop Frye does not appear to have argued against the granting of the Governor-General's Award to this work, but Frye and some others, from what they had to say in their reviews, probably felt that it was a matter of minor if authentic poetry receiving its due. As for *The Channel Shore* and *The Township of Time*, they were quietly if respectfully received, though again it needs to be emphasized that the lasting chord resounded in the hearts and minds of the reading public. To judge from what was said in the journals, magazines, and newspapers, there was the strong perception of CB as writing well of "a simpler Canadian way of life" that "lacked the latest fashionable gambits in psychology" (positive but not very progressive commentary), writing equally well of "the backwaters which the busy world has passed by" (certainly qualified praise), or as having created a territory that reeked too much of the East Coast and was too filled with Nova Scotia virtues and nostalgia (damning without the praise). Consider what Norah Story had to say of *The Channel Shore* in her edition of *The Oxford Companion to Canadian History and Literature* (winner of the Governor-General's Award in 1967): "[Bruce's] novel ... set in a fishing village, brings out the frustration that leads young men in Nova Scotia to leave that province."[4]

Why the relegation of CB over the years, why his disappearance from the critical sense almost altogether at a time when Canadian literature was coming into its own through the efforts of small publishing houses, the New Canadian Library productions, and the support of various and excellent literary journals, little magazines, and individual artists by federal and provincial cultural bodies? CB's work should have been a part of the burgeoning of literary expression in this country and the growth of Canadian academic studies, part of the tremendous preoccupation with our political and social identity and our cultural diversity during the 1960s and 1970s. But it was not to be. My own feeling is that it is CB's very artistic strengths that have negatively influenced so many of those in charge of the Canadian literary canon.

In his deservedly and widely acclaimed *The Mountain and the Valley* (on almost everyone's list of great Canadian novels), Ernest Buckler does not really write about Nova Scotia. He writes about the country of David Canaan's mind more than anything else, a private rural region with familiar trappings that does not loudly proclaim itself as a place where anyone else should be. The community of Entremont does not rival any other community in Canada, nor contain facts and history that are other than personal and the property of an individual who, for all his potential, dies unfulfilled on an unnamed "mountain" top. But CB, by contrast, is an intense conveyor of the details of recognizable time and place, of the parameters of geography, social life, and individual and collective behaviour with which we are all familiar, and which exist within the larger context of time's vagaries and acceptance of a world that does inexorably change; the private experience of his characters merges successfully with the community experience in which CB has considerable faith and which he so obviously insists transcends limited perceptions of region.

CB's quiet but firm insistence in his art that Nova Scotia has an elemental place in the lifetime of the nation, as a past, present, and therefore future force, has been something of a threat to those whose views of Canadian literature have looked first at Toronto and then west and south from there (with an occasional glance over the shoulder at a few chosen Quebecois poets and novelists in translation). The Atlantic region of the country has been viewed as a politically and economically minor, if authentic, territory; as history, effectively portrayed in Thomas Raddall's novels, or as rural *cul de sac*, effectively *containing* David Canaan. The cultural view of the area has suffered accordingly — how else explain that Dorothy Roberts, Elizabeth Brewster, Milton Acorn, Alden Nowlan and Don Domanski are the sole 20th-century, Maritime representatives born after 1900 (out of a total of ninety-five such poets) in *The New Oxford Book of Canadian Verse*, edited by Margaret Atwood?[5] It has only been in the past few years, through the increase in the number of small publishing houses, independent journals, magazines, and places of review, and the appearance of more writers, like

Alistair MacLeod, who cannot be ignored because the universal implications of their writing arise profoundly out of its allegiance to the East Coast, that the impact of literary creativity in the Maritimes on the national scene has begun to demand, among other things, a review of CB's creative talents and a recognition of the lasting quality of his work.[6]

Notes

I Heritage

1. Guysborough Anglican Church Record Book, March 28, 1805 (in the Public Archives of Nova Scotia, hereafter referred to as PANS). James Bruce, "about 40 years," was buried on this date. CB refers to the death of his great-great-grandfather in a letter to Thomas Raddall of November 1, 1951, and in a letter to his son Harry on February 14, 1970.

2. CB, "The Township of Time," *Echoes* (Autumn, 1955), p.4. *Echoes*, the "National Magazine" of the Imperial Order Daughters of the Empire, was published four times a year. It had begun as a pamphlet in 1902.

3. CB to A.C. Jost, June 19, 1951.

4. "The Township of Time," *Echoes*, p.5.

5. This information on the settlement of the Chedabucto Bay region up to the time of the American Revolution is taken from A.C. Jost, *Guysborough Sketches And Other Essays* (Kentville: The Kentville Publishing Company Limited, 1950).

6. Boylston was named after Benjamin Hallowell's eldest son, Ward Nicholas Boylston, who took the name of his maternal uncle "having attained his twenty-first birthday, having [been] promised ... very considerable estates in Boston" (Jost, p.60).

7. The information on the loyalist settlement of Nova Scotia and the Chedabucto region in particular is taken from Jost and from Neil MacKinnon, *This Unfriendly Soil: The Loyalist Experience in Nova Scotia 1783-1791* (Kingston and Montreal: McGill-Queen's University Press, 1986).

8. MacKinnon, pp.29-30.

9. *Ibid.*, pp. 41-42.

10. Jost, p.150.

11. MacKinnon, p.42.

12. *Ibid.*, p.148.

13. *Ibid.*, p.11. It is worth quoting part of a letter from John Wentworth, Surveyor-general of the woods, to Governor John Parr on March 5, 1788: "There are not thirty of the privates living within one hundred miles of Chedabucto, five or six officers only are in this country, the rest are abroad: many of the Privates Sold their lotts for a dollar, or a pair of Shoes, or a few pounds of Tobacco — but most for a Gallon of New England rum, and quit the country without taking any residence." (MacKinnon, pp. 171-172).

14. Records of the Guysborough Agricultural Society, January 27, 1821. (PANS)

15. Jost, p.53.

16. MacKinnon, p.147.

17. CB, "Words Are Never Enough," in *The Mulgrave Road*(Toronto: Macmillan of Canada, 1951), p.27.
18. Thomas Raddall to CB, November 1, 1951.
19. Jost, p.283.
20. CB to Harry Bruce, February 14, 1970: "About 2 miles northwest of where we are now."
21. CB to Jost, July 19, 1951.
22. CB to Thomas Raddall, December 17, 1950.
23. CB, "The Standing Woods," in *The Mulgrave Road: Selected Poems of Charles Bruce* (Porter's Lake, Nova Scotia: Pottersfield Press, 1985), p.69.
24. CB wrote to Harry Bruce on February 14, 1970 that Catherine "may have been an adopted daughter."
25. "The Standing Woods," p.70.
26. "The Township of Time," *Echoes*, p.4.
27. Mrs. Hazel Oliver to author, December 3, 1985.
28. Jost, p.302.
29. *Ibid.*, p.348.
30. Author's interview with Mrs. Anna MacKeen, August 18, 1984.
31. James C. Tory was elected three times to the Nova Scotia Legislature, in 1911, 1916, and 1920, and was Minister without Portfolio in the administration of Premier George Murray in 1921. He was Lieutenant-Governor of Nova Scotia from 1925-1930. Henry Marshall Tory (1864-1947) was "principal founder" of the University of Alberta, the University of British Columbia, and Carleton University. He was the National Research Council's first full-time president (1927-1935) and was "the most famous educator of his day." *The Canadian Encyclopedia* (Edmonton: Hurtig Publishers, 1985), pp.1836-1837.
32. "The Township of Time," *Echoes*, p.5.
33. CB to Harry Bruce, February 14, 1970.
34. CB to Thomas Raddall, August 2, 1954.
35. CB, "Our Place," *Globe* Magazine, Toronto *Globe and Mail*, June 12, 1971.
36. "The Standing Woods," p. 71.
37. "The Township of Time," *Echoes*, p.5. Charles Joseph was "said not to know the taste of tobacco or liquor." (CB in his unpublished essay "A Hill For Looking," Dalhousie University Archives).
38. "The Township of Time," *Echoes*, p.5.
39. CB, *Currie Head*, unpublished manuscript, Dalhousie University Archives, pp.55-56. Hereafter referred to as CH.
40. Author's interview with Clayton Hart, September 1, 1985. Hart, who was born in 1918, remembers Will Bruce's kindly nature, and that "You could tell him anything and he would put it in a stone wall." Will obviously could keep a secret.
41. CB to Harry Bruce, April 5, 1970.
42. *Ibid.*
43. *Ibid.*

44. Author's interview with Mrs. Anna MacKeen, Mrs. Carrie Macmillan, Mrs. Zoe Schulze, and Miss Bessie Bruce, August 18, 1984.

45. "A Hill For Looking," unpublished autobiographical essay in Dalhousie University Archives.

46. Author's interviews with Harold MacIntosh and Clayton Hart, August 31 and September 1, 1985.

47. Author's interview with Mrs. Agnes Bruce, May 5, 1984.

48. The original Micmac name for the settlement was "Assugadich," meaning Clam Ground. "Shoreham" means "village by the shore." Port Shoreham became the official name of the community on April 4, 1901, according to the records of the Nova Scotia Legislature (PANS).

49. "A Hill For Looking."

50. "A Hill For Looking."

II Boyhood

1. Interview with Charles Bruce's sisters, August 18, 1984.

2. These anecdotes are from my interviews with Harold MacIntosh and Wilbur Cummings on August 31 and September 1, 1985. As for "lee-o," CB writes in *Currie Head* that teams of boys stood on opposite sides of the schoolhouse and threw a ball back and forth: "Whoever started play shouted 'Lee-O!'"

3. In a letter to me in November of 1985, Anna (Bruce) MacKeen states that she went to Saskatchewan in 1927 and that her sister Bess had gone to Edmonton "a few years before that." Carrie went to the United States in 1925 and Zoe at about the same time, where they have lived since.

4. *Shoreham Searchlight*, Wednesday, March 5, 1919. Dalhousie University Archives.

5. *Weekend Magazine*, August 7, 1971.

6. CB describes Salter in another unpublished autobiographical essay "The Back of the Book," p.1 (Dalhousie University Archives). The *North Sydney Herald* was a weekly paper in 1919, but became a daily from 1920 -1928.

7. The *Evening Echo* was the evening edition of the Halifax *Morning-Chronicle*.

8. "The Back of the Book," unpublished essay by CB in the Dalhousie University Archives, p.2. The war poem published in *The Family Herald* was entitled "Their Share."

9. "The Back of the Book," p.3.

10. "Tin Pigs and Raisins," *Canadian Homes and Gardens*, (December 1954), p.50.

11. *Ibid.*

12. Bliss Carman, "Low Tide on Grand Pré," in *Canadian Poetry, Volume One*, editors Jack David and Robert Lecker (Toronto: General Publishing Company, Limited, 1982), p.75.

13. A.E., "The Voice of the Waters," in *The Divine Vision And Other Poems* (London: Macmillan and Company, Limited, 1904), p.68.

14. *Canadian Poetry, Volume One,* pp. 75 and 79.

15. *The Divine Vision,* pp. 15, 68, 3. I have not mentioned the realism to be found in G.D. Roberts, Lampman, and Duncan Campbell Scott's poetry, nor the attempt by the latter two poets especially to deal with a changing world (see Lampman's "In November" and "The City at the End of Things," and Scott's "The Onondaga Madonna.")

16. *The Divine Vision,* p.8.

17. *Ibid.,* p.21.

18. CB, *The Channel Shore* (Toronto: Macmillan of Canada, 1954), p.243.

19. "The Back of the Book," p.4.

20. CB, "Earthbound," in *The Bard,* February 22, 1922.

21. CB, "The Ships of Home" (April 22, 1922), "The Builder" (October 22, 1922), "Sea Windows" (December 23, 1922), and "After Grass" (no date). All in *The Bard.*

22. "A Hill For Looking."

23. Interview with CB's sisters, August 18, 1984.

24. "A Hill For Looking." CB seems to admit through Stan Currie's similar memory in *Currie Head* that he might have confused the name of Will's friend with that of another man at a later date. The impact of CB's recollection is not much lessened by this possibility; he seems to have wanted it to be his earliest memory.

25. "About the only machine we used was an ancient horse-drawn raker which I remembered chiefly for the fact that for storage purposes it had to be dismantled each fall and put together again each summer. The thing was a Chinese puzzle." ("A Hill for Looking")

26. CB, "The Two Communities: 1. Space," first broadcast on CBC Radio in the summer of 1956 and published in the *CBC Times* for the week of August 19-25, 1956.

27. Letter to author from Mrs. Anna MacKeen, November 1985.

28. Will Bruce to CB, September 27, 1922.

29. *Ibid.,* December 3, 1922.

30. "The Back of the Book," p.6.

31. CB, "Lost Hours," in the Halifax *Morning-Chronicle,* November 9, 1923.

32. Annie Campbell Huestis to CB, October 29, 1923.

33. Robert Norwood to CB, November 22, 1923.

34. Andrew Merkel to CB, October 11, 1923.

35. "Infidel," from "The Back of the Book," p.12. The poem appeared in the Mount Allison student newspaper, *The Argosy* (January 15, 1927), with the first of these two lines reading "He walks unmindful; and his ways are wild"; it was published in CB's first book, *Wild Apples* (in the spring of 1927), with this first line as "The transient riches of his days are wild."

36. Mount Allison Alumni Dinner Speech, May 13, 1952. This speech preceded the toast that CB was invited to propose to the university.

III The Bard

1. In 1882 Mount Allison granted the first B.A. degree awarded to a woman in Canada (to Harriet Starr Stewart).
2. *The Argosy*, Volume 1, Number 1, October 6, 1923.
3. CB's unpublished notes, Dalhousie University Archives.
4. Mount Allison Yearbook, 1927.
5. CB's "Junior Year Notebook," October 10, 1925. Dalhousie University Archives.
6. CB to Thomas Raddall, May 30, 1952.
7. The *Monthly Argosy* first appeared in 1872.
8. "The Hill-Dwellers," *The Argosy*, November 10, 1923.
9. *The Argosy*, November 8, 1924. In addition, there was an essay by CB on the history of St. Valentine's Day, February 14, 1925.
10. *Ibid.*, March 7, 1925.
11. Author's interview with Charles Blue, November 20, 1985.
12. George J. Trueman to Will Bruce, December 29, 1924.
13. CB to Vera Campbell, April 3, 1971. The others were Lawton Scovill, Charles Blue, Tom Nicholls (later publisher of the Hamilton *Spectator*), and Ross Flemington (later President of Mount Allison).
14. Ernest Hemingway, *The Sun Also Rises* (New York: Charles Scribner's Sons, 1926, 1970), p.148.
15. David G. Pitt, *E.J. Pratt, The Early Years*, (Toronto: The University of Toronto Press, 1985), pp.257-258.
16. "The Back of the Book," p.16.
17. CB, Valedictory Address, Mount Allison University, May 1927. Published in the 1927 Yearbook.
18. CB, Mount Allison Alumni Dinner Speech, May 13, 1952.
19. With the exception of the following times: December 1, 1939-December 1,1940 when CB was Acting Superintendent of CP in New York City; March 3, 1944-July 2,1945 when he was Superintendent of CP's London, England Bureau.
20. CB's own term for the sentiments of the poem, "The Back of the Book," p.11.
21. "The Back of the Book," p.12.

IV On The Road

1. At the *Morning-Chronicle* CB was probably paid in the vicinity of $15.00-$20.00 per week.
2. Jack Brayley, from a memoir of CB, a copy of which was given to me during an interview with Mr. Brayley on July 15, 1985.
3. Telephone interview with Mrs. Agnes Bruce, January 16, 1986, and interview with her in her Toronto home, May 5, 1984.
4. "A Hill For Looking," Dalhousie University Archives.
5. CB's unpublished notes, Dalhousie University Archives.

6. "Brooklyn," in *Tomorrow's Tide* (Toronto: The Macmillan Company of Canada, Limited, 1932), p.12. The other poems discussed here that were published in the same book are "Caution" (p.11), "Resurrection in October" (p.8), "Rainfire" (p.10), and "Not Now" (p.13).

7. Neither Will nor Sarah attended the wedding; an aunt was Agnes's family representative, and Charles Blue was CB's best man.

8. Interview with Gillis Purcell, July 23, 1985. For information on Canadian Press staffing and operations see M.E. Nicholls, *The Story of The Canadian Press* (Toronto: The Ryerson Press, 1948).

9. "By The Canadian Press: A Word for the Good Reporter," published in booklet form very probably in March or April of 1931.

10. Interview with Jack Brayley, July 15, 1985.

11. CB, letter to F.B. Watt [this may have been F.W. Watt] October 16, 1946.

12. CB's unpublished notes, Dalhousie University Archives.

13. "Lunenburg," in *Tomorrow's Tide*, p.24.

14. *Port and Province*, Volume 1, Number 1, (May 1932), p.30.

15. "The Two Communities 1. Space" and " 2. Time" in *CBC Times* (August 19-25 and September 1, 1956).

16. *Modern Canadian Poetry*, editor Nathaniel A. Benson (Ottawa: Graphic Publications, 1930). Poems published here were "The Immortals," "In Praise of Earth," "Resurrection in October," "A Song of Snow," "Wild Apples," and "Altar-Fires." *Songs of the Maritimes*, editor Elizabeth Ritchie (Toronto: McClelland and Stewart Limited, 1931) contained "The Immortals" and "Infidels."

17. Letter to CB, December 12, 1932.

18. *Canadian Homes and Gardens*, December 1954.

19. CB's unpublished notes, Dalhousie University Archives.

20. Poems referred to were published in *Tomorrow's Tide* (Toronto: The Macmillan Company of Canada Limited, 1932): "Ragwort" (p.14), "The Bystanders" (p.15), "Reinforcement for the City under the Star" (p.19), "Essay on Sociology" (p.21), "Parable on Peace" (p.22), "Tomorrow's Tide" (p.1), "Lunenburg" (p.24), "Spirit of a Province" (p.4), "Recapitulation" (p.28), "To Harold Raine" (p.23).

21. Evelyn S. Tufts, "New Books at a Glance." There is no record in the Dalhousie University Archives of where this review was published.

22. No source except CB's unpublished notes, Dalhousie University Archives.

23. *The Commonweal*, October 1933.

24. *The New York Herald-Tribune*, August 27, 1933.

25. "Tomorrow's Tide," in *Tomorrow's Tide*, p.1.

26. Charles G.D. Roberts to CB, March 7, 1933.

27. CB to George J. Trueman, August 8, 1934.

28. H.M. Wood to CB, August 11, 1934.

29. CB to C.A. Munro, June 11, 1937.

30. "An Ear to the Ground," in *Grey Ship Moving* (Toronto: The Ryerson Press, 1945), p.21.

31. Letter from the editor of *The Canadian Magazine* to CB, July 2, 1935. I have not been able to determine if and when the poem was actually published. The editor told CB, "...it may be some time before [the poem] sees the light of day." "Fisherman's Son" consists of two related sonnets, and the second sonnet was published under the title "Seance" in *Canadian Poetry Magazine*, Volume 3, Number 2 (October 1938).

32. "Fisherman's Son I & II" in *Grey Ship Moving*, pp.27-28. The poem was later reprinted, with alterations to two lines in CB's *The Mulgrave Road* in 1951.

33. J.F.B. Livesay to CB, March 14, 1938.

34. "Words Are Never Enough," in *Grey Ship Moving*, pp.15-17. Also reprinted, with a few slight changes, in *The Mulgrave Road*.

35. *Canadian Poetry Magazine*, Volume 4, Number 1 (July 1939), pp.11-13; *Anthology of Canadian Poetry*, editor Ralph Gustafson (Harmondsworth: Penguin Books Limited, 1942); *Book of Canadian Poetry*, editor A.J.M. Smith (Toronto: W.J. Gage and Company, Limited, 1943)--other poems by CB in this collection were "Immediates," "Alternatives," and "The Steelyards."

36. Leo Kennedy, "Direction for Canadian Poets," *New Frontier*, Volume 1, Number 3 (June 1936), p.22.

37. According to CB, in "The Back of the Book," p.44. Kennedy does not seem to have made any public declaration of the error as the *Literary History of Canada*, published in 1965, refers to his "vehement article in *New Frontier* [which] called upon Canadian poets to recognize 'immediates' and serve the social good with their pens." *Literary History of Canada*, editor Carl F. Klinck (Toronto: University of Toronto Press, 1965), p.754.

38. "Immediates" and "Alternatives," in *Grey Ship Moving*, pp.18-19.

39. Leo Kennedy to CB, January 5, 1937,

40. CB to Leo Kennedy, February 9, 1937.

41. "Deep Cove," in *New Frontier*, Volume 2, Number 2 (June 1937), pp.15-16.

42. "Return and Introduction," in *Grey Ship Moving*, p.25.

43. "The Back of the Book," p.40. CB writes, "Sometime in the 1940's, when I had not been back to Nova Scotia in years...."

44. "In the Long Evenings of Long Summers," in *Canadian Poetry Magazine*, Volume 13, Number 1 (Fall 1949), p.8.

45. Charles G.D. Roberts, "Life and Art," in his *Collected Poems* (Wolfville, Nova Scotia: The Wombat Press, 1985), p.231.

46. J.F.B. Livesay in unidentified newspaper clipping, Dalhousie University Archives.

47. CB to J.F.B. Livesay, August 1, 1940.

48. J.F.B. Livesay to CB, July 28, 1940.

49. Interview with Gillis Purcell, July 23, 1985.

50. Interview with Jack Brayley, July 15, 1985.

51. CB to J.F.B. Livesay, May 20, 1940.

52. *Ibid.*, April 16, 1940.

53. Leon Edel had belonged to the Montreal group of poets in the 1920s. An indication of his respect for CB can be found in Edel's asking him for a recommendation for a Nieman fellowship at Harvard in 1950.
54. Leon Edel to CB, April 9, 1941.
55. A.J.M. Smith, *Book of Canadian Poetry*.
56. CB to Leon Edel, February 14, 1941.
57. "Finds Former Poet in Editor's Chair," in *Grey Ship Moving*, p.26.
58. Dorothy Livesay to CB, May 29, 1941.
59. CB to Dorothy Livesay, June 21, 1941.
60. From an unidentified newspaper review of *Personal Note* in CB's files, Dalhousie University Archives.
61. According to Gillis Purcell, CB wrote the poem "because of and for Sam Robertson," a CP war correspondent who was killed on April 30, 1941 when the troopship *Nerissa* was torpedoed in the North Atlantic. Interview with Gillis Purcell, July 23, 1985.
62. "Personal Note," in *Grey Ship Moving*, pp.29-34.
63. *Voices of Victory: Representative Canadian Poetry in War Time*, editor Keith Knowlton (Toronto: Macmillan of Canada, 1941).
64. *London [Ontario] Free Press*, November 8, 1941.
65. James C. Tory to CB, December 18, 1941.
66. "The Steelyards" was published in Smith's *Book of Canadian Poetry* in 1943 and in *Canadian Poetry Magazine* in September of 1946.

V Homeward Bound

1. A letter from a *Harper's* editor, Elizabeth Lawrence, to CB of September 16, 1946 refers to the "stories" of Anna, Grant, Hazel, and Chance.
2. Elizabeth McKee to CB, August 13, 1946.
3. CB to Elizabeth McKee, September 3, 1946.
4. CB to Elizabeth Lawrence; no date, but probably his reply to her letter to him of April 1, 1947.
5. CB's unpublished manuscript of CH in the Dalhousie University Archives.
6. Hugh Currie says this about his brother Steve in CH, p.87, and Will Bruce says almost the same thing about James C. Tory in "A Hill for Looking."
7. Elizabeth Lawrence to CB, April 1, 1947.
8. CB to Elizabeth Lawrence, no date.
9. See CH, p.121, and the Mount Allison student newspaper, *The Argosy* (I do not have the exact week in October of 1927).
10. Gillis Purcell to author, October 29, 1985.
11. Alan Bruce (July 23, 1985) and Harry Bruce (November 24, 1985) have both attested to this.
12. CB received $40.00 per week when he joined CP in New York on January 9, 1928. When he became General News Editor on Toronto on November 1, 1937 he made $75.00 per week. As General Superintendent

of CP he began on August 1, 1945 at $105.50 per week and by 1961 (the last available salary information) he was making $346.15 per week.

13. CH, p.269. These words are actually used to describe the character of Starbuck in Melville's *Moby Dick*.

14. Bill Graham is, of course, a central figure in *The Channel Shore*. Stan Currie learns in CH (p.317) that during World War Two Bill is "a war correspondent [for the Halifax *Globe*] with the Canadian troops in training."

15. CB to Elizabeth Lawrence, September 19, 1946.

16. CB to Elizabeth Lawrence; no date, but probably his reply to her letter of April 1, 1947.

VI Interlude

1. *Canadian Printer and Publisher*, February 1944.

2. CB to GIllis Purcell, March 6, 1944.

3. CB to Gillis Purcell, June 9, 1944.

4. CB to Gillis Purcell, February 2, 1945.

5. *Toronto Star Weekly*, July 15, 1944, and *Saturday Night*, September 9, 1944.

6. CB's story for CP, which was carried in many Canadian newspapers, was filed in Brussels.

7. CB to Gillis Purcell, March 19, 1945. The reference to Lincoln's Inn Fields is in an undated London notebook.

8. CB to Harry Bruce, July 6, 1944. No other mention of a post-D-Day landing by CB exists to my knowledge.

9. Sand Lake was near Kearney, Ontario (Haliburton region). The family went up by train for parts of several summers during the 1940's, though often CB was there only on weekends. Harvey Bruce, born in 1950, recalls holidays there when he was quite young. All the Bruce sons state that CB seemed able to relax at Sand Lake, though Harvey insists that CB was most happy when he "was doing something" (Interview with Harvey Bruce, July 19, 1985).

10. CB's CP story, February 10, 1945.

11. CB to British Poetry Society Secretary, June 9, 1945.

12. CB told Andrew Merkel that this is what he would do at the Poetry Society in a letter to Merkel on April 4, 1945.

13. CB's London notes, no date.

14. In *Grey Ship Moving*, p.14.

15. "Grey Ship Moving" in *Grey Ship Moving*, pp.1-2.

16. CB, "The Back of the Book," p.49.

17. Edith Frye to CB, January 17, 1945.

18. "Three of the neglected names in this group [the 'native tradition'] will bear much re-reading: Raymond Knister, Kenneth Leslie, and Charles Bruce. The latter, together with E.J. Pratt, has been singled out by the *Manchester Guardian* as a convincing poet." Dorothy Livesay in *Canadian Forum*, Volume XXIV, Number 279 (April 1944), p.21.

In December 1943 in *Canadian Forum* (Volume XXIII, Number 275, p.209) Northrop Frye wrote, "The vocabulary and diction correspond: the snap and crackle of frosty words, some stiff with learning and others bright with concreteness, is heard wherever there is the mental excitement of real creation, though of course most obviously where the subject suggests it: in, for instance, Charles Bruce's 'Immediates':

> An ageless land and sea conspire
> To smooth the imperfect mould of birth;
> While freezing spray and drying fire
> Translate the inexplicit earth."

Frye also quotes here from P.K. Page's "The Stenographers." CB was in no mean company.

19. Edith Frye to CB, March 8, 1945.

20. Lorne Pierce to CB, March 24, 1945. It seems that CB had sent Pierce the manuscript without informing Edith Frye.

21. Wilfred Gibson to CB, May 5, 1945.

22. Montreal *Gazette*, March 2, 1946.

23. Halifax *Daily Star*, March 9, 1945.

24. Alan Creighton, *Canadian Forum*, Volume XXV, Number 302 (March 1946), p.293.

25. E.K. Brown, "Letters in Canada, *The University of Toronto Quarterly*, Volume XV, Number 3 (April 1946), p.273.

26. "1945" in *Grey Ship Moving*, p.13.

27. Of course, "1945" might have been a poem with a narrative voice that is not CB's. The "we" and the "your" might be fictions altogether or refer to other people familiar to the poet. But it was CB who wrote that "poetry is simply the most personal of all arts, the form of writing in which what you say is what you are or nothing at all" (*Canadian Author and Bookman*, June 1948). The poem was republished in *The Mulgrave Road* under the title "Of This Late Day."

28. CB to Frank B. Watt, October 16, 1946.

29. CB to Norman Smith, February 19, 1946.

30. W.A. Deacon had said in a *Globe and Mail* review of *Grey Ship Moving* (no date, but certainly just before mid-September of 1946), "If he [Bruce] had labored at technique as an exercise, there would be more lines of printable quality." CB replied to Deacon on September 14, 1946: "... for myself, subject, emotion, and craftsmanship are interwoven .... My own experience has been that there is a direct relationship between quality of craftsmanship and strength of feeling .... Frankly I doubt whether anyone in Canada has been more concerned with craftsmanship in the last few years than I have."

31. Others were aware of his talents. *Grey Ship Moving* finished second in the 1945 Governor-General's Awards in poetry to Earle Birney's *Now Is Time*.

32. Michael Gnarowski, *The Making of Modern Poetry in Canada*, p.26.

33. *Ibid.*, p.38.

34. *Ibid.*, p.39.

35. Louis Dudek, "The Role of the Little Magazines in Canada," Gnarowski, p.207.
36. Michael Gnarowski, "The Role of the 'Little Magazines'in the Development of Poetry in English in Montreal," in Gnarowski, p.221; and Louis Dudek (see footnote 36).
37. Gnarowski, p.221.
38. Desmond Pacey, "The Writer and His Public 1920-1960," in *Literary History of Canada*, p.490.
39. John Sutherland, *Northern Review*, Volume I, Number 6 (August-September, 1947).
40. John Sutherland, Introduction to *Other Canadians* (Montreal: First Statement Press, 1947). Reprinted in Gnarowski, p.60.
41. A.J.M. Smith, "Contemporary Poetry" in *The McGill Fortnightly Review*, December 15, 1926. Reprinted in Gnarowski, p.28.
42. Quoted by CB from Miller Williams in *The Saturday Review of Literature* ("The Back of the Book," p.45).
43. *Canadian Poetry Magazine*, Volume 14, Number 2 (Winter 1950).
44. *Canadian Author & Bookman*, Volume XXIV, Number 2 (June 1948).
45. *Ibid.*
46. *Ibid.*
47. CB to Carolyn Willett, February 26, 1952. She was a fourth-year journalism student at Carleton University who was writing a thesis on "The Poetry of Nova Scotia." CB is actually quoting to her part of a reply to the Ottawa *Journal* reviewer of *The Mulgrave Road*.
48. *Ibid.*
49. CB to Al Purdy, October 19, 1950. The fifth stanza of Purdy's submission read as follows: "I envy you for what you took/And did not ask, and saw no crime/In taking women by a brook/You laughed as long as you had time." CB suggested the last two lines be changed to "In taking without bell or book,/She after she — when you had time." Purdy agreed to alter the first of these two lines to read "In taking (minus bell or book)." "Extroverts" appeared in *Canadian Poetry Magazine*, Volume 14, Number 2 (Winter 1950), p.26.
50. CB to *The Saturday Review of Literature*, August 31, 1949.
51. William Carlos Williams, *Paterson* (New York: New Directions Books, 1963), p.6.

VII Homeward Bound II

1. Author's interview with Alan Bruce, July 23, 1985.
2. CB to Lorne Pierce, July 18, 1946.
3. After some discussion, Pierce's choice of Winifred Fox won out. She had illustrated Evelyn M. Richardson's Governor-General's Award-winning biography *We Keep A Light* (Toronto: The Ryerson Press, 1946).
4. All quotations are from *The Flowing Summer* (Toronto: The Ryerson Press, 1947).These lines can be found on p.2.

5. E.K. Brown, "Letters in Canada," *University of Toronto Quarterly*, Volume XVII, Number 3 (April 1948), p.261.

6. *Queen's Quarterly*, Volume LIV, Number 2 (Summer 1947), p.278, and Halifax *Herald*, April 17, 1947.

7. *The Mulgrave Road* herafter referred to in notes as TMR.

8. At least twenty-seven poems were published during this five-year period in journals or magazines. Twenty of the twenty-four new poems in *The Mulgrave Road* had appeared previously in: *Maclean's (2), Saturday Evening Post (7), Saturday Night (4), Harper's (2), Canadian Poetry Magazine (2), Chambers's Journal (1), Ladies' Home Journal (1), Poetry, A Magazine of Verse (1)*.

9. *Maclean's*, April, 1946.

10. TMR, p.18.

11. TMR, p.19, CB's italics.

12. CB to Glenda Whidden, October 4, 1964.

13. TMR, "Back Road Farm," p.3.

14. TMR, "Biography," p.5.

15. TMR, "Tidewater Morning," p.4.

16. TMR, "Coast Farm," p.6.

17. TMR, "Eastern Shore," p.14.

18. TMR, "Disapproving Woman," p.9.

19. TMR, "Coast Farm," p.6.

20. TMR, "Wool," p.11.

21. TMR, p.17.

22. TMR, p.12.

23. "Nova Scotia Fish Hut," TMR, p.1.

24. TMR, pp.20-21.

25. "Habits and images" became "In questioning speech, all things" (line 14). As well, line 16 is divided in two to become lines 16-17.

26. TMR, "Planes of Space and Time," p.30.

27. CB to Carolyn Willett, February 26, 1952.

28. TMR, p.31.

29. *Saturday Night*, December 1, 1951, pp.24-25. Also Prime Minister Lester Pearson used "a few lines" from the poem in his remarks at the official lighting of the Centennial Flame on Parliament Hill at midnight, December 31, 1966-January 1, 1967 (Letter from Lester Pearson to CB, March 3, 1967).

30. TMR, pp.33-36.

31. Toronto *Globe and Mail*, October 27, 1951; *Maritime Advocate and Busy East*, April 1952.

32. Unidentified review of TMR in CB's notes, Dalhousie University Archives.

33. Burns Martin, *Canadian Poetry Magazine*, Volume 15, Number 4 (Summer 1952).

34. *The Varsity*, November 6, 1951.

35. Toronto *Telegram*, November 17, 1951.

36. CB, "The Two Communities: 1. Space," *CBC Times*, August 19-25, 1956, and "People: Nova Scotia's Best Export," *Saturday Night*, August 4, 1956.

37. CB to Northrop Frye, March 13, 1953.

38. *University of Toronto Quarterly*, Volume XXI, Number 2 (January 1952), pp.253-254.

39. CB to Northrop Frye, March 13, 1953.

40. See "Note For a Textbook" in *Poetry (Chicago)* [reported in a letter from CB to Mrs. R. Woodruff, April 2, 1952]; "Back Road Farm" and "Lake Superior Coast" in *Harper's*; and "Stories" in *The Poetry Review* (London).

41. Hartley Prichard, *Maclean's*, July 1953.

42. Actually, the magazine was not always staid. As has been said, Dorothy Livesay's "Day and Night" was published in it in 1936, and Earle Birney was the Editor from 1946-1948.

43. *Canadian Poetry Magazine*, Volume 12, Number 2 (December 1948). CB wrote that Klein's "glass-clear diction and strictly disciplined technique produce the outward form of a poetry that, in common with a good deal of verse now being written — rarely of such quality — somehow puzzles and disturbs while it seldom stirs." He said that "Portrait of the Poet As Landscape," arguably Klein's masterpiece, was "as clinically revelatory as the successive colored cut-outs in an old-fashioned 'Doctor's Book.'" CB then went on to announce that "Poetry in Canada has achieved a singular felicity in the expression of a cool, objective and slightly contemptuous anger. We have found an effective way to pinpoint stupidity, ugliness, and social exploitation. Could we have, now and then, a cool, objective recognition of the other qualities that inform this flesh and its behaviour? Even a touch of warmth, perhaps. Or have we lost the will to see?"

44. *Canadian Poetry Magazine*, Volume 12, Number 2 (December 1948), pp.9-10, and Volume 13, Number 1 (Fall 1949), p.8.

45. *Canadian Poetry Magazine*, Volume 14, Number 4 (Summer 1951, p.11.

46. "The Ark Refloated" (*Canadian Poetry Magazine*, Volume 14, No.4, Summer 1951); "Lines for a Copybook" is in CB's typescript, Dalhousie University Archives.

47. "The Boatbuilder," *Saturday Night*, May 28, 1955.

48. "The Boy Was Saying Something," *Saturday Night*, May 26, 1956.

49. "The Independent," *Saturday Night*, November 13, 1954; "Late Marriage," *Saturday Night*, June 5, 1954; "Upstairs Room," *Maclean's*, November 1, 1953; "Poem Without Title," *Canadian Poetry Magazine*, Volume 16, Number 4, (Summer 1953); "Wave," *Saturday Night*, June 11, 1955.

50. Charles Bruce, *The Ottawa Journal*, September 11, 1954.

51. In addition CB revised various stories for CBC Radio plays, gave talks on writing, and wrote several significant essays.

52. It obviously was in need of extensive revision, but this was prevented by CB's death in December of 1971.

VIII Second Fictions

1. Howard Moorepark to CB, January 20, 1949.
2. Elizabeth Lawrence to Howard Moorepark; contained in a letter from Moorepark to CB, March 8, 1949.
3. CB to Howard Moorepark, March 9, 1949.
4. CB to Lorne Pierce, November 8, 1950.
5. CB to Lorne Pierce, November 24, 1950.
6. CB, "The Road 1918," in *The Township of Time* (Toronto: Macmillan of Canada, Limited, 1959), p.155. Hereafter referred to as TT.
7. CB, "The Sloop," in TT, p. 191.
8. CB mentions that Will wrote to Sarah from Boston in the summer and fall of 1901 in a letter from CB to Harry Bruce, April 5, 1970.

IX Yesterday, Today, and Tomorrow

1. Lorne Pierce to CB, November 22, 1950.
2. John Gray to CB, February 25, 1952.
3. John Gray to CB, August 6, 1952.
4. CB's notes, Dalhousie University Archives.
5. CB wrote to Lorne Pierce on November 8, 1950: "As this so far is a reasonably secret job of work, would you be good enough to address any correspondence about it to me at the personal address given above [P.O. Box 403, Adelaide Street P.O., Toronto]."
6. CB's notes, Dalhousie University Archives.
7. "The Township of Time," *Echoes* (Autum 1955).
8. Epigraph to *The Channel Shore*.
9. *The Channel Shore*, p.3.
10. Perhaps there was something of himself in James Marshall, given Harry Bruce's recounting of the train trip to Mount Allison University in May of 1952.
11. Montreal *Star*, July 10, 1954, and Montreal *Gazette*, July 27, 1954.
12. Saskatoon *Star-Phoenix*, July 31, 1954.
13. Claude Bissell, "Letters in Canada," *University of Toronto Quarterly*, Volume XXIV, Number 3 (April l955), pp. 260-261.
14. Bissell wrote a glowing forward for the New Canadian Library edition of Buckler's novel in 1961.
15. Fred Cogswell, Fredericton *Daily Gleaner*, November 6, 1954.
16. Kaye Rowe, Brandon *Sun*, January 2, 1958. She had received a copy of the 1957 Macmillan reprint.
17. *The United Church Observer*, December 1, 1954.
18. CB's reply to *The United Church Observer* is referred to in several of his letters, but no copy of the reply exists in the Dalhousie University Archives.
19. W.A. Deacon, Toronto *Globe and Mail*, April 2, 1955.

20. W.A. Deacon, Toronto *Globe and Mail*, July 10, 1954.
21. See especially "The Two Communities: 1. Space" and "People: Nova Scotia's Best Export."
22. CB's notes, Dalhousie University Archives.
23. CB, unpublished speech, Dalhousie University Archives.
24. CB to James Taylor, March 15, 1949.
25. CB to James J. Talman, Chief Librarian at the University of Western Ontario and Chairman of the Governor-General's Awards for 1956 (July 18, 1956).
26. CB to James J. Talman, February 24, 1958.
27. CB to W.A. Deacon, September 14, 1946.
28. CB, unpublished speech, Dalhousie University Archives. This speech was on newspapers and reporting and the relationship between journalism and what CB called the "re-creative writing" of fiction.
29. "Marshall and Son" aired on CBC Radio's "Wednesday Night" on July 13, 1955.
30. "The Wind in the Juniper" aired on CBC Radio's "Vancouver Theatre," March 10, 1950; on "Maritime Theatre," April 5, 1951; and on CBC Winnipeg on November 18, 1954. "Tidewater Morning" was heard on CBC's "Summer Stage" on June 27, 1954. CBC had purchased "Schoolhouse Hill" for broadcast on Robert Weaver's *Canadian Short Stories* on June 30, 1950. Another radio play, "The Unexpected Magic," based on the short story "The Red Pig" (or perhaps yielding the story) was heard on "Summer Theatre" on June 18, 1950.
31. From the announcer's introduction to "Marshall and Son," obviously written by CB.

X Hearsay History

1. The manuscript of *No Left-Handed Reaping Hook*, the map, and many pages of notes to the intended novel, are in the Dalhousuie University Archives.
2. "The Two Communities: 2. Time," *CBC Times*, September 1, 1956.
3. "The Two Communities: 1. Space," *CBC Times*, August 19-25, 1956.
4. *Ibid.*
5. "The Township of Time," *Echoes*.
6. "The Two Communities: 2. Time."
7. *Maclean's*, September 1, 1949.
8. Quotations are taken from the version of the story ("The Wind in the Juniper 1945") published in *The Township of Time* in 1959. Here the reference is to p. 205.
9. It was first published in the Toronto *Star Weekly*, April 30, 1955.
10. In April of 1958 John Gray at Macmillan wrote CB that he had read "the first five stories of *People From Away*," and in May of that year he enclosed a contract for the book but added, "It doesn't seem to be an ideal selling title." On May 30, 1958, Gray replied very positively to CB's suggestion

that the book's title be changed to *The Township of Time*. CB at this time indicated that he still had at least two stories to write for the chronicle.

11. "The Township of Time," *Echoes*.

12. CB spent considerable time in the Provincial Archives of Nova Scotia, looking in particular at the *Manchester and Guysborough Township Book* that recorded births, marriages, and deaths between 1782 and 1869. The records of the Anglican church in early Guysborough were also useful to him. In 1951-52 he carried on a correspondence with Dr. A.C. Jost, author of *Guysborough Sketches and Other Essays*, about his own family genealogy and ways of life in late 18th and early 19th century in the Chedabucto Bay region.

13. See letters from CB to Dr. A.C. Jost between June of 1951 and January of 1955; see, as well, CB's letters to his friend Thomas Raddall, together with Raddall's helpful replies, between January of 1947 and September of 1957 (Dalhousie University Archives).

14. "(Stone fences clamber still beyond Dunoon/ Where the cock-pheasant calls from the yellow gorse,/ And narrow and dark in its loch the resilient sea/ Goes curving home to the steep low heart of the hills.)" *The Township of Time*, p. 14.

15. It is difficult to say when "People From Away" was first written.

16. *The Channel Shore*, p.3.

17. CB, unpublished speech, Dalhousie Archives. All quotations in this paragraph are from this speech.

18. *The Flowing Summer*, p.28.

19. CB, "Suspense," *The Dalhousie Review*, Number 32, Autumn 1952, pp. 197-200.

20. CB also kept in touch in the late 1940's and early 1950's with Alex McMaster, a Port Shoreham fisherman, asking him questions about fishing grounds and equipment through the years. See letter to McMaster from CB, January 6, 1947, and McMaster's reply, March 7. 1947.

21. See footnote 30, Chapter IX.

22. I have been using this image of art flowing into life and life flowing into art throughout my text. Certainly I owe the concept to my reading of Malcolm Lowry's *Dark As the Grave Wherein My Friend Is Laid* (Toronto: General Publishing Company, 1968) and specifically to p. 43 of that novel.

23. Harper Brothers to Willis Wing (an American literary agent), December 22, 1958.

24. Ottawa *Citizen*, November 28, 1959.

25. *Time*, February 8, 1960.

26. Ottawa *Citizen*, November 28, 1959 and London *Free Press*, October 3, 1959.

27. Winnipeg *Tribune*, January 9, 1960.

28. Montreal *Gazette*, October 17, 1959.

29. Sally Creighton, CBC Radio, October 25, 1959.

30. F.W. Watt, *University of Toronto Quarterly*, Volume XXIX, Number 4 (July 1960), pp. 473-474.

31. Fred Cogswell, Fredericton *Daily Gleaner*, November 6, 1954.

XI World Enough and Time

1. CB to Gillis Purcell; no date, but sometime in 1952.

2. CB to Norman Smith, April 3, 1958. ·

3. CB to Thomas Raddall, September 23, 1960.

4. Author's interview with Gillis Purcell, July 23, 1985.

5. Author's interview with Jack Brayley, July 15, 1985.

6. CB wrote from Newfoundland under a by-line for CP. His sympathy for the economic plight of the Newfoundland people is obvious as he comments on the difficulties with "transitional grant payments" from Ottawa. He also wrote a moving tribute to Newfoundland entitled "This Island — Stranger Amongst Us?" that appeared in various Canadian newspapers.

7. CB's journalism notes, Dalhousie University Archives.

8. CB to Alan Harvey, February 24, 1958.

9. CB to J.A. Falconer, Manager, CBC Radio Script Bureau, June 8, 1953.

10. CB's notes for the Marvell script, Dalhousie University Archives.

11. I have been unable to pin down the exact date of the broadcast. The contract for the script was dated October 16, 1953 and stated that CB was to receive $300.00 upon completion. The script was to be submitted by April 1, 1954.

12. Edited by Carl F. Klinck, who seems to have had a blind spot regarding CB. Nor was any information on CB's life and work provided in the first edition of the *Canadian Encyclopedia* (Edmonton: Hurtig Publishers, 1985). An article on his accomplishments will appear in the second edition of the encyclopedia to be published in 1988.

13. Desmond Pacey, *Creative Writing in Canada* (Toronto: Ryerson Press, 1961), pp. 180-181, 234.

14. Exceptions are: *Ninety Seasons*, editors Robert Cockburn and Robert Gibbs (Toronto: McClelland and Stewart Limited, 1974) with "Stories," "Back Road Farm," "Biography," "Eastern Shore," "The Other Shore," and "Words Are Never Enough"; *Poems of a Snow-Eyed Country*, editors Richard Woollatt and Raymound Souster (Toronto: Academic Press, 1980) with "Words Are Never Enough."

15. CB to Norman MacKenzie, June 12, 1962.

16. CB to Thomas Raddall, September 23, 1960.

17. CB to Alan Harvey, November 30, 1960.

18. Author's Interview with Alan Bruce, July 23, 1985.

19. Harry Bruce, *Movin' East* (Toronto: Methuen, 1985), p.226.

20. CB to St. Clair Balfour, July 1, 1963. Balfour was the grandson of William Southam, company founder.

21. CB, "Memorandum" to St. Clair Balfour, October 1, 1966.

22. St. Clair Balfour to CB, May 9, 1967.

23. CB to St. Clair Balfour, March 23, 1967.

24. CB to St. Clair Balfour, January 8, 1965.
25. CB, *News and the Southams* (Toronto: Macmillan of Canada Limited, 1968), pp. 77-78.
26. *Ibid.*, pp.83-84.
27. *Ibid.*, p.84.
28. *Ibid.*, p.405.
29. *Ibid.*
30. Speech by William Aberhart at Edmonton, October 18, 1935. Quoted in *News and the Southams*, p.298.
31. *News and the Southams*, p.306.
32. CB to St. Clair Balfour, May 23, 1968.
33. Author's interview with Mrs. Agnes Bruce and Andrew Bruce, July 22, 1985.
34. CB to Thomas Raddall, January 9, 1967.
35. Calgary *Herald*, May 10, 1968.
36. Ottawa *Journal*, August 10, 1968.
37. A.C. Cummings to CB, May 28, 1968; R.W. Southam to CB, June 3, 1968.
38. *News and the Southams*, p.410.
39. Lieutenant-General R.W. Moncel to CB, November 28, 1966; Fraser MacDougall to CB, December 5, 1966.
40. Eric Dennis to CB, June 2, 1967; CB to Eric Dennis, June 6, 1967.
41. Eileen Brownridge, Brandon University Alumni Association, to CB, June 28, l967; CB to Eileen Brownridge, July 7, 1967.
42. CB to Ross Munro, February 8, 1966.
43. CB to Denis Harvey, October 17, 1966.
44. CB to John Gray, February 8, 1968.
45. *Ibid.*, February 20, 1968.
46. CB, "The Back of the Book," p.49.
47. John Gray to CB, July 7,1969.
48. CB to John Gray, July 9, 1969.
49. Robert Cockburn to CB, July 22, 1967.
50. CB to Robert Cockburn, March 3, 1971.
51. *Ibid.*, March 30, 1971.
52. *Ibid.*, April 19, 1971.
53. CB, "The Explorer," unpublished manuscript, Dalhousie University Archives.
54. CB to the Canada Council, May 6, 1969.
55. At least this is stated in a letter to CB from Anne-Marie Hogue, Arts Division of the Canada Council, July 11, 1969. She states that "no assistance can be given for use in 1970-71." This is curious as I myself received a short-term artist's grant from the Canada Council in the spring of 1970, and I know that full-term artist's grants were also given out that same spring.
56. CB to Canada Council, September 2, 1971.

57. CB to Fraser MacDougall, May 20, 1971.
58. Author's interview with Alan Bruce, July 23, 1985.
59. Author's interview with Harold MacIntosh, August 31, 1985.

XII Another Shore

1. CB, unpublished manuscript, Dalhousie University Archives.
2. CB to Thomas Raddall, January 21, 1951.
3. CB, "Young Avenue," *Saturday Night*, October 16, 1948.
4. John Moss, *Journal of Canadian Fiction*, Volume 1, Number 1 (Winter 1972), p.7.
5. Author's interview with Harold MacIntosh, August 31, 1985.
6. CB to Charles Blue, May 31, 1985.
7. Author's interview with Harry Bruce, November 24, 1985.

Conclusion

1. Richard C. Davis, "Tradition and the Individual Talent in Charles Bruce," *The Dalhousie Review*, Volume 59, Number 3 (Autumn 1979), pp. 443-451.
2. John Moss, *Patterns of Isolation* (Toronto: McClelland and Stewart Limited, 1974), pp.166-189. See also Janice Kulyk Keefer's *Under Eastern Eyes, A Critical Reading of Maritime Fiction* (Toronto: University of Toronto Press, 1987), pp.55-61 and 231-233. For an alternative reading of *The Channel Shore* along economic and class lines see Erik Kristiansen, *New Maritimes*, September-October 1988, pp.31-33.
3. CB's work is absent, for example, from the following:
   The Oxford Anthology of Canadian Literature, edited by R. Weaver and W. Toye (Toronto: Oxford University Press, 1973).
   Literature in Canada, edited by D. Daymond and L. Monkman (Toronto: Gage Educational Publishing Limited, 1978).
   An Anthology of Canadian Literature in English, edited by D. Bennett and R. Brown (Toronto: Oxford University Press, 1983).
   Canadian Writers and Their Works, Volumes 1-10 (Fiction and Poetry), edited by R. Lecker, J. David, and E. Quigley (Toronto: ECW Press, 1985) — Thomas Raddall and Ernest Buckler are included. This is a series of criticial essays and bibliographical material.
4. *The Oxford Companion to Canadian History and Literature*, edited by Norah Story (Toronto: Oxford University Press, 1967), p. 112.
5. *The New Oxford Book of Canadian Verse*, edited by Margaret Atwood (Toronto: Oxford University Press, 1982).
6. It is fascinating and somewhat disturbing that while CB is included in *The Atlantic Anthology, Volume II, Poetry*, edited by Fred Cogswell (Charlottetown: Ragweed Press, 1985), there is no excerpt from his fiction in *Volume I, Fiction* (1984), also edited by Cogswell.

INDEX